It would be hard to imagine clinical practice or research that would not be enhanced by familiarity with the incredible precision and utility of Structural Analysis of Social Behavior (SASB) as a lens for understanding inter- and intrapersonal behavior. Critchfield and Benjamin have written an essential book articulating SASB's elegant theory and its many past and potential applications. This is a must-read for any clinician or clinical scientist who has ever wanted a more parsimonious yet powerful way of understanding how humans interact and how to use that knowledge to enhance therapeutic processes.
—**Julia Mackaronis, PhD,** Licensed Clinical Psychologist, Praxis Psychotherapy

Critchfield and Benjamin have succinctly captured decades of pioneering work and research demonstrating, with clinical examples and empirical support, how Interpersonal Reconstructive Therapy and Structural Analysis of Social Behavior can be utilized for case conceptualization and the psychotherapeutic process. This volume is likely to be a classic in the field and a must-read for students and practitioners, as well as offering an elegant system for psychotherapy researchers.
—**Jeffrey J. Magnavita, PhD,** Founder, Glastonbury Psychological Associates, PC, and CEO, Strategic Psychotherapeutics, LLC, Glastonbury, CT, United States

In this book, the authors translate half a century of cumulative work on Structural Analysis of Social Behavior, which is extensively used in psychotherapy research, and present it in a more user-friendly form. Now, students, professors, clinicians, supervisors, and researchers of any level or persuasion can collaborate in broadening and building upon such a solid structural foundation for evolving human relating, AT BEST.
—**Nuno Conceição, PhD,** Faculty of Psychology, University of Lisbon, Lisbon, Portugal; Past President, Society for the Exploration of Psychotherapy Integration

Structural Analysis of Social Behavior (SASB) is a dimensional assessment system and an interpretative model created by Lorna Smith Benjamin to read personality disorders. It is a "secret lens" which can be used to view and identify behavior patterns. SASB allows its users to analyze the subject's interpersonal space and view the world from their perspective: a necessary requirement in order to provide the help needed. Critchfield and Benjamin's book masterfully summarizes SASB theory, explaining its application while connecting it to Interpersonal Reconstructive Therapy through the case formulation process. The authors scientifically present ample research material on SASB application to the field of psychopathology and psychotherapy. This is the fully-fledged SASB handbook.

**—Francesco Colacicco**, Psychologist, Psychotherapist, and Director, Istituto Dedalus, and Teacher, Centro Studi di Terapia Familiare e Relazionale, Rome, Italy; Member of European Family Therapy Association (EFTA) and Italian Society of Psychology and Relational Psychotherapy (SIPPR)

As a mental health practitioner, educator, scholar, or trainee, if you want to know how to do what you do—in an evidence-based manner that is nonreductionistic—there is no better resource than this powerfully illuminating book. To master the SASB model and method—to see why our clients suffer and how they may heal—there are no better guides than Drs. Ken Critchfield and Lorna Benjamin. Ken and Lorna are not only the brains behind SASB, they are consummate scientists and master therapists, who value craft and rigor in equal measure, a unique gestalt that helps SASB clinicians of all stripes become transformative agents of in-depth change.

**—Craig N. Shealy, PhD**, Executive Director, International Beliefs and Values Institute (IBAVI); Developer of the Beliefs, Events, and Values Inventory (BEVI)

Structural Analysis of Social Behavior (SASB) is the most fully developed and researched model of human behavior. This volume is the definitive and comprehensive guide for clinicians new to SASB as well as researchers experienced with the system. It is eminently accessible, practical, and carefully organized to be equally useful as a learning and training resource as well as a reference source. It is one of those "core" books that informs when first read, and will keep on serving you at each stage of your career!

**—Adam O. Horvath, EdD**, Professor Emeritus, Simon Fraser University, Vancouver, BC, Canada

For experienced interpersonalists, the interpersonally curious, and everyone in between, Critchfield and Benjamin provide an accessible yet detailed overview of 50 years of theory, research, and clinical application. Because the authors have been gifted scholars, clinicians, and teachers for decades, all readers will leave an encounter with this superbly organized, clinically rich volume with a much more detailed understanding not only of Structural Analysis of Social Behavior and Interpersonal Reconstructive Therapy, but also of their own work, even if they don't think of their personal conceptual approach as particularly interpersonal.

**—Timothy W. Smith, PhD**, Distinguished Professor of Psychology, The University of Utah, Salt Lake City, UT, United States

# Structural Analysis of Social Behavior

**SASB**

# Structural Analysis of Social Behavior

**SASB**

A Primer for Clinical Use

Kenneth L. Critchfield • Lorna Smith Benjamin

AMERICAN PSYCHOLOGICAL ASSOCIATION

Copyright © 2024 by the American Psychological Association. All rights reserved. Except as permitted under the United States Copyright Act of 1976, no part of this publication may be reproduced or distributed in any form or by any means, including, but not limited to, the process of scanning and digitization, or stored in a database or retrieval system, without the prior written permission of the publisher.

The opinions and statements published are the responsibility of the authors, and such opinions and statements do not necessarily represent the policies of the American Psychological Association.

Published by
American Psychological Association
750 First Street, NE
Washington, DC 20002
https://www.apa.org

Order Department
https://www.apa.org/pubs/books
order@apa.org

Typeset in Charter and Interstate by Circle Graphics, Inc., Reisterstown, MD

Printer: Sheridan Books, Chelsea, MI
Cover Designer: Anthony Paular Design, Newbury Park, CA

**Library of Congress Cataloging-in-Publication Data**

Names: Critchfield, Kenneth, author. | Benjamin, Lorna Smith, author.
Title: Structural analysis of social behavior (SASB) : a primer for clinical use / authored by Kenneth L. Critchfield and Lorna Smith Benjamin.
Description: Washington, DC : American Psychological Association, [2024] | Includes bibliographical references and index.
Identifiers: LCCN 2023044983 (print) | LCCN 2023044984 (ebook) | ISBN 9781433837913 (paperback) | ISBN 9781433837920 (ebook)
Subjects: LCSH: Interpersonal relations. | Social psychology. | BISAC: PSYCHOLOGY / Psychotherapy / General | PSYCHOLOGY / Interpersonal Relations
Classification: LCC HM1106 .C758 2024 (print) | LCC HM1106 (ebook) | DDC 302—dc23/eng/20240110
LC record available at https://lccn.loc.gov/2023044983
LC ebook record available at https://lccn.loc.gov/2023044984

https://doi.org/10.1037/0000403-000

*Printed in the United States of America*

10 9 8 7 6 5 4 3 2 1

*To all those patients who might become free of their cages.*
*And, of course, to Lorna.*

# Contents

| | |
|---|---|
| *Acknowledgments* | *ix* |
| *Preface* | *xiii* |

## I. BASIC PRINCIPLES — 3

1. Introduction to Structural Analysis of Social Behavior — 5

2. The Structural Analysis of Social Behavior Models: Comprehensive Description of the Interpersonal Domain — 25

3. Application of Structural Analysis of Social Behavior Technology — 63

## II. USING STRUCTURAL ANALYSIS OF SOCIAL BEHAVIOR TO PUT CLINICAL THEORY INTO CLINICAL PRACTICE: AN OVERVIEW — 97

4. Structural Analysis of Social Behavior as Precise Description: Applications in Diverse Theoretical Frameworks — 99

5. Interpersonal Reconstructive Therapy — 119

## III. OBSERVING, ASSESSING, AND FORMULATING PATIENT PATTERNS — 145

6. Formulation Using Structural Analysis of Social Behavior Intrex Questionnaires — 147

viii • *Contents*

7. Using Structural Analysis of Social Behavior to Formulate
   Patterns From Clinical Interviews     171

## IV. TREATMENT: CONNECTING WITH PATIENTS AND OPTIMIZING INTERVENTIONS USING STRUCTURAL ANALYSIS OF SOCIAL BEHAVIOR-BASED FOCUS ON PSYCHOTHERAPY PROCESS, CASE FORMULATION, AND THERAPY GOALS     197

8. Directing In-Session Relational Processes Toward
   Therapeutic Goals     199

9. Actively Applying the Interpersonal Reconstructive Therapy
   Case Formulation     223

10. Tracking Change and Assessing Outcomes     239

*References*     *263*

*Index*     *281*

*About the Authors*     *289*

# Acknowledgments

A large number of folks have been supportive and influential in the writing of this book. At the top of the list is Susan Reynolds at APA Publishing who was there with us at the beginning of this project. She kept on believing, encouraging, checking in, and understanding our process across the years. She was also the one to give the much-needed message: "Okay, this is your last deadline!" Our editor for the final steps was Krissy Jones, who was immensely helpful and encouraged us through the process of review, revision, and finalizing everything.

This work owes much to the support of Ross Van Vranken (executive director) and Tom Woolf (clinical services director) at the University of Utah Neuropsychiatric Institute (now the Huntsman Mental Health Institute) for steady support of the Interpersonal Reconstructive Therapy (IRT) Clinic across all its years in operation. As codirector of the IRT Clinic, Tom offered key perspectives, including pragmatic grounding in the realities (i.e., challenges) of mental health care system functioning. As a wise clinician himself, he helped crystallize language of the "healing image." The patients and clinicians who worked with us in the IRT Clinic may see themselves here and there in the examples provided in this book. Even with a strong clinical model like Structural Analysis of Social Behavior (SASB) and IRT, our patients are our most important instructors and informants about whether the work is helpful. We have been fortunate in their generosity in providing their data, which ultimately is a lens on their personal lives. That trust and faith in our use and interpretation of their data, as well as the safeguards x • *Acknowledgments*

around it, are deeply appreciated. We hope that this book will be recognized as the kind of offering they would want to see.

Our ongoing research with SASB and IRT was assisted and advanced by trainees at the University of Utah, James Madison University, and the Ferkauf Graduate School of Psychology at Yeshiva University. Students who have contributed the lion's share of work toward coding our database notably include Matt Davis, Emily Traupman, Sheryl Schindler, Jonathan Broadwell, Karen Stovall, Andriana Hench, Megan Mischinski, Kathia Bonilla, Paulihna Cechak, Ali Kenny, Felicia Romano, and Fabrice Ndzana. Doctoral trainees have innovated, adapted, and extended SASB and IRT ideas in recent years, both clinically and in terms of our research frontier, and include Molly Bowman, Bridget Smith, Kirstin Drucker, Mariafé Panizo, Julia Dobner-Pereira, Eliza Stucker-Rozovsky, and Priyata Thapa. We gratefully acknowledge funding received from the Society for Advancement of Psychotherapy (APA Division 29) as well as from the Society for Psychotherapy Research to support trainees in applying SASB to session material and exploring hypotheses, testing key propositions, and optimizing IRT.

Colleagues and members of the SASB "tribe" that contributed in large and small ways to the development of this book include Kathleen Levenick, Francesco Colacicco, Paola Ciapanna, Andrea Ferrazza, and the fabulous trainees at Instituto Dedalus; Jeffrey Magnavita, Lynne Knobloch-Fedders, Lindsey Harvell-Bowman, Craig Shealy, and Marjorie Klein; Michael Constantino, Henny Westra, and their students using SASB to study motivational interviewing with cognitive behavior therapy; Fulvia Ronchi, Randi Ulberg, Per Høgland, Elizabeth Skowron, Nuno Conceição, Michael Westerman, Heather Gunn, Alexandre Vaz, Nadja Hebenstreit, Christie Karpiak, Tim Smith, Karla Moras, Ed Teyber, Aaron Pincus, Robert Mestel, and Paula Miceli; and Chris Molnar and the Philadelphia Behavior Therapy Association. Some of these individuals may be surprised to find their names listed here. Conversations with them have deepened my [KLC] appreciation for the work we are all doing and helped refine my ability to talk, think, and write about its potential.

Thanks to my [KLC] work with SASB and IRT, I have had the honor to supervise and consult with many truly talented therapists, whose questions and circumstances have helped me develop and grow as a clinician and clinician-educator. In this, I wish to acknowledge contribution of the IRT peer consultation group convened by the IRT Institute as well as all those using SASB in research and clinical settings across the globe. In working with Lorna Smith Benjamin's ideas (and with her personally), I have many times thought of the phrase "standing on the shoulders of giants." I am grateful to her and know that many others feel the same way for the fact of her life and work, as well as her ability to articulate and provide precision that can optimize what we try to do in psychotherapy.

Personal and professional lives have their many interfaces. Linda Kidd, Lorna's daughter, has been constructive and supportive of this work in ways that are beyond words. I [KLC] am also very grateful to my wife, Anikó, and daughter, Míra, for their support and allowing me to steal time away when needed.

# Preface

This book is intended primarily for clinicians engaged in psychotherapy. I (K.L.C.) am certain that other audiences will find it informative as well. It summarizes an approach to measuring and conceptualizing interpersonal relationships that has benefitted from 50 years of use and development. This approach can be applied to a wide range of clinical activities and processes. In fact, it can be applied to just about any topic that can be thought of in interpersonal or relational terms. In this book, our emphasis is on clinical case conceptualization, in-session relating, therapeutic decision making, and tracking the change process in therapy. If you are a clinician or clinician-in-training, our overall objective for this book is to enhance your ability to perceive patient patterns, their origins, and their reasons for persisting. Usually, the enhanced awareness provides a basis for hope and clarity about how to pursue change for each patient, including those with high complexity and severity.

The idea for this book dates back roughly 20 years. The outline and some early chapter drafts date back that far. I had returned to the University of Utah for a postdoctoral position focused on Lorna Smith Benjamin's research with Interpersonal Reconstructive Therapy (IRT). She asked if I would be interested in helping write "the SASB book." Since then, it has been refined and informed (and delayed!) by 10 years of working together in the IRT clinic, which included teaching graduate trainees how to use the methods described in this book to treat "complex" patients who had typically been hospitalized for suicidality and already had multiple prior treatment attempts. We continued to work together after I left Utah and have many times joked about being fused together in this work.

xiv • *Preface*

Lorna's model and approach long precede my involvement with her, and I cannot claim credit. Lorna first published the Structural Analysis of Social Behavior (SASB) model with an accompanying description in 1973. That means it arrived in print the same year that Hip-Hop was invented and Pink Floyd's *Dark Side of the Moon* was released. But Lorna had developed the basic model well before that, as an observational coding system for use in Harry Harlow's primate lab at the University of Wisconsin–Madison. Its application to psychotherapy happened not long after. Clinically, Lorna's practice was influenced by the work of important figures passing through Madison in the 1960s. Lorna reportedly turned down an invitation to work with John Bowlby at Tavistock, who she met as part of his visits to Harlow's lab while attachment theory was first being articulated. She was supervised by Carl Rogers for a brief period, and she was also deeply influenced by the family therapist, Carl Whitaker, among others. In addition, Lorna has always been an autodidact, deepening her own understanding of therapy processes by making rough, handwritten transcripts of her clinical work and studying them to test ideas about how to optimize treatment processes. This included applying the SASB lens to that material.

I only come into the story much later in Lorna's career, after she had taken a position at the University of Utah. As luck would have it, I discovered SASB as an undergraduate who was given special permission to take a graduate course in psychopathology, taught by Dr. Benjamin. I thought she made a compelling case for her model's utility for organizing and making sense of a wide range of psychiatric problems. It appealed to the dawning sense I had at the time (influenced by developmental psychologist Alan Fogel's research) that there was a kind of "emotional logic" behind peoples' lives and problems. I was hooked—and inspired to pursue graduate training in clinical psychology. Although Lorna Benjamin was not my major professor back then, I was supervised by her for a time and was very involved in SASB-based psychotherapy process research. A few years later, she invited me back as a postdoctoral fellow to help her empirically test the approach to therapy she had recently decided to name "Interpersonal Reconstructive Therapy (IRT)."

That brings us up to about 20 years ago. I started teaching classes in SASB for our clinic trainees, and Lorna asked me to take the lead in writing this book. At about the same time, she began writing what would become *Interpersonal Reconstructive Therapy for Anger, Anxiety, and Depression: It's About Broken Hearts, Not Broken Brains* (Benjamin, 2018). Our time-in-production is a sure sign of incurable perfectionism in both of us. Even so, I think both books are much richer than if they had been written on their original timelines. I know I benefitted immensely from the opportunity to discuss therapeutic principles, theory, practice, research strategies, teaching methods, and clinical decision making in many settings (including informally across many lunches!) with the use of SASB integrated throughout.

I am writing this preface with the singular pronoun "I." And that feels very strange for me, and hard. We were a "we" through the time of writing this book, and that "we" carries a lot of meaning about our connection, collaboration, and friendship over the years—our interdependence, our attachment, and the way Lorna has become part of my personal and professional "family in the head." Unfortunately, she began having noticeable difficulties with her memory a few years ago, a problem that progressed until she could no longer go back and forth with our drafts. Her work is (obviously!) at the core of everything discussed here. We discussed the various details all along the way. She is even the clinician in several of the examples provided. She was part-way through reviewing my full drafts when the problems became too severe.

It is not an easy thing to have a big piece of your life's work go to press without your final approval or full control. Not long ago, she was asked to make some comments for a book about aging as a psychologist. Her memory problems had progressed, and so she was interviewed by her daughter Linda and had this to say about it:

> . . . I am very grateful for the many unsolicited thank you notes I have been receiving from patients and trainees thanking me for helping them and the work we did together. I got one the other day saying, "thank you for saving my life." Receiving these notes is a reassuring reality that with both trainees and patients the impact of the work continues. . . . Unlike problems that one can work on and change in psychotherapy, problems that come with aging are 100% created by reality. Many problems dealt with in therapy can be solved by changing perceptions and situations. Father time is a non-responsive patient. (Benjamin, 2023, p. 236)

I believe I have done justice to Lorna's ideas here, especially in terms of laying out ways that clinicians can use them in work with their patients, and to traverse the space between individual application of the SASB model and aggregate research findings about the related clinical topics. Lorna is a hard act to follow and really had a sight line on what was important for clinical practice 50 years in advance. As part of revising and finalizing these chapters, I frequently returned to her early writing and was amazed at how she had already described, with elegance and clarity, the points I "was noticing" in our examples and data. Fifty years later, we benefit from additional research validation of her ideas, plus many repeated examples of its underlying principles in clinical practice. Her careful work to develop, measure, and test her own theory bears good fruit.

As "heir apparent" to Lorna's work (she would use that phrase, and I would take a deep breath), I see that there is more work to be done by way of researching, teaching, and extending ideas linked to SASB and IRT. It will take a community of us to fill her shoes and carry the work forward. The good news is that there are new generations and new growth. I'm hoping this book will be a contribution that helps further stimulate and grow the community of practitioners and researchers interested in SASB and IRT. We wish to attract committed skeptics as well as dedicated practitioners. The emphasis in this book is on practice, but science and practice are closely wedded in SASB and IRT and we need to keep challenging and working to validate the method and its underlying principles, to enhance and optimize our ability to help others.

In one of her last published efforts, Lorna was asked to write about her personal history, as a brief autobiography in a collection of related works focused on "understanding the people who understand people." She wrote,

> Writing an autobiography violates every related standard I can recall from childhood. For example: "Don't be self-centered. Do what needs to be done and don't complain. Don't get any ideas to the effect you are special. Don't whine or expect help: just get the job done." . . . That is the sort of message my two older (foster) brothers and I received on an everyday basis. Everybody hustled and even in our advanced years, everybody still is "productive" and, heaven forbid, not dependent. (Benjamin, 2022, p. 340)

And so, despite what you might infer by the personal and historical tone of this preface (a lot of 2-2: Disclose), I share her sentiment about this work. It is not about her. It is not about us. What it is about is "the work" of helping people by getting clear about underlying principles. We both hope you will learn about, practice, and weigh the value of SASB and IRT ideas on their own merits.

And if you like the ideas, don't be a stranger.

—*Ken Critchfield, PhD*
*New York City*

# Structural Analysis of Social Behavior

**SASB**

PART I BASIC PRINCIPLES

# 1 INTRODUCTION TO STRUCTURAL ANALYSIS OF SOCIAL BEHAVIOR

*In a science of persons, we state as axiomatic that: 1. behaviour is a function of experience; 2. both experience and behaviour are always in relation to some one or something other than self.*

—Laing et al., 1966

Relationships, perhaps more than any other single factor, are at the heart of lived experience, including the "problems of living" captured in part by clinical diagnosis (Stein, 2021).[1] The *Structural Analysis of Social Behavior* (SASB; Benjamin, 1974, 2000) provides an elegant and sophisticated framework for tracking patterns described by patients within and across relationships. Throughout this book, SASB is presented as a tool for instructing mental health clinicians. It applies especially to psychotherapists working with patients who experience interpersonal problems, including the variety of affective, cognitive, and behavioral disturbances that flow from and contribute to those problems. However, the applications of SASB extend far

---

[1] The clinical material used in this book is adequately disguised to protect patient confidentiality.

https://doi.org/10.1037/0000403-001
*Structural Analysis of Social Behavior (SASB): A Primer for Clinical Use,* by K. L. Critchfield and L. S. Benjamin
Copyright © 2024 by the American Psychological Association. All rights reserved.

beyond the clinic. It is of potential use in any setting involving relationships and social interactions. Anyone interested in the workings of human relatedness—from business negotiation to diplomacy, to the courtroom, to the workplace, to parenthood, and so on—will find that SASB facilitates recognition and objective assessment of relationship patterns and provides a path for improving problematic interactions.

A central assumption of this book is that beliefs, expectations, and values learned through loyalty and love guide our interactions and patterns of relating with ourselves and others. Put simply, our early experiences shape what we often think of as personality. Benjamin (2018) used a natural biological perspective rooted in principles of evolution to explain how and why learning that derives from the crucible of important early relationships organizes our nervous system. Specifically, our learning history informs rapid perception and evaluation of safety versus threat cues. It also shapes the relational behaviors and patterns built from those behaviors that we use, adaptively or maladaptively, to seek safety. In line with this developmental perspective, we will emphasize how to use SASB with patients[2] to identify connections between current symptoms and early and present relational patterns, and to help choose and adopt more adaptive ways of being. The importance of interpersonal patterns, their sources, and their links to symptoms is illustrated next with a brief clinical example.

Sarah is a married, college-educated, working mother in her mid-30s who lives in a rural community. She was hospitalized and referred to our inpatient clinic for consultation after experiencing multiple psychiatric and somatic complaints, including significant and persistent suicidal ideation. Over the course of a clinical interview, Sarah described strong anxiety and depression directly tied to her attempts to comply with the many demands of her boss at work. Among other things, he demanded that she do the work of several people (including handling his personal finances) but kept her in a position that, at least on paper, required less than the number of hours qualifying for benefits. When she asked her boss for relief in the form of a lessened workload, help from others in the office, better pay, or benefits,

---

[2] The term *patient* will be used throughout this book to refer to individuals who seek mental health care from any of the variety of professions that offer assessment, diagnosis, counseling, or psychotherapy. Other terms, such as *client*, are also commonly used and have been offered as an alternative to the medicalized doctor–patient relationship. I (K.L.C.) use these terms interchangeably in my teaching and practice. However, in this book, the choice of *patient* is largely based on a frame offered by my coauthor (L.S.B.), who notes that the word can also be heard as a reminder for clinicians to appreciate how often the folks we work with need to be patient with our ongoing attempts to truly hear and be of help to them.

he acknowledged the problems but did nothing. Sarah responded to her boss's unreasonable demands by becoming self-critical and redoubling her efforts to perform. She dutifully pushed on, despite onset of carpal tunnel pain, missed social opportunities, and less time at home with her family, including her two small children. With each failed attempt to get recognition and relief, Sarah became more anxious, depressed, and overwhelmed. Her attempts to work harder were accompanied by increased self-criticism and diminished self-care. Over time, she began to see her situation as hopeless, escalating to the point of significant suicidal ideation.

When Sarah was interviewed in the hospital, she described an early history that paralleled the adult experience at work. Her memories of her father included that he was very controlling and made extreme demands of her and her siblings. When any of them deviated from their father's wishes or failed to perform to his standards, he enforced compliance with harsh physical punishment, rejection, and long silences that could last for days. He was otherwise emotionally distant. Unlike her siblings, Sarah succeeded at avoiding punishments by anticipating her father's demands and working hard to comply. It was a strategy that worked for her in that context, and she was able to spend more time with her father, something that she desired very much. Her siblings called her "Daddy's favorite." Although she was only a child, her closeness with her father allowed her to be a mediator between her parents when they eventually divorced.

Sarah's strategy of hard work, self-discipline, and compliance was once essential to gaining her father's favor, avoiding his punishments, and providing service to the family. Applied in the workplace, this same strategy led rapidly to burnout with another controlling but neglectful figure, her boss. Understanding the parallels between past and present turned out to be key in helping her see that she had healthier alternative strategies as an adult in the workplace. This same understanding was key to helping Sarah reduce her suicidality, self-criticism, and sense of failure. It ultimately gave her the ability to work through old feelings, wishes, and fears that were both triggered by, and maintaining parallels in, her adult life.

## ON LEARNING SASB AS A CLINICIAN

SASB is a model for describing, organizing, and making predictions about interpersonal behavior. The model, shown in Figure 1.1 and elaborated in more detail in Chapter 2, is organized around two fundamental axes. The horizontal axis captures a range of behavior from the extremes of love to the extremes of hate. The vertical axis ranges from the extremes of enmeshment

8 • Basic Principles

**FIGURE 1.1. Structural Analysis of Social Behavior (SASB) Simplified Cluster Model (With Two-Digit Codes)**

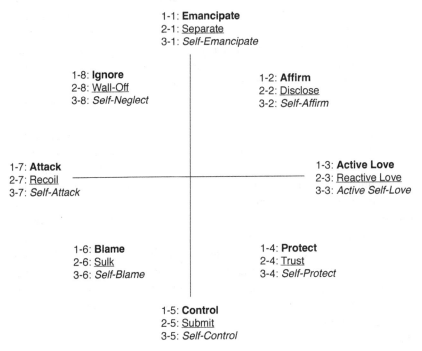

*Note.* Each position reflects a combination of the primary organizing dimensions of focus (font type), affiliation (horizontal axis), and interdependence (vertical axis). The figure combines two figures: Adapted from *Interpersonal Diagnosis and Treatment of Personality Disorders* (2nd ed., p. 55) by L. S. Benjamin, 1996, Guilford Press. Copyright 1996 by Guilford Press; with numeric codes added from "Use of the SASB Dimensional Model to Develop Treatment Plans for Personality Disorders: I. Narcissism," by L. S. Benjamin, 1987, *Journal of Personality Disorders*, 1(1), p. 53 (https://doi.org/10.1521/pedi.1987.1.1.43). Copyright 1987 by Guilford Press. Adapted with permission.

and interdependence to those of extreme separateness, differentiation, and independence. A third distinction tracks the attentional focus of a behavior as being toward others, toward the self (in interaction with others), or intrapsychically (termed *introject*).[3] The resulting chart of behavior can be used to clarify and describe relational patterns in ways that make sense of presenting problems and symptoms. For example, Sarah's relationship with her

---

[3] A two-digit numbering system is additionally shown in Figure 1.1 and is used to note structural placement of each behavior on the model. This aspect of the model is described in detail in Chapter 2. It is included here in anticipation that Figure 1.1 will be used as a go-to resource and reference throughout the book.

father, her boss, and herself can be characterized by various positions that include several at the bottom of the model. Her father and boss were controlling (1-5: **Control**) and blaming (1-6: **Blame**), to which Sarah responded with submission (2-5: <u>Submit</u>), forcing herself to comply and criticizing herself for her limitations (3-5: *Self-Control* and 3-6: *Self-Blame*). Several behaviors at the top of the model are also invoked in Sarah's case. The fact that her father and boss's demands were unreasonable and neglected her needs and capacities (1-8: **Ignore**) is mirrored in her willingness to push beyond healthy limits (3-8: *Self-Neglect*). These behaviors occur in Sarah's narrative in recognizable patterns and sequences that make sense of her presenting symptoms. These patterns involve input from others, responses to them, and implications for self-concept and self-treatment.

We expect that most clinicians interested in this book will already have an intuitive understanding of patient patterns and relational themes like Sarah's. It is important to ask what SASB offers over and above a good clinician's experience, training, and intuition. The answer is that SASB's high degree of behavioral specificity can place observations about relational patterns into a precise set of structural relations that extend and offer clarity about their implications. This clarity can, in turn, enhance clinical perception and formulation. Let us consider an example of a problematic behavior in the present. Say that a patient engages in a reckless process of staying out late and drinking, which results in missing important meetings (3-8: *Self-Neglect*), including canceling therapy sessions, and being reluctant to talk about their feelings (2-8: <u>Wall-Off</u>). These behaviors might be understood in light of recent events with a similar interpersonal position, such as (a) a roommate going out with mutual friends and not inviting the patient (1-8: **Ignore**); (b) the patient perceiving her therapist as not appreciating the importance of this (1-8: **Ignore**); while (c) the patient's internalized experience of their mother in childhood is as being depressed, withdrawn, and self-medicating with opiates while the patient was left to fend for themself (1-8: **Ignore**, 2-8: <u>Wall-Off</u>, and 3-8: *Self-Neglect*). The simple observation that all these clinically salient behaviors "code" into the upper-left portion of Figure 1.1 suggests an avenue for collaborative exploration of how these diverse-seeming experiences may come together and make sense.

Another distinct benefit of SASB for clinicians is enhanced recognition of patterns within the therapy relationship itself. SASB facilitates tracking within the here-and-now process of the therapeutic relationship and guides the clinician to appropriate responsiveness. Examples provided throughout this book are designed to make clear the many practical implications of being able to see recurring patterns through the lens provided by SASB.

Our experience teaching and applying the model over decades suggests that a better articulated sense of their patients' interpersonal patterns offers clinicians a much-improved ability to empathically track the complexity of patients' experience and use that understanding to guide therapeutic action. Accurate empathy is itself associated with better outcomes, particularly in the context of an interpersonal approach to treatment (Crits-Christoph et al., 2010). In addition, a more precise articulation of patterns can help therapists and patients use the resulting awareness to mobilize the will for change. Awareness and agentic choice are key elements of the Interpersonal Reconstructive Therapy (IRT; Benjamin, 2003, 2006, 2018) approach to treatment described in Chapter 5. They have also been proposed as transtheoretical elements involved in all approaches to therapeutic change (Gorlin & Békés, 2021; Williams & Levitt, 2007).

In sum, SASB provides clear language and a structured set of concepts that can help anchor clinical intuition and reduce the likelihood of missing or misunderstanding what is happening in patients' lives or in the here-and-now process of therapeutic interaction. The need to be specific when discussing complex therapeutic principles is a long-standing challenge in mental health. In 1958, Fritz Heider, a pioneering social psychologist, discussed this issue in *The Psychology of Interpersonal Relations*:

> . . . though nonscientific language in the hands of a master is unsurpassed for the description of even the most subtle relationships, it lacks the features of a real system . . . the relations between terms are only crudely defined and understood. Though we know the meanings of words like "promise," "permit," or "pride" we do not know them in the same way we know the meaning of words like "two" and "four," or of words like "speed" and "acceleration." The words referring to interpersonal relations are like islands separated from each other by impassable channels. We do not know how to reach one from the other, we do not know whether they contain a certain number of basic principles of variation, or basic elements, different combinations of which produce the manifold of qualitative differences. (p. 8)

SASB provides a bridge over Heider's "impassable channels" by placing basic principles of interpersonal behavior into a systematic framework that is directly applicable to clinical settings. Some key advantages of the SASB model derive from it being first developed by Benjamin to study primate social behavior in rhesus monkeys while working with her major professor, Harry Harlow (Benjamin, 1961, 1973). Patterns indicative of parent–child attachment, as defined by Bowlby (1969), were of particular relevance. The remainder of this chapter focuses on briefly reviewing the history and

Introduction to Structural Analysis of Social Behavior  •  11

intellectual tradition that has informed interpersonal theory in general and the SASB model in particular. The model is detailed in Chapter 2.

## BRIEF REVIEW OF HISTORY: INTERPERSONAL THEORY LEADING TO DEVELOPMENT OF SASB

Harry Stack Sullivan has been widely recognized as the father of interpersonal psychiatry. Sullivan wrote in 1940, "The field of psychiatry is the field of interpersonal relations—a personality can never be isolated from the complex of interpersonal relations in which the person lives and has his being" (p. 10). Going against dominant theories of the time, Sullivan viewed psychopathology, including schizophrenia, in terms of characteristic patterns of relating with others. He saw the origins and motivation to maintain those patterns as being a function of early experiences with caregivers (and other important people) through a process of social learning:

> But, I shall insist that, however like some average people I may be in many respects, I am nonetheless the product of a unique course of acculturation. . . . From infancy each of us is trained to think in this way. If one was fortunately born, the parents have been fairly consistent in their expressed appraisals, and one has elaborated a dependable self. However absurdly it may be related to one's manifest behavior, one is relatively secure in dealing with others. If one's parents have been less reassuring or if experience subsequent to childhood has demonstrated the serious deficiency of a once-trusted illusion as to one's personality, the case is quite otherwise. "I did not think you were that kind of a person" comes to be a very painful remark the deeper implications of which do not engage one's attention. One becomes as realistically as possible a member of the group made up of the right kind of people and acts as rightly as possible in those restricted interpersonal contexts in which one still has freedom to participate. (Sullivan, 1939, pp. 932–933)

Sullivan's work both influenced and was influenced by emerging themes about the nature and structure of the self in the 1930s. G. H. Mead's approach to social psychology, as well as neo-Freudian and early object-relations modifications to psychoanalysis, emphasized the role of other people in relation to a concept of the self, including how primary survival needs—to belong and to relate—shape us (J. R. Greenberg & Mitchell, 1983). At that time, the main clinical implication of a social view of the self was that personality and pathology are both intimately connected to past and present experiences with others. Sullivan (1938) described psychopathology as having "a developmental history which is in turn completely understandable in terms of the functional adequacy of the person in the

12 • *Basic Principles*

series of interpersonal situations through which he has had to live" (p. 79). Like Sullivan, we view psychopathology as reflecting ongoing attempts to implement patterns of relating with the self and others in settings where they are no longer adaptive. However, like Heider, Sullivan (1953) noted the need for a reliable science of observing and describing relationships:

> . . . the fabulous difficulty of teaching psychiatry, as I have seen it over the years, is that it is quite easy to learn certain things—that is, to get so you can talk about them—but it is extremely difficult to get any two people to mean just the same thing when they talk about what they have supposedly learned. (p. 3)

## Measurement: Capturing Interpersonal Patterns, Personality, and Processes of Self

Working separately but at about the same time as Sullivan, Murray (1938) generated the list of human needs shown in Table 1.1. Later, Freedman and colleagues (1951) placed a subset into a circular order that provides a measurement framework. Initially, Murray organized needs in two broad categories: those related to basic physical survival (*vicerogenic* or primary needs) and those related to psychological functioning (*psychogenic* or secondary needs). Consistent with the expectation of Sullivan and others, many of the psychological needs involved other people.

### Structure of the Interpersonal Domain: Inventing the Wheel

In Murray's (1938) initial presentation of the list, human relational needs were grouped according to themes of status (achievement and recognition, defense of status, and avoidance of humiliation), power (assertion of power, reactions to power through submission, separation, or opposition), aggression (giving, receiving, and avoiding it), affiliation (seeking, giving, exchanging, or withholding it), and knowing (the need to know and be known; see Table 1.2).

Freedman et al. (1951) and Leary (1957) combined these basic themes with clinical observations to form a two-dimensional, circular structure referred to as the *interpersonal circle* (IPC). As can be seen in Figure 1.2, the IPC involves two dimensions; the first (horizontal) ranges from hate to love, while the second (vertical) ranges from dominate to submit. In pioneering work, the structure was used to map clinical concepts and diagnoses relative to their respective interpersonal tendencies (Leary, 1957). Others refined the IPC further (e.g., Kiesler, 1983; Lorr et al., 1965; Plutchik & Conte, 1997; Wiggins, 1979; Wiggins et al., 1988). From initial charting, the interpersonal domain showed systematic and useful connections to clinical work.

*Introduction to Structural Analysis of Social Behavior* • 13

**TABLE 1.1. Murray's List of Needs**

| Primary (viscerogenic) needs | | Secondary (psychogenic) needs | | | |
|---|---|---|---|---|---|
| | | Inanimate | | Human | |
| Air | Harmavoidance | Acquisition | Superiority | Dominance | Affiliation |
| Water | Noxavoidance | Conservance | Achievement | Deference | Rejection |
| Food | Heatavoidance | Order | Recognition | Similance | Nurturance |
| Sex | Coldavoidance | Retention | Exhibition | Autonomy | Succorance |
| Lactation | Sentience | Construction | Inviolacy | Contrarience | Play |
| Urination | Passivity | | Infavoidance | Aggression | Cognizance |
| Defecation | | | Defendance | Abasement | Exposition |
| | | | Counteraction | Blame avoidance | |

*Note.* Data from Murray (1938).

**TABLE 1.2. Murray's People-Oriented Needs, Organized by Theme**

| Status | Power | Aggression | Affiliation | Knowing |
|---|---|---|---|---|
| Gaining | Dominance | Aggression | Affiliation | Cognizance |
|   Superiority | Deference | Abasement | Rejection | Exposition |
|   Achievement | Similance | Blame avoidance | Nurturance | |
|   Recognition | Autonomy | | Succorance | |
|   Exhibition | Contrarience | | Play | |
| Protecting | | | | |
|   Inviolacy | | | | |
|   Infavoidance | | | | |
|   Defendance | | | | |
|   Counteraction | | | | |

*Note.* Data from Murray (1938).

**FIGURE 1.2. Interpersonal Circle for (A) Observed Behaviors and (B) Using Trait Terms**

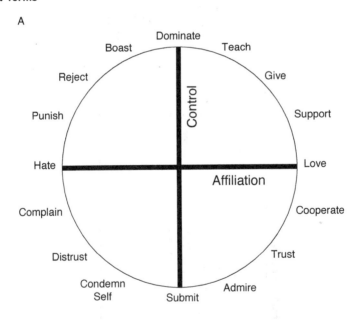

**FIGURE 1.2. Interpersonal Circle for (A) Observed Behaviors and (B) Using Trait Terms (*Continued*)**

*Note.* Panel A (observed behaviors) has been simplified from the original to emphasize illustrative verbs for each model position, and labels for the underlying dimension have been added. Adapted from "The Interpersonal Dimension of Personality," by M. B. Freedman, T. F. Leary, A. G. Ossorio, and H. S. Goffey, 1951, *Journal of Personality*, 20(2), p. 151 (https://doi.org/10.1111/j.1467-6494.1951.tb01518.x). Copyright 1951 by John Wiley and Sons. Adapted with permission. Panel B (trait terms) has been simplified from the original to show general category labels in adaptive and maladaptive forms (with the latter in parentheses), plus the addition of labels for the underlying dimensions. Adapted from *Interpersonal Diagnosis of Personality: A Functional Theory and Methodology for Personality Evaluation* (p. 65), by T. Leary, 1957, Ronald Press. Copyright 1957 by Timothy Leary and reprinted in 2004 by Wipf and Stock Publishers (https://www.wipfandstock.com). Adapted with permission.

## Structure Revisited: Solving the Problem of Autonomy

Leary (1957) predicted that additional developments would follow: "We cannot doubt that more complex formal systems will eventually add new spatial dimensions to the organization of personality" (p. 64). SASB builds on the IPC with an additional distinction requiring reorganization of the conceptual space. The distinction hinges on recognition that expressions of autonomy, separateness, and other forms of agency are missing, especially those that are nonhostile and neither dominate nor submit to others (i.e., to either dominate or submit denotes a lack of separateness from the other person or persons).

16 • *Basic Principles*

As a specific example, like many humanist and existentialist writers, poet Rainer Maria Rilke recoiled from a view of the world in which human relationships allow only for varying degrees of domination or submission. He once wrote in a letter to a friend, "I beg all those who love me to love my solitude too" (Leppmann, 1984, p. 237). The IPC does not provide a clear language for the condition described by Rilke's request: to be allowed distance in a context of warm relatedness that does not involve significant control or submission by anyone else involved. The same can be said for clinically relevant goals that invoke humanistic and existential themes, such as developing a well-differentiated, healthy sense of self through the letting go of old wishes, fears, relationships, hurts, identities, and so on. These involve a very different stance than simply becoming more or less dominating or submissive in relation to others or to the self.

### Insights About Autonomy From Parent-Child Interaction Research

A structural model of behavior that more clearly embraced the issue of autonomy was developed at about the same time as the IPC, but in a different area of psychology. Schaefer (1959, 1965) developed a circular model of parental behavior shown in Figure 1.3. Like the IPC, Schaefer's model had a horizontal dimension ranging from loving, affiliative parenting to aggressive, disaffiliative parenting. Also similar was a vertical dimension describing degrees of control or domination.

For Schaefer, the conceptual opposite of parental control was to grant autonomy. Like the IPC, the Schaefer model has had a long history in research. For example, the same essential dimensions underlie the Parental Bonding Instrument (PBI; Parker et al., 1979). The PBI has been widely used in clinical and epidemiological research to link early experiences with parents to anxiety and depressive disorders, delinquency, drug and alcohol abuse, personality disorders, and schizophrenic relapse (Parker, 1990). As such, the model is clearly useful for understanding clinical phenomena. Items measuring the opposite pole of parental control are clear examples of an autonomy-granting stance and include "let me decide things for myself" and "gave me as much freedom as I wanted."

### What Is the Opposite of Control? Integration of Models to Produce SASB

The IPC and Schaefer models each capture something about control that is not directly covered in the other. A parent may permit a child to go their own way rather than controlling them (Schaefer model), but a parent may

**FIGURE 1.3. Schaefer's Circle**

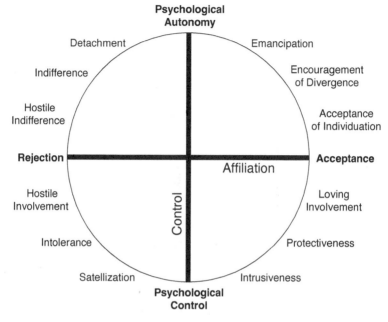

*Note.* The figure omits from the original a proposed third dimension for lax versus firm control and adds labels to identify the underlying dimensions. Adapted from "A Configurational Analysis of Children's Reports of Parent Behavior," by E. S. Schaefer, 1965, *Journal of Consulting Psychology, 29*(6), p. 557 (https://doi.org/10.1037/h0022702). Copyright 1965 by the American Psychological Association.

also submit and comply with a child's insistent demands (IPC model). SASB incorporates the constructs of both models, as shown in Figure 1.4.

The reorganized structure involves two parallel planes defined by their interpersonal focus. One plane consists of behaviors that are primarily about something that happens to the other person (prototypically parentlike, involving transitive actions). The other plane includes behavior concerned with what is happening with the self in relation to others (prototypically childlike, involving intransitive states). The resulting structure creates complementary pairings of behavior that share the same combination of underlying dimensions (referred to as *affiliation* and *interdependence*) but differ by focus.

The model includes positions for important themes from the clinical literature. At extreme poles of the model, these positions include sexuality, aggression, power, and separateness. The ability to track each of these behavioral positions in ways that were anchored in an assessment of underlying constructs that existed separate from language was necessary to apply to primate

18 • *Basic Principles*

**FIGURE 1.4. Control, Submission, and Freedom in the Schaefer, Structural Analysis of Social Behavior (SASB), and Interpersonal Circle Models**

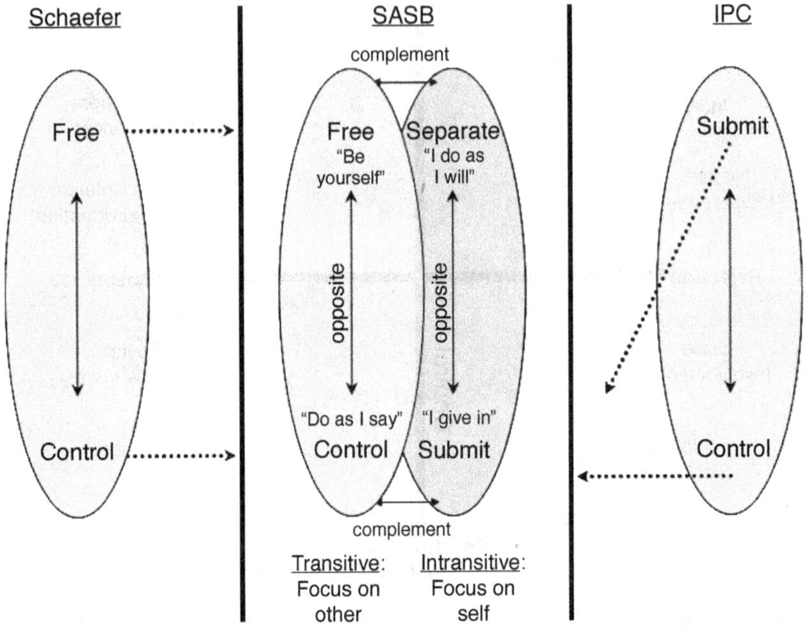

*Note.* Dotted lines indicate the location of conceptual parallels integrated into the SASB model.

nonverbal behavior in the context of Harlow's laboratory. Benjamin (1973, 1974, 1979) later developed the model for analysis of clinical processes, including narrative descriptions involving a wide range of developmental contexts. As will be described in more detail in Chapter 2, the extensions of the model explicitly incorporate self-treatment into its framework with a plane of behavior termed *introject*. This surface reflects Sullivan's (1940) sense of introjection as reflecting the behavior of others taken in and applied to the self. For example, as can be seen in Figure 1.1, each position focused on others (e.g., 1-2: **Affirm**, 1-5: **Control**, and 1-8: **Ignore**) has a parallel behavior involving self-treatment (e.g., 3-2: *Self-Affirm*, 3-5: *Self-Control*, and 3-8: *Self-Neglect*).

When used in clinical practice, SASB provides a language that can be used to focus, summarize, and reflect a patient's relational narrative in lay terms. An accurate model can correctly shape clinical perception and language, providing seamless connection with everyday language to enhance clinical discernment and allow clinicians to provide accurate empathy.

*Introduction to Structural Analysis of Social Behavior* • 19

**TABLE 1.3. Contrasts Between Use of SASB and IPC When Coding Autonomy**

| Source | Referent | Rated item | IPC description | SASB description |
|--------|----------|------------|-----------------|------------------|
| MMPI item | Rater to family | 1. I have been quite independent and free from family rule. | Dominance | 2-1: Separate |
| Therapy transcript | Mother to speaker | 2. I think it makes her retract, withdraw from me when I am dependent on her. | Hostile dominance | 2-8: Wall-Off |
| Therapy transcript | Speaker to mother | 3. . . . especially my mother, tried to push me a little which I resented and probably went out of my way to do the opposite. | Dominance | 2-1: Separate |
| TAT card response | Child to mother | 4. I think she'll run away, but it isn't from the school—because she hates her mother who is unkind and doesn't show her any love. My own experience tells me she runs away. | Hostile submission | 2-8: Wall-Off |

*Note.* Coded segments are underlined in rated items. IPC codes and illustrative clinical material are from Freedman et al. (1951). SASB descriptors are from the model shown in Figure 1.1. IPC = interpersonal circle; MMPI = Minnesota Multiphasic Personality Inventory; SASB = Structural Analysis of Social Behavior; TAT = Thematic Apperception Test.

These enhancements can be seen in Table 1.3, which shows differing results when SASB and IPC are applied to examples of clinical material provided by Freedman and colleagues (1951) in their initial presentation of the IPC. The examples were selected to highlight the way each model addresses differentiated interpersonal behavior. In each instance, the SASB-based description can be seen to land closer to the qualitative material being described. More than this, the distinctions have profound implications for therapeutic decision making. Clinicians might be set down very different paths if, as in the first three examples of Table 1.3, expressions of separateness (including simple disagreement) are mistaken for the exertion of power over another person. The final example invokes parent–child relationships. A child who responds to a parent by shouting an angry "no" or by avoiding and fleeing (i.e., separating or walling off) is not engaging in the same pattern as a child who complies fearfully or resentfully (i.e., sulking or submitting).

20 • *Basic Principles*

Returning to the example of Sarah, the response she learned with her father and then carried forward to her adult workplace was one of submitting to the demands of others. If key distinctions between enmeshed and differentiated behavior are not made clear, Sarah may think the only options she has are to continue submitting or to flip the script and somehow find a way to oversee her boss. However, for Sarah, a more effective approach would be to learn to assert herself and explore "empowered" interpersonal territory that she has less familiarity with per history, which involves being self-possessed and able to be separate enough from those who make inappropriate demands of her that she can decide for herself what solutions best fit the situation. Subsequent chapters of this book will unpack such distinctions further to guide readers through the process of "coding" behavior using SASB to characterize clinical material accurately and precisely, to develop clinical case formulations, to monitor treatment processes and outcomes, and to guide therapist behavior. For now, the goal is just to get acquainted with SASB's underlying structure and concepts and obtain a sense of how they relate to clinical work.

## COGNITIVE AND AFFECTIVE PARALLELS TO SOCIAL BEHAVIOR

SASB's structural elements build on a rich scholarly tradition in interpersonal measurement. Benjamin's theory extends beyond this domain, however, to include consideration of the cognitive and affective precedents of interpersonal behavior. As will be described in detail in Chapter 2, these domains have a parallel structure based on cognitive and affective appraisals of focus, affiliation, and interdependence. Benjamin (2018) argued that due to natural biology, cognition, affect, and behavior have evolved in tandem such that they can be measured and tracked using parallel conceptual models. For example, the cognitive and affective parallels of 1-6: **Blame** would be cognitions involving condemnation and feelings characterizable as scorn. These models are extensions of the SASB model reviewed earlier and efforts to operationalize and test them using questionnaire and observational coding methods are underway (described in Chapter 2).

### Interactive Context

As an observational coding system, SASB has potential to be applied microanalytically to track relational behavior moment by moment. This includes the sequential patterning of behavior between two people, including their inputs and responses to each other over time. In other words, SASB can be used to track what happens in a relationship, including the therapy relationship, in real time. The interactive context of two or more people influencing each other in sequence is often key to understanding clinically relevant patterns, and this is at the core of a SASB-based understanding of patient patterns as well as the interactive flow of therapy sessions. For example, one patient may recoil and withdraw from others (2-7: <u>Recoil</u>) but only in response to perceived control (1-5: **Control**). A different patient may respond in the same way but only recoils in response to perceived abandonment (1-8: **Ignore**). The interactive, *input-response* nature of this information could be used differentially, for example, to help understand, predict, and defuse marital conflicts or to detect and address signs of a rupture in the therapeutic alliance. Additional contextual factors can also prove important for understanding when or why characteristic patterns will be enacted (e.g., only in relation to people outside the family, or with a certain gender, age, or role). As will be illustrated in examples throughout this book, a SASB-based definition of personality is usually thought of in contextualized terms that involve a process of interacting with others.

Interactive context can be captured not only through behavioral observation and narrative description but also with the SASB-based Intrex questionnaires (Benjamin, 2000), as will be explained in subsequent chapters. Intrex instruction sets can be tailored to capture specific state-by-trait-by-situation ratings. For example, the Intrex standard series asks patients how they and a significant other relate to one another (both partners are rated) when their relationship is at its best and again for when it is at its worst. The issue of how to handle the interface between moment-by-moment observation in sessions, repeating patterns acted out and described by patients, and specific states or circumstances that produce one pattern or another will be repeating themes in the examples used in this book.

## SASB's History and Track Record in Clinical Research

The SASB model has now had more than 50 years of application in research and clinical practice. A 2006 summary cited a wide range of representative topics researched using SASB's interpersonal lens (Benjamin, Rothweiler, & Critchfield, 2006). The list has grown considerably since then. In addition to interpersonal and psychodynamic approaches, the list of topics using SASB in published research includes diverse theoretical orientations, including cognitive behavior therapy (Critchfield et al., 2007; Hara et al., 2022; Karpiak & Benjamin, 2004), patient-centered (Wong & Pos, 2014), and emotion-focused (L. S. Greenberg & Malcolm, 2002) approaches, as well as application to a range of integrative methods (e.g., Bennett & Parry, 1998;

Critchfield et al., 2017). Across the various orientations, SASB has been directed toward questions of case conceptualization (Bennett & Parry, 1998; Critchfield et al., 2015), the impact of specific interventions (Ahmed et al., 2012; Vittengl et al., 2004), in-session processes of relating (e.g., alliance, rupture and repair processes, resistance episodes; Eubanks et al., 2019), the role of therapist and patient interpersonal histories to in-session relating (Hilliard et al., 2000), analysis of session content (e.g., dreams; Frick & Halevy, 2002), therapeutic change in relationships (Bedics et al., 2005), self-concepts (Bodlund & Armelius, 1994; Forsén Mantilla, Clinton, & Birgegård, 2019; Forsén Mantilla, Norring, & Birgegård, 2019; Jeanneau & Armelius, 2000), and more. Multiple modalities of treatment have also been explored, including application to individual, couple (Knobloch-Fedders, Caska-Wallace, et al., 2017), group (Canate, 2012; Dobner-Pereira, 2021; Tasca et al., 2011), and family (Stern et al., 2023; Woehrle et al., 2023) settings across a spectrum of diagnostic labels and severities.

Benjamin has long advocated for an interpersonal approach to diagnosis and case conceptualization (Benjamin, 1993, 2018; Benjamin, Wamboldt, & Critchfield, 2006; McLemore & Benjamin, 1979). Accordingly, Benjamin and others have applied SASB to topics of differential diagnosis (Panizo Jansana, 2020; T. L. Smith et al., 2003), category definition (Benjamin, 1993, 2018), and relational context for all major diagnostic groups, including mood disorders (Knobloch-Fedders, Critchfield, & Staab, 2017), psychosis (Armelius & Granberg, 2000; Harder, 2006), posttraumatic stress disorder (Knobloch-Fedders, Caska-Wallace, et al., 2017), substance use disorders (Florsheim & Moore, 2008; MacDonald et al., 2007), eating disorders (Monell et al., 2020), anxiety disorders (Erickson & Pincus, 2005), adolescent and adult suicidality (Harvell-Bowman et al., 2022; Ness et al., 2018), and personality disorder (Ruiz et al., 1999).

SASB's uses have also extended beyond psychopathology and its treatment to include issues in normative development (Beveridge & Berg, 2007), parenting (Bowman, 2018; Skowron et al., 2011), dating (Eastwick et al., 2010), spirituality (Stucker-Rozovsky, 2022; Vespa et al., 2018), teaching of psychology (Paddock et al., 2001), intergenerational patterns of relating (Critchfield & Benjamin, 2008, 2010; Cushing, 2003; Woehrle et al., 2023), medical health problems (T. W. Smith, Baron, Deits-Lebehn, et al., 2020; T. W. Smith, Baron, & Grove, 2014; Vespa et al., 2018, 2021), sleep (Gunn et al., 2017), behavioral genetics (McGonigle et al., 1993), and sports performance (Conroy, 2003; B. E. Smith, 2018). The range of applications and uses of the SASB model over 50 years speaks to the transtheoretical relevance of the interpersonal domain. As a descriptive system, SASB clearly provides valuable information across topics of key interest in human affairs.

## ORGANIZATION OF THIS BOOK

This book is intended to support clinical use and application of SASB. As such, each section focuses on a different topic of relevance to clinicians. Chapters 1 through 3 compose Part I and will give readers a basic understanding of SASB theory and application needed for more sophisticated uses of the model. Following the historical overview provided in this chapter, Chapter 2 presents several versions of the SASB model with examples of their varied clinical uses. Chapter 3 provides instructions for how to gather questionnaire and observational data to be interpreted through SASB's lens.

Part II comprises two chapters that address how SASB can be integrated and applied within existing clinical models. Chapter 4 focuses on transtheoretical use, while Chapter 5 provides an overview of IRT (Benjamin, 2003, 2006, 2018). IRT is the clinical method that Benjamin derived from observations made with the SASB lens. Our initial case discussion of Sarah suggests key components of the IRT perspective, which understands current interpersonal patterns in light of prior learning in close attachment relationships that continue to govern behavior via the internalized *family in the head*. IRT represents an integrative approach to treatment that incorporates elements of cognitive behavior, dynamic, and humanistic therapies. Use of techniques from each of these perspectives is guided by a comprehensive conceptual framework guided by a SASB-based case formulation. Subsequent chapters use clinical material from IRT sessions to illustrate principles of conceptualization and intervention.

Part III focuses on observing, assessing, and formulating patient patterns. SASB is used to develop and apply case formulation via the questionnaire-based method (Chapter 6), followed by the interview-based method (Chapter 7). The conceptualization method in part tracks evidence of the role that internalized relationships play when patterned repetitions are observed in interpersonal behavior across developmental context (e.g., acting like an important other person; expecting others to behave the same as others once did; treating oneself as other did). This includes patterns that can be enacted in the therapy relationship itself. In these chapters, repeating interpersonal patterns with the self and others are the primary lens through which (a) personality is understood and (b) symptoms and problems "make sense" and form the basis for therapeutic decision making.

In Part IV, Chapters 8 through 10 turn attention to treatment processes guided by IRT principles, with each topic cued to a SASB-based understanding of patient problems, the therapist's choice of intervention and in-session manner of delivery, and therapeutic outcomes. We provide diverse case examples from patients referred to the IRT clinic due to high levels of diagnostic

24 • *Basic Principles*

complexity, severity, and nonresponse to prior treatment attempts. Clinicians will gain an understanding of SASB-based methods to organize that complexity and enhance patient motivation for change. Names and details are changed to protect confidentiality, but the SASB-based descriptions are true to the original cases. The therapy perspective includes the idea noted earlier in the case of Sarah, that psychopathology often reflects misdirected attempts to adapt to new circumstances by using old interpersonal strategies and views.

As described in Chapter 5 and illustrated with additional case examples, maladaptive patterns (with the self and others) often resist change because they are linked to attachment with important others. In IRT, a key hypothesis is that the persistence of problem patterns represents continued attempts to receive real or imagined love, acceptance, security, or restitution from key attachment figures or their internalized representations. Behaviors enacted out of this motivation are termed *gifts of love* (Benjamin, 1993). A gift of love is suggested in the case of Sarah, described earlier. Sarah stated in her clinical interview, "I tried to get Dad to love me by doing all that he said," and went on to link this to her desire to keep working to the point of extreme burnout and serious contemplation of suicide. The IRT approach uses SASB not only to increase the accuracy of case conceptualization but also to use awareness to help patients like Sarah to give up the gift of love motivation and choose more adaptive ways of being. The associated change process can be difficult and entail substantial grief as a person comes to terms with problematic aspects of the internalized attachment. In Sarah's case, it would mean giving up the assignment she had accepted to get her father's love and affirmation by doing the impossible in relation to her boss. Strategies for detecting, working with, and therapeutically responding to similar attachment-linked patterns, as well as summaries of evidence for that approach, will be provided in these final chapters focused on treatment processes and outcomes (Chapters 8–10).

In summary, it is our hope that readers finish this book feeling comfortable with a new clinical tool, SASB, that they can use to enhance specificity, empathy, and efficacy in their work across theoretical orientations and clinical settings. Readers will learn how to use SASB and IRT methods to help even the "stuck" and "complex" patients with whom they work to access motivation and internal permission to change, even when it means letting go of wishes to finally be loved and accepted by an internalized family in the head.

# 2 THE STRUCTURAL ANALYSIS OF SOCIAL BEHAVIOR MODELS

*Comprehensive Description of the Interpersonal Domain*

The Structural Analysis of Social Behavior (SASB) can be thought of as a set of related models. These include the full, cluster, and quadrant models. Each has the same underlying structure and logic but offers a different degree of resolution. Each version involves the same, three-component structure of (a) focus (other, self, or introject), (b) affiliation (love vs. attack), and (c) interdependence (enmeshment/closeness vs. differentiation/distance). This chapter describes a variety of SASB models and different degrees of resolution to articulate elements of the underlying theory, moving toward a "happy medium" model that is well suited for many applications. The chapter concludes with a description of Benjamin's parallel models for cognition and affect. The hope is that readers will become comfortable with the underlying concepts and structure of the models and then be ready to follow and apply their use to diverse topics and sustained clinical examples in the chapters that follow.

---

https://doi.org/10.1037/0000403-002
*Structural Analysis of Social Behavior (SASB): A Primer for Clinical Use*, by
K. L. Critchfield and L. S. Benjamin
Copyright © 2024 by the American Psychological Association. All rights reserved.

26 • *Basic Principles*

## BASIC STRUCTURE OF SASB: FOCUS, AFFILIATION, AND INTERDEPENDENCE

### Focus

*Focus* describes who a given behavior is directed toward (i.e., is to, for, or about). Focus tracks one of the key issues that needs to be determined quickly in any interaction: "Is this primarily about you or me?" Benjamin (1974) argued that the focus distinction, along with the other two SASB dimensions (affiliation and interdependence), is linked to our evolutionary heritage as social animals. An issue of central importance is to answer the question: "Is this about you, about me, or about my relationship with myself?" Focus is used to determine which of the three SASB planes can be used to represent a given behavior.

As illustrated graphically in Figure 2.1, behavior that is to, for, or about another person with whom someone interacts is termed *focus on other*. These behaviors consist of transitive actions and can be thought of as prototypically parentlike, active, or initiating in nature. This focus includes behaviors like control, emancipation, active love, and attack. These behaviors are concerned with what is happening to the other person, rather than with the actor.

By contrast, behaviors that are to, for, or about the self in relation to others are termed *focus on self*. These behaviors are concerned with what is happening

**FIGURE 2.1. Focus**

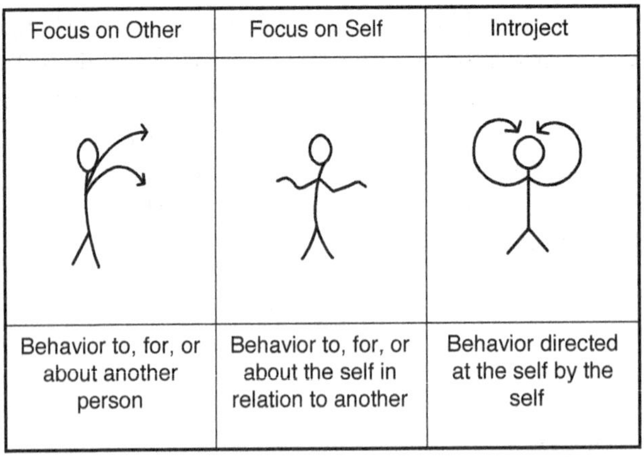

| Focus on Other | Focus on Self | Introject |
|---|---|---|
| | | |
| Behavior to, for, or about another person | Behavior to, for, or about the self in relation to another | Behavior directed at the self by the self |

*Note.* From "Use of the SASB Dimensional Model to Develop Treatment Plans for Personality Disorders: I. Narcissism," by L. S. Benjamin, 1987, *Journal of Personality Disorders, 1*(1), p. 48 (https://doi.org/10.1521/pedi.1987.1.1.43). Copyright 1987 by Guilford Press. Reprinted with permission.

to the person doing the behaving, rather than the other person. These behaviors are prototypically childlike, reactive, or responsive to the (real or imagined) initiations of others. They reflect intransitive states and include behaviors like submit, separate, reactive love, and recoil.

*Introject* is the term used for self-treatment (i.e., behaviors directed toward the self by the self). These behaviors are intrapersonal or intrapsychic in nature and do not require that others be directly involved. They are about the self in relation to the self. Examples include self-control, self-emancipate, self-love, and self-attack.

### Affiliation and Interdependence

Each SASB surface is organized around two dimensions: affiliation and interdependence. *Affiliation* is represented on the horizontal axis and consists of a dimension that ranges from extremes of hostility (on the left) to extremes of friendliness (on the right). This dimension captures a range of behaviors extending from murderous attack, annihilation, and recoiling in fear at one pole to loving, tender sexuality, and ecstatic response at the other.

*Interdependence* (vs. independence) defines the vertical dimension and ranges from extremes of enmeshment (e.g., control and submission) at the bottom pole to extremes of differentiation (e.g., emancipating and separating) at the top.

## THE FULL MODEL: PUTTING THE THREE DIMENSIONS TOGETHER

The full SASB model is the most detailed version and is presented in Figure 2.2. Close inspection of this model is useful for getting an intuitive feel for each underlying dimension as it interacts with the others. As shown in Figure 2.2, focus distinguishes the three planes (other, self, and introject), while specific behaviors reflect unique combinations of affiliation and interdependence to form a diamond-shaped structure. The numbering system will be described later, but first we discuss how the underlying dimensions work together.

### Getting a Feel for Focus in Combination With Affiliation and Interdependence

Figure 2.3 strips detail out of the full model to help readers get a sense of how the underlying dimensions of affiliation and interdependence change based on whether focus on other, focus on self, or introject is considered.

28 • Basic Principles

FIGURE 2.2. Structural Analysis of Social Behavior (SASB) Full Model

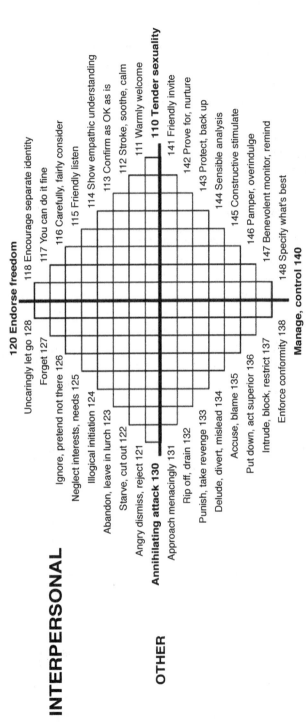

**FIGURE 2.2. Structural Analysis of Social Behavior (SASB) Full Model (Continued)**

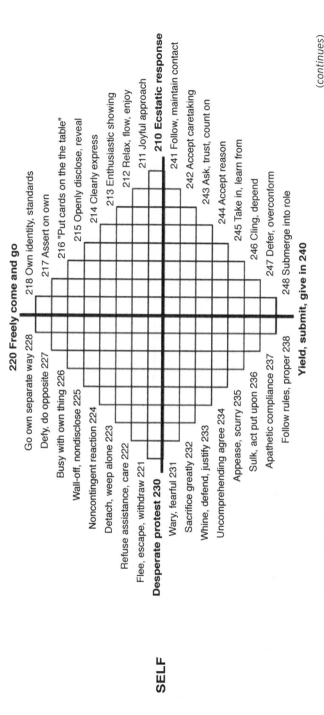

(continues)

30 • Basic Principles

FIGURE 2.2. Structural Analysis of Social Behavior (SASB) Full Model (*Continued*)

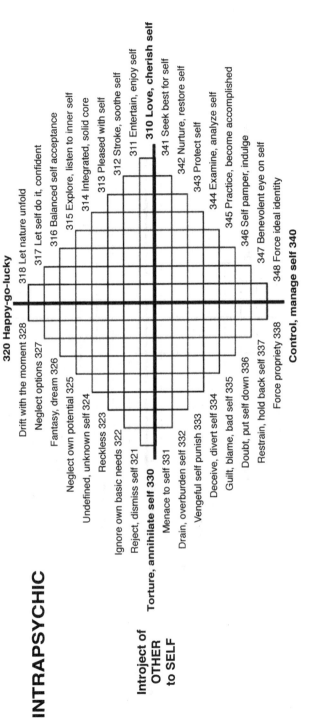

*Note.* From "Structural Analysis of Differentiation Failure," by L. S. Benjamin, 1979, *Psychiatry*, 42(1), p. 6 (https://doi.org/10.1080/00332747.1979.11024003). Copyright 1979 by Taylor & Francis. Reprinted with permission.

## FIGURE 2.3. Underlying Dimensional Structure for All Structural Analysis of Social Behavior (SASB) Model Versions

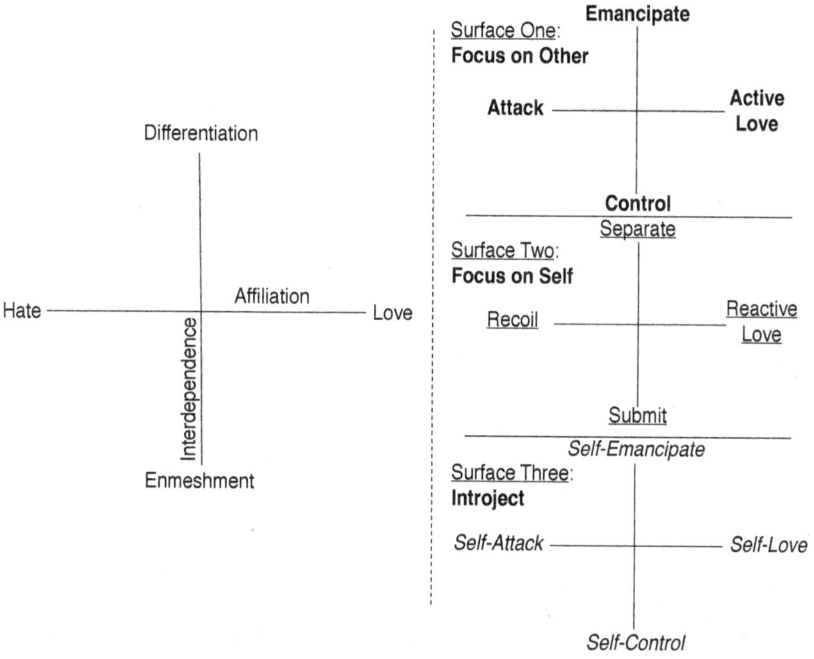

*Note.* Pictured with focus collapsed (left) and separate (right).

On the left of Figure 2.3, the structure of the SASB model is displayed when focus is not considered. It offers the broad terms we have used already to describe the overarching structure: *love versus hate* and *enmeshment versus differentiation*. When focus is introduced, three separate structures emerge. Some consideration of how their language differs should give a stronger sense of the focus distinction. For example, the lower right of each diamond involves warm enmeshment. Each region contains behavior that respectively involves protection (focus on other), trust (focus on self), and self-protection (introject). The difference in focus can be illustrated with a simple example: If you offer an umbrella to another in the rain; this is different from accepting the umbrella and different from pulling out the umbrella you remembered to bring for yourself.

Comparing language at each pole, the part of the model representing differentiation (i.e., relational distance) is now divided into one part characterized as emancipating others and another part characterized as separating

32 • *Basic Principles*

from others. In this context, focus is the distinction between letting someone be free to do as they please (focus on other) versus taking leave of someone else to go act independently (focus on self). To keep the distinction in mind, it might be useful to recall that focus on other is parentlike (surface 1) and focus on self is childlike (surface 2). A parentlike example at this location on the model would be to give a child permission, while a childlike example might be to take off on one's own or otherwise assert their own separation.

For the extreme of friendliness, the language of dual focus offers "active" versus "reactive" love. This can be thought of as expressions that give versus receive affectionate behavior. Focus on other might consist of giving a warm compliment or a backrub, while focus on self would be to show sincere signs of enjoying or taking pleasure in what is offered, perhaps through laughter, smiles, or other expressions of delight that fit a warm context. Interpersonal hostility also has a complementary pairing that differs by focus. Directed toward another, hostility involves threat, attack, and destructive action. The complementary position focused on self involves recoiling away from another person in a way that shows fear or perception of a direct threat, including fleeing and freezing behaviors.

At the bottom poles of the model, *control* and *submit* both describe complementary aspects at the extreme of interdependent enmeshment that is neither hostile nor friendly. These might be understood as a context in which performance and discipline are essential. To direct the actions of another person—for example, in roles such as a coach, teacher, musical conductor, military commander, boss, or even medical provider (e.g., surgeon)—requires focus to be on the other person or persons and/or their behavior. To be well coordinated in the role as an athlete, student, musician, soldier, employee, surgical patient, and so on requires a conforming submission of the self in relation to the other. A similar pair of complementary behaviors is positioned at the top of the model (extreme of differentiation) in the form of freeing or emancipating another person (focus on other), paired with taking leave or separating or asserting one's own values or identity in a way that is neither friendly nor hostile. The phrase "live and let live" captures some of the character of this warmth-neutral independence. Here, one person "let's go" of another, through forms (including tacitly) of allowing, facilitating, or inviting the other person to do as they wish. The complementary position of neutral, self-focused separation might be imagined as two coworkers working simultaneously on their separate tasks before reconvening together, or as small children engaged in parallel play.

As can be seen by inspecting the respective labels, focus-on-other behaviors often have the "feel" of an individual holding or exerting relative power or authority, whereas focus-on-self behaviors prototypically have the feel of being lower in a hierarchy. The model was developed in part with parent–child prototypes in mind, per Schaefer's (1965) model. Imagining other relationships involving power differentials, such as boss–employee, teacher–student, therapist–patient, or commanding officer–subordinate, can also be useful prototypes to consider when making decisions about where a given behavior codes into the model. It may helpful to ask: "What kind of role does it seem like this person is playing right now?" Readers should keep in mind, however, that although these prototypes give a "feel for focus," the distinction is not actually defined by power differentials. Instead, focus is defined by the difference between transitive action (i.e., attentional focus is on another person) and intransitive action (attentional focus is on the self). Prototypes based on power differentials can be useful for understanding SASB's structure; however, in practice, it is possible for behavior to occur in ways that run counter to each prototype. A child can be parentlike and try to exert control (1-5: **Control**) over a parent, a therapist can sulk (2-6: <u>Sulk</u>) in relation to a patient, and so on.

Finally, surface 3 (introject) uses language that should help make clear that these behaviors have reference primarily to the person doing the behaving, but otherwise mirror the focus-on-other set of constructs (i.e., control the self vs. free the self, love the self vs. attack the self). These behaviors consist of transitive action directed by the self, toward the self. This surface allows tracking of an individual's relationship with themselves, without involvement of others. The poles include allowing oneself to do, be, or feel as one wishes (top); to engage in loving action to the self (right); to manage, control, monitor, or constrain the self (bottom); or to destructively attack, reject, or deplete the self (left).

### Sensing Unique Blends of Affiliation and Interdependence Around Each Model Surface

SASB's underlying dimensional structure can be sensed through close inspection of the model positions. Figure 2.4 extracts two contrasting regions from the full model's focus-on-other surface. As one reads across the sequence of behaviors listed in the upper right, it is possible to sense how these behaviors are shifting toward more warmth or less warmth simultaneously with more distance or less distance. Behaviors in proximity to one another are more similar than those farther away.

Another sampling of behavior is provided in the lower left of Figure 2.4. For these behaviors, more versus less hostility can be perceived as changing

**FIGURE 2.4. Behaviors Organized by Their Underlying Dimensions (Focus on Other as an Example)**

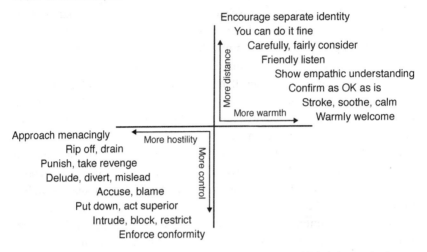

*Note.* The focus-on-other plane is shown with added arrows and labels to emphasize underlying dimensional constructs. The figure shows only half of the items from the full model (see Benjamin, 1979, p. 6) to narrow in on their structural and conceptual patterning.

simultaneously with more versus less control. Behaviors that have the opposite values for both underlying dimensions (i.e., 180° apart) should readily be perceived as opposites. For example, "Accuse, blame" contrasts the structurally opposite position of "Friendly, listen." Meanwhile, "Put down, act superior" is maximally different from "Carefully, fairly consider."

## Logic of the Diamond

The diamond-shaped structure produced for each surface has implications for both theory and measurement (Benjamin, 2005). Each position on the full model (Figure 2.2) involves a unique proportional contribution of the underlying dimensions. The way this occurs is consistent with the mathematical formula for a diamond: $|x| + |y| = 1$. For example, to return to Figure 2.2, the behavior labeled "120 Endorse freedom" (the top of the top-most diamond) contains a maximum amount of emancipation directed toward others, while also being at the neutral point regarding friendliness/hostility. If we count the boxes shown in the model to express this fractionally, this behavior is nine of nine possible units away from the center in the direction of independence (i.e., nine positive units on the $y$-axis, or nine ninths of independence) and zero of nine units for affiliation ($x$-axis; zero ninths of affiliation).[1] The adjacent point to the right, "118 Encourage separate identity," involves eight of nine units of independence and one unit of friendliness. The same pattern continues for each model position and follows the logic that the units of $y$ and the units of $x$ added together (after taking the absolute value to drop any minus signs) will always equal the same number. In the first example, $|9/9| + |0/9| = 1$; and in the second, adjacent example, $|8/9| + |1/9| = 1$.

One of the reasons Benjamin (1974, 2005) chose the diamond shape is her assertion that as a matter of evolutionary survival, humans have needed to rapidly assess and respond to key questions about social encounters: "Who is this about? Are we in a friendly or hostile space? Are we connected or separate?" Use of a diamond is consistent with the idea that a perceptual process would be focused simply on the basic, linear intensity of each underlying dimension. The structure of a circle, by contrast, is mathematically defined by squaring the underlying dimensions (i.e., $x^2 + y^2 = 1$), implying the need for additional layers of cognitive or perceptual complexity that would be inconsistent with Benjamin's (2018) articulation of a natural biological view of interpersonal behavior.

A more important point for the current chapter is that the diamond shape emphasizes the underlying dimensions. The *primitive basics* of love, aggression, power, and separate territory are always at the poles and are believed to have been essential to our survival and evolution as social, herd animals (Benjamin, 2005, 2018). The diamond shape graphically emphasizes the primacy of these primitive basics (Benjamin, 1974, 2005). Unlike a purely circular structure, SASB's underlying axes cannot be arbitrarily rotated. In SASB theory and practice, it is the underlying dimensions that are emphasized, rather than the categories of behavior listed at the perimeter. For example, if one person says to another, "I hear you, I'm listening," then the SASB rater should not simply decide this represents "115 Friendly listen" on the full model based on the word "listen." Instead, as described in greater detail in Chapter 3, each underlying dimension needs to be determined and checked to see whether the meaning is captured well by the resulting code. The fact that a single statement might be imagined at various points around the SASB model helps underscore that determination of underlying dimensions is key. For example, the same "I hear you, I'm listening" could be said in a manner

---

[1] The reason for use of nine units here anticipates SASB's thematic tracks as will be discussed later in connection with Table 2.1.

36 • *Basic Principles*

**FIGURE 2.5. Structural Analysis of Social Behavior (SASB) Quadrant Model**

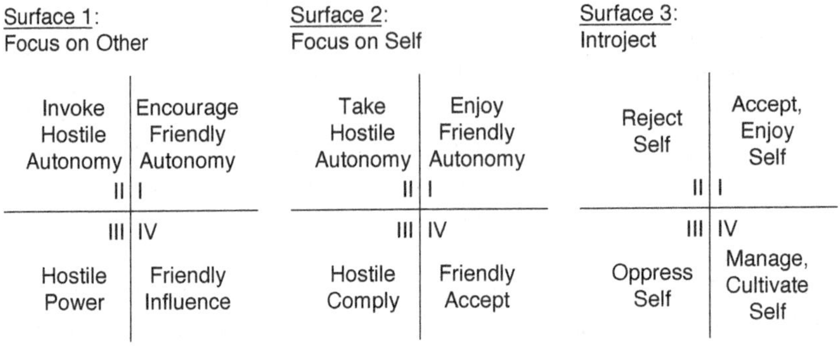

Surface 1:
Focus on Other

Surface 2:
Focus on Self

Surface 3:
Introject

| Invoke Hostile Autonomy | Encourage Friendly Autonomy | Take Hostile Autonomy | Enjoy Friendly Autonomy | Reject Self | Accept, Enjoy Self |
|---|---|---|---|---|---|
| II | I | II | I | II | I |
| III | IV | III | IV | III | IV |
| Hostile Power | Friendly Influence | Hostile Comply | Friendly Accept | Oppress Self | Manage, Cultivate Self |

*Note.* From "Structural Analysis of Differentiation Failure," by L. S. Benjamin, 1979, *Psychiatry, 42*(1), p. 13 (https://doi.org/10.1080/00332747.1979.11024003). Copyright 1979 by Taylor & Francis. Reprinted with permission.

and a context that fits any of the following: (a) "115 Friendly listen" (e.g., a sensitive therapist encouraging a patient to express); (b) "238 Follow rules, proper" (e.g., a person confirming they are hearing their instructions for a task); (c) "135 Accuse, blame" (e.g., said angrily to emphasize how a partner is not doing these things); and (d) "126 Ignore, pretend not there" (e.g., said mindlessly to a partner in the other room while otherwise engaged on social media).[2] Still other positions are possible.

## THE QUADRANT MODEL

The quadrant model comes directly from the logic outlined earlier about the likely need for rapid perception of interpersonal behavior using a binary logic for each dimension. In this version, only three binary distinctions are included: (a) What is the focus? (other, self); (b) Is it friendly or hostile? (yes or no); and (c) Are we together or separate? (yes or no). A parallel surface includes introject and is shown in Figure 2.5.

In addition to descriptive labels, the quadrants are organized with a number from I to IV in counterclockwise order (following mathematical conventions). As might be expected, the quadrant model is a simple application that emphasizes the simultaneous combination of underlying dimensions

---

[2]Some of these examples involve potential complex codes as well, involving more than one simultaneous position. The point here is that the underlying dimensions, rather than surface level "words," of the model are the emphasis. Coding of complex behavior will be discussed later in this chapter.

The Structural Analysis of Social Behavior Models • 37

(and so can miss extreme behavior at the poles). Despite its coarse resolution, this model can be highly useful for rapidly organizing and tracking behavior in a real-time conversation without getting "lost in the weeds" (e.g., in clinical work with groups, couples, or families). The quadrant labels also help round out an understanding of the types of behavior represented in each of SASB's broad regions. More specific clinical applications will be noted in later chapters.

## THEMATIC TRACKS WITHIN EACH QUADRANT

As shown in Figure 2.2, the full model includes all regions of the quadrant model but defines eight numbered positions within each quadrant, plus another for each pole. Each position on the full model has a descriptive label and a three-digit number that tracks the various conceptual and structural connections of the model. To decode these, the first full model digit identifies the surface (1 = focus on other, 2 = focus on self, and 3 = introject). A second digit indicates the position on the quadrant model (counterclockwise from 1 to 4). The final, third digit ranges from 0 to 8 and identifies the primary theme or track for each behavior (see Table 2.1). Tracks are labeled as 0 at each pole. Numbers 1 through 8 move away from the horizontal poles in both vertical directions.

The track descriptions suggest some of the more nuanced aspects of SASB-based interpersonal measurement. These will not be emphasized in this book beyond noting their existence as part of the full model, although clinician readers will likely easily perceive their clinical utility. For example, behaviors at the poles are considered the primitive basics, while varying

**TABLE 2.1. Structural Analysis of Social Behavior Full Model Track Descriptions**

| Track | Description |
|:---:|:---|
| 0 | Primitive basics |
| 1 | Approach–avoidance |
| 2 | Need fulfillment |
| 3 | Attachment |
| 4 | Logic, communications |
| 5 | Attention to self-development |
| 6 | Balance in relationship |
| 7 | Intimacy–distance |
| 8 | Identity |

Note. From "Structural Analysis of Differentiation Failure," by L. S. Benjamin, 1979, Psychiatry, 42(1), p. 7 (https://doi.org/10.1080/00332747.1979.11024003). Copyright 1979 by Taylor & Francis. Reprinted with permission.

38 • *Basic Principles*

blends of the underlying dimensions reflect a range of clinical and developmental themes invoked by social relationships.

## THE CLUSTER MODEL: A HAPPY MEDIUM FOR CLINICAL PRACTICE AND RESEARCH

The SASB cluster model provides an intermediate level of resolution between the quadrant and full models, using eight regions defined by collections or *clusters* of behavior. The cluster model is presented in Figures 2.6 and 2.7. One or two words are used to describe the behaviors involved in each cluster, and a two-digit code is assigned. As in the full model, the first number refers to the surface (1 = focus on other, 2 = focus on self, and 3 = introject). The second number moves clockwise from 1 through 8, starting at the top of each surface.

The level of detail in the cluster model allows for careful plotting of patterns for research and clinical assessment, without being burdensome. The descriptive labels involve lay language that is useful for reflecting behaviors and themes in clinical processes and narratives. The balance between user-friendliness and precision has led the cluster model to be the primary version implemented in output of the SASB-based Intrex questionnaire and in the observational coding approach (both described in Chapter 3).

The cluster model with single-word descriptors (Figure 2.7) will be the primary reference for clinical data and examples presented in this book. This is done partly for convenience of exposition and partly so that readers can have this scaffolding as they practice making discernments based on the model. However, readers are reminded that SASB is ultimately defined by its underlying dimensions rather than being a set of categories defined by specific words. Throughout this book, we will use the convention of applying different typefaces to show the focus distinction (other in **bold**, self in underline, and introject in *italics*) while also providing the numeric positions. Figure 1.1 in Chapter 1 places all three SASB surfaces in one simplified presentation of this model. Readers are encouraged to access it often as a convenient reference. Additionally, Table 2.2 presents a precise mapping of the cluster model with the full model.

## SIMPLE VERSUS COMPLEX BEHAVIORS

Up to this point, examples and illustrations have emphasized single points on the SASB models. However, humans regularly engage in complex and mixed behavior, such as simultaneously expressing friendliness and hostility,

**FIGURE 2.6. Structural Analysis of Social Behavior (SASB) Cluster Model (Two-Word Descriptors)**

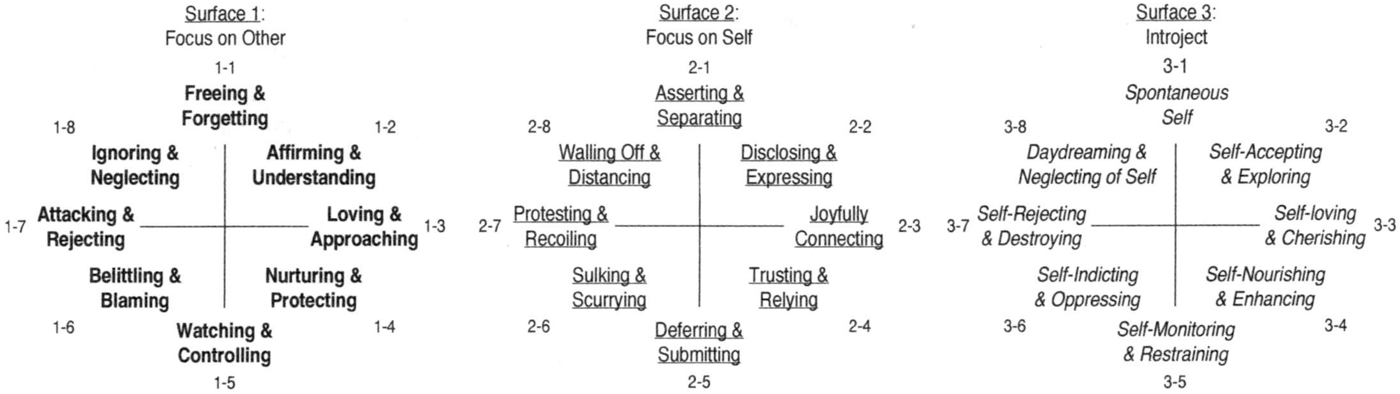

Surface 1:
Focus on Other

1-1 Freeing & Forgetting

1-2 Affirming & Understanding

1-3 Loving & Approaching

1-4 Nurturing & Protecting

1-5 Watching & Controlling

1-6 Belittling & Blaming

1-7 Attacking & Rejecting

1-8 Ignoring & Neglecting

Surface 2:
Focus on Self

2-1 Asserting & Separating

2-2 Disclosing & Expressing

2-3 Joyfully Connecting

2-4 Trusting & Relying

2-5 Deferring & Submitting

2-6 Sulking & Scurrying

2-7 Protesting & Recoiling

2-8 Walling Off & Distancing

Surface 3:
Introject

3-1 Spontaneous Self

3-2 Self-Accepting & Exploring

3-3 Self-loving & Cherishing

3-4 Self-Nourishing & Enhancing

3-5 Self-Monitoring & Restraining

3-6 Self-Indicting & Oppressing

3-7 Self-Rejecting & Destroying

3-8 Daydreaming & Neglecting of Self

*Note.* From "Use of the SASB Dimensional Model to Develop Treatment Plans for Personality Disorders: I. Narcissism," by L. S. Benjamin, 1987, *Journal of Personality Disorders, 1*(1), p. 53 (https://doi.org/10.1521/pedi.1987.1.1.43). Copyright 1987 by Guilford Press. Reprinted with permission.

**40** • *Basic Principles*

**FIGURE 2.7. Structural Analysis of Social Behavior (SASB) Cluster Model (Single-Word Descriptors)**

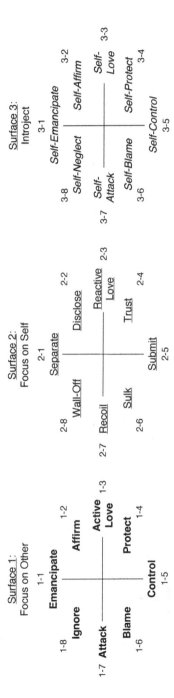

*Note.* The figure combines two figures: Adapted from *Interpersonal Diagnosis and Treatment of Personality Disorders* (2nd ed., p. 55), by L. S. Benjamin, 1996, Guilford Press. Copyright 1996 by Guilford Press; with numeric codes added from "'Use of the SASB Dimensional Model to Develop Treatment Plans for Personality Disorders: I. Narcissism," by L. S. Benjamin, 1987, *Journal of Personality Disorders*, *1*(1), p. 53 (https://doi.org/10.1521/pedi.1987.1.1.43). Copyright 1987 by Guilford Press. Adapted with permission.

The Structural Analysis of Social Behavior Models • 41

**TABLE 2.2. Mapping the Cluster and Structural Analysis of Social Behavior (SASB) Full Model Positions**

| Cluster model | Full model |
| --- | --- |
| | **Surface 1: Focus on Other** |
| 1-1: **Emancipate** | 127: Self forgets all about other, their agreements, plans |
| | 128: Without concern, self lets other do and be anything at all |
| | 120: Self peacefully leaves other completely on other's own |
| | 118: Self leaves other free to do and be whatever other thinks is best |
| | 117: Believing other does things well, self leaves other to do them other's own way |
| 1-2: **Affirm** | 116: Self lets other speak freely and hears other even if they disagree |
| | 115: Self really hears other, acknowledges other's views even if they disagree |
| | 114: Self clearly understands other and likes other even if they disagree |
| | 113: Self likes other and thinks other is fine just as other is |
| 1-3: **Active Love** | 112: Self gently, lovingly soothes other without asking anything in return |
| | 111: Full of happy smiles, self lovingly greets other just as other is |
| | 110: With loving tenderness, self connects sexually if other wants it |
| | 141: Self warmly and cheerfully invites other to be in touch as often as other wants |
| | 142: Self provides for, nurtures, and takes care of other |
| 1-4: **Protect** | 143: Self lovingly looks after other's interests and takes steps to protect other |
| | 144: With kindness and good sense, self figures out and explains things to other |
| | 145: Self gets other interested and teaches other how to understand and do things |
| | 146: Self pays close attention to other to figure out and take care of other's needs |
| 1-5: **Control** | 147: For other's own good, self checks on and reminds other of what to do |
| | 148: For other's own good, self tells other exactly what to do, be, and think |
| | 140: Self controls other in a matter-of-fact way. Self takes charge of everything |
| | 138: Self makes other follow self's rules and ideas of what is right and proper |
| | 137: Self butts in and takes over. Self blocks and restricts other |

(continues)

42 • *Basic Principles*

**TABLE 2.2. Mapping the Cluster and Structural Analysis of Social Behavior (SASB) Full Model Positions (*Continued*)**

| Cluster model | Full model |
|---|---|
| 1-6: **Blame** | 136: Self puts other down, tells other that other's ways are wrong and self's are better |
| | 135: Self accuses and blames other. Self tries to get other to admit that other is wrong |
| | 134: Self misleads other, disguises things, and tries to throw other off track |
| | 133: Self harshly punishes and tortures other. Self takes revenge |
| 1-7: **Attack** | 132: Self rips other off. Self tears, grabs all self can from other |
| | 131: Looking very mean, self follows other and tries to hurt other |
| | 130: Self murders, kills, and destroys other; self leaves other as a useless heap |
| | 121: Self angrily leaves other out. Self refuses to have anything to do with other |
| | 122: Self could help, but leaves other to go without what other really needs |
| 1-8: **Ignore** | 123: When needed most, self abandons other, leaves other alone with trouble |
| | 124: Self ignores the facts and offers other unbelievable nonsense and craziness |
| | 125: Self neglects other, other's interests, or needs |
| | 126: Self just doesn't notice or pay attention to other at all |
| | **Surface 2: Focus on Self** |
| 2-1: <u>Separate</u> | 227: To do own thing, self does the opposite of what other wants |
| | 228: Self goes own separate way apart from other |
| | 220: Self freely comes and goes; does own thing separately from other |
| | 218: Self has a clear sense of who self is separately from other |
| | 217: Self speaks up, clearly and firmly states self's own separate position |
| 2-2: <u>Disclose</u> | 216: Self is straightforward, truthful, and clear with other about self's own position |
| | 215: Self freely and openly talks with other about their innermost self |
| | 214: Self expresses themself clearly in a warm and friendly way |
| | 213: Self is joyful, happy, and very open with other |

The Structural Analysis of Social Behavior Models • 43

**TABLE 2.2. Mapping the Cluster and Structural Analysis of Social Behavior (SASB) Full Model Positions (*Continued*)**

| Cluster model | Full model |
| --- | --- |
| 2-3: Reactive Love | 212: Self relaxes, lets go, enjoys, feels wonderful about being with other |
| | 211: Self is very happy, playful, joyful, delighted to be with other |
| | 210: Self joyfully, happily, very lovingly responds to other sexually |
| | 241: Self warmly happily stays around, keeps in touch with other |
| | 242: Self warmly, comfortably accepts other's help and caregiving |
| 2-4: Trust | 243: Self trusts other, comfortably counts on other to come through when needed |
| | 244: Self willingly accepts, goes along with other's reasonable suggestions and ideas |
| | 245: Self learns from other, comfortably takes advice and guidance from other |
| | 246: Self trustingly depends on other to meet every need |
| 2-5: Submit | 247: Self checks with other about everything because self cares greatly what other thinks |
| | 248: Self feels, does, thinks, becomes what they think other wants |
| | 240: Self gives into other, yields and submits to other |
| | 238: Self mindlessly obeys other's rules, ideas about how things should be done |
| | 237: Self gives up, helplessly does things other's way without views of self's own |
| 2-6: Sulk | 236: Self caves in to other and does things other's way, but self sulks and fumes about it |
| | 235: To avoid other's disapproval, self bottles up rage and resentment and complies |
| | 234: Full of doubt and tension, self sort of goes along with other's views anyway |
| | 233: Self whines, unhappily protests, tries to defend themself from other |
| 2-7: Recoil | 232: Self very hatefully, bitterly, resentfully, chooses to let other's needs prevail |
| | 231: Self is very tense, shaky, wary, fearful with other |
| | 230: In great pain and rage, self screams and shouts that other is destroying self |
| | 221: Boiling over with rage and fear, self tries to escape, flee, hide from other |
| | 222: Self furiously, angrily, hatefully refuses to accept other's offers to help out |

*(continues)*

44 • *Basic Principles*

**TABLE 2.2. Mapping the Cluster and Structural Analysis of Social Behavior (SASB) Full Model Positions (*Continued*)**

| Cluster model | Full model |
|---|---|
| 2-8: <u>Wall-Off</u> | 223: Self bitterly, angrily detaches from other, asks nothing; self weeps alone about other |
| | 224: Self reacts to what other says or does in strange, unconnected, unrelated ways |
| | 225: Self walls themselves off from other, doesn't hear, doesn't react |
| | 226: Self is too busy and alone with their "own thing" to be with other |
| **Surface 3: Introjective Focus** | |
| 3-1: *Self-Emancipate* | 327: Self lets important matters, choices, slip by without paying much attention |
| | 328: Self lets self drift with the moment. Self has no internal direction, goals |
| | 320: Self lets self go along with today as it is and doesn't plan for tomorrow |
| | 318: Without concern, self lets self be free to turn into whatever they will |
| | 317: Self freely, easily, confidently lets self do whatever comes naturally |
| 3-2: *Self-Affirm* | 316: Knowing their faults and strong points, self comfortably lets self be as is |
| | 315: Self comfortably lets self hear and go by their own deepest inner feelings |
| | 314: Self understands and likes self just as they are. Self feels solid, "together" |
| | 313: Self lets self feel glad about and pleased with themself just as self is |
| 3-3: *Active Self-Love* | 312: Self gently and warmly appreciates self just for being themself |
| | 311: Self likes self very much, and feels good when able to just "be" with self |
| | 310: Self tenderly, lovingly cherishes and adores themself as is |
| | 341: Self keeps self open to people, places, things that would be very good for self |
| | 342: Self naturally and easily provides for, nurtures, and takes care of themself |
| 3-4: *Self-Protect* | 343: Self comfortably looks after their own interests and protects themself |
| | 344: To help self, self tries to figure out what really is going on within self |

The Structural Analysis of Social Behavior Models • 45

**TABLE 2.2. Mapping the Cluster and Structural Analysis of Social Behavior (SASB) Full Model Positions (*Continued*)**

| Cluster model | Full model |
| --- | --- |
| | 345: Self practices and works on developing worthwhile skills, ways of being |
| | 346: Self puts much energy into figuring what self is going to need and how to get it |
| 3-5: *Self-Control* | 347: Self keeps an eye on self to be sure to do what should and ought to be done |
| | 348: Self tries very hard to make themself be like an ideal |
| | 340: Self has a habit of keeping very tight control over themself |
| | 338: Self puts much energy into being sure self follows standards and is proper |
| | 337: Self very carefully watches, holds back and restrains self |
| 3-6: *Self-Blame* | 336: Self puts self down, tells self that they have done everything wrong |
| | 335: Self accuses and blames self until self feels guilty, bad, ashamed |
| | 334: Self makes self do or be things known to be not right for self; self fools self |
| | 333: Self harshly punishes, tortures, "takes it out" on themself |
| 3-7: *Self-Attack* | 332: Self tears away at and empties self by greatly overburdening themself |
| | 331: Self thinks up ways to hurt and destroy self; self is their own worst enemy |
| | 330: Self lets themself murder, kill, destroy, reduce themself to nothing |
| | 321: Self angrily rejects self as worthless and leaves what happens to fate |
| | 322: Self lets their own serious sickness and injury go unattended |
| 3-8: *Self-Neglect* | 323: Self recklessly, carelessly lets self end up in self-destructive situations |
| | 324: Self ignores and does not bother to know their real self |
| | 325: Self neglects self, doesn't try to develop good skills, ways of being |
| | 326: Self lets self daydream instead of doing what they need to do for self |

*Note.* Data adapted from SASB coding resource figures included in Benjamin (2000).

46 • *Basic Principles*

connection plus disengagement, or mixed focus, all in the same words or actions. For example, sarcasm can be used by close friends to express warm connection through criticism. Formally, this is called *complex behavior*, in the sense that it involves simultaneous use of multiple SASB positions.[3] The cheery comment, "Nice hair!" (upon seeing a friend who just arrived and took off a hat, leaving their hair a mess), might be an example of something friendly (implicitly, a friendly greeting: "Hello! Welcome. I like you and see you there") paired with something more hostile (implicitly, a put-down: "Your hair is a mess and you should do something about it"), or 1-2: **Affirm** and 1-6: **Blame**. The emphasis on one part of the message or the other may be expressed by the relative intensity of each part.

Like sarcasm, many forms of humor involve simultaneous, paradoxical juxtaposition of contrasting behaviors. Other forms are less interpersonally risky and can be benign or even enhance a sense of warmth. For example, a therapist's sincere disclosure celebrating a patient's progress can include a complex focus. The statement, "I'm really happy to see how you are making so many positive changes in your life," combines 2-2: <u>Disclose</u> ("I'm really happy" has attentional focus on the therapist) with 1-2: **Affirm** ("you are making so many positive changes in your life" has attentional focus on the patient).

Less benign examples are commonly encountered in clinical narratives, such as that of Sarah from Chapter 1. Her father treated her in ways that were simultaneously controlling (i.e., strong enmeshment/interdependence) and neglectful (i.e., highly distant and disconnected), which qualifies for both labels: 1-5: **Control** plus 1-8: **Ignore**. Sarah's self-treatment at work paralleled this complexity. Sarah forcing herself to do more work despite clear costs to her health and family life can be described as simultaneous 3-5: *Self-Control* plus 3-8: *Self-Neglect*. As needed, complex combinations of multiple SASB positions can be helpful in attempts to characterize expressions of paradox, ambivalence, double binding messages, and more. SASB's ability to clearly capture what makes complex messages so difficult to untangle (let alone identify an adequate response) is one of its strengths.

---

[3] Additional rules apply in formal application of complex codes in research settings. One such constraint is that complex codes cannot be from adjacent clusters on the same surface (e.g., 1-5: **Control** plus 1-6: **Blame**). In these instances, the coder must choose one or the other cluster as being most accurate (these often fall close to the boundary between clusters when the full model is consulted). Consultation and formal training for research use is available via the Interpersonal Reconstructive Therapy Institute (https://irtinstitute.com). The current description provides readers with a basic introduction to the topic sufficient to follow and learn more in context of examples provided in later chapters.

### Underlying Dimensions Take Precedence Over Descriptive Labels

Across the various models, different terms are used to indicate the same or similar locations. This is allowable in part because the model is not organized around language as such. Instead, the various labels serve as approximate descriptions of the underlying dimensions. Model points can clarify the potentially multiple meanings of any given word or phrase. For example, "I trust you" may indicate friendly submission ("I agree and am happy to take your advice") or friendly autonomy ("I'm happy with you making your own decisions"). These two potential meanings are captured in SASB as the difference between 2-4: Trust (full model track 245) and 1-1: **Emancipate** (full model track 117). Interpersonal behavior will thus be clarified using both numeric codes and descriptive labels throughout the examples given in this book.

## USING SASB TO DESCRIBE PATTERNS OF INTERACTION

An overview of formal coding procedures for research or training use is provided in Chapter 3. This section provides an overview emphasizing how SASB's structure enhances not only description of specific interpersonal behaviors but also interactive patterns.

### Specifying Referents and Assigning a SASB-Defined Region

As will be described in Chapter 3, the first step is to identify the specific people, or *referents*, involved in the interaction. For example, a person may describe an interaction with their father, in which case the two referents would be self and father. The behavior of both referents could be characterized and compared using SASB by assigning specific regions of the model to each behavior. For convenience, the process of characterizing or assigning positions on the SASB model will subsequently be referred to as *coding*. For example, during a phone call, the person begins to tell her father her thoughts and feelings about a new romantic relationship (2-2: Disclose). The father responds by changing the topic to her schoolwork (1-8: **Ignore**), and he goes on to say that she should focus more on her studies rather than new relationships (1-6: **Blame**). The person says she has to go and ends the call (2-8: Wall-Off). The most fine-grained level of analysis would involve the specific sequence of their interactions (which behaviors tended to immediately follow which other behaviors). A less fine-grained version would be to look at an aggregated profile for how each person behaved toward the

48 • *Basic Principles*

other within a period of time. The image of two people interacting provides a context for understanding common patterns, or *predictive principles*, that have been named and are described in the next few paragraphs.

## Predictive Principles Linked to SASB's Structure

Some examples of predictive principles are similarity, complementarity, introjection, opposition, and antithesis. Each is described next.

### Similarity

Similarity is the most simply stated of the predictive principles because it involves two interactants behaving in precisely the same way. For example, similarity can be observed as blame (1-6: **Blame**) from one person countered by blame from another, as control (1-5: **Control**) responded to with counter-control, as friendly disclosure (2-2: <u>Disclose</u>) by friendly disclosure, and so on. Similarity commonly occurs but usually does not persist comfortably or stably for long periods. For example, it is common enough to see a therapist initially check in at the beginning of a session ("How are you today?" [1-2: **Affirm**]), followed by a reversal of focus by the patient after their own brief response ("I'm fine. And how has your week been?" [2-2: <u>Disclose</u> and 1-2: **Affirm**]). Both partners seem to want to focus on the other (in this case, in a context that is reciprocal and friendly). In the therapeutic context, the focus will typically return to the patient and resolve an implicit tension around who the interaction should be about. In other settings, the focus may oscillate to involve reciprocity of focus over time. For example, among friends, one may disclose how their week has been for several minutes while the other affirms, and then the affirming listener becomes the disclosing speaker for the next several minutes. In that example, both have been similarly disclosing and affirming when the whole exchange is considered.

Similarity also applies to parallels in the introjective focus of a behavior. For example, two people are engaging in reckless behavior (3-8: *Self-Neglect*) by driving drunk. An example from the friendly side of the circumplex might include creative self-expression (3-2: *Self-Affirm*) perhaps through collaborative engagement with music or art, by self-enhancement (3-4: *Self-Protect*) by studying together to learn a language or other skill, and so on.

### Complementarity

Complementary interactions (see Figure 2.8) are hypothesized to be among the most stable. Carson (1969), Benjamin (1974, 1993), Kiesler (1983), and others noted that each interpersonal behavior differentially invites or "pulls for" a specific response. For example, control (1-5: **Control**) invites another to

**FIGURE 2.8. Structural Diagrams Illustrating Three Predictive Principles: Complementarity, Opposition, and Antithesis**

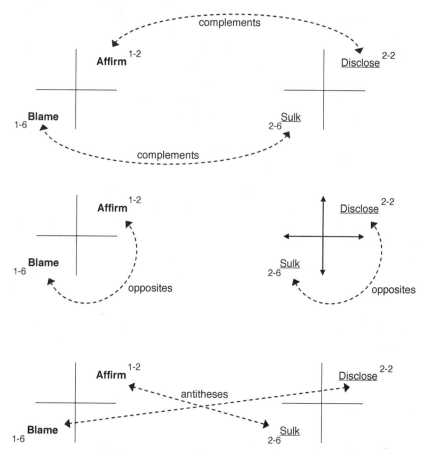

submit (2-5: <u>Submit</u>). Friendly disclosure (2-2: <u>Disclose</u>) invites another to affirm (1-2: **Affirm**). In terms of the SASB structure, complementary behaviors are those that are identical in terms of underlying dimensions and differ only in terms of their focus (other vs. self). In sequences, the pull toward complementarity can begin on either interpersonal surface. For example, sulking (2-6: <u>Sulk</u>) will pull for blaming (1-6: **Blame**), just as blaming a person can produce a sulking response.[4] Sarah's response to her boss in

---

[4] Tracking complementarity may sometimes seem to risk "blaming the victim" for their plight in the narrative. Clinicians are encouraged to think in terms of patterns and interactive cycles when characterizing patient narratives. The question of "how it works" should be the primary focus, rather than "who is to blame."

50 • *Basic Principles*

Chapter 1 also demonstrates this principle. By resolving to comply and work harder (2-5: Submit), Sarah increases the likelihood that her boss will continue assigning her work (1-5: **Control**).[5] Using the logic of complementarity can aid in understanding many clinical processes. For example, a patient who is quiet and appears to sullenly go along with the therapist (2-6: Sulk) may see the therapist as critical (1-6: **Blame**); a patient who appears to wall-off (2-8: Wall-Off) may experience their therapist as ignoring (1-8: **Ignore**) them. Asking about and responding to these possibilities can help identify ruptures or other relationship processes that need attention to find productive collaboration (Eubanks et al., 2019; Muran et al., 2018).

While the principle of complementarity predicts that one behavior pulls for another, it does not necessarily mean that the effect is strong in every context or that another person will necessarily respond in kind. For example, in a conflict, one partner may respond to blame with sulking; another time, they may respond with assertion, disclosure, or counter-blaming. The prediction of complementarity is only that the corresponding response tendency is increased. This is supported by data. In a sample of 97 couples discussing a conflict, Knobloch-Fedders and colleagues (2014) observed that complementary responses (demand/submit) were more common than noncomplementary responses (demand/withdraw). The effect size was not so large that one partner's behavior determined the other; rather, it changed the likelihood of a specific response.

### Introjection

Like complementarity, introjection can appear in stable patterns over time. Introjection occurs when interpersonal behavior is paralleled in self-treatment. Clinical examples of introjection can sometimes be vivid and specific, such as when words heard from others ("You're worthless, stupid" [1-6: **Blame**]) are directly reflected in self-talk when the person is alone ("I'm worthless, stupid" [3-6: *Self-Blame*]). Other examples are less obvious. For example, a patient's self-neglect (3-8: *Self-Neglect*) might be a cue that their therapist's recent vacation was perceived as an abandonment (1-8: **Ignore**).

As with all the predictive principles, introjection can occur anywhere on the SASB model, including in more healthy or adaptive regions. Therefore, introjection applies when affirmation and encouragement (1-2: **Affirm**) are

---

[5] The same logic applies to complex codes. When Sarah resolves to work harder despite being overwhelmed and to handle it all by herself (2-5: Submit plus 2-8: Wall-Off), it pulls for her boss to pile on more demands in ways that further neglect her needs (1-5: **Control** plus 1-8: **Ignore**). Since the boss's demands pulled for Sarah's complementary response to begin with, it is likely the cycle will persist.

followed by forms of self-acceptance and empowerment (3-2: *Self-Affirm*). Like complementarity, introjective self-treatment can pull for a parallel response from others: Self-treatment expressed as confidence in one's own abilities (3-2: *Self-Affirm*) is more likely to result in affirmation by others (1-2: **Affirm**) than is thoughtless or reckless behavior (3-8: *Self-Neglect*) or self-criticism (3-6: *Self-Blame*).

## Opposition

Opposite behaviors are those that share the same focus but have opposite dimensionality, 180° apart on a given surface. These sets include affirming (1-2: **Affirm**) a person who returns blame (1-6: **Blame**) or providing helpful structure (1-4: **Protect**) to a person who actively ignores (1-8: **Ignore**). As can be imagined from these examples, opposite behaviors are typically not sustained interactively for very long unless other forces are holding them in place (e.g., a history suggesting the other person is not behaving authentically, in good faith, or with full information, or that their behavior is an exception to the rule). Health care providers trained in basic deescalation techniques will recognize one version: An upset patient blames (1-6: **Blame**) the care team for a long stint in the waiting room and may be somewhat comforted by an affirming (1-2: **Affirm**) response that acknowledges the reality of the inconvenience despite the hostile tone in which the complaint was made.

## Antithesis

Antithetical behaviors are maximally different on all three dimensions. An antithetical behavior is sometimes referred to as an *antidote* because it pulls (via complementarity) for a response that is opposite from the other person's behavior. The antidote can sometimes be used strategically to shift a person away from one kind of behavior pattern or role to another. For example, a patient who is critical of the therapist and therapy (1-6: **Blame**) naturally pulls for a complementary response of sulking and defensive explaining by a therapist (2-6: *Sulk*, and potentially also 3-6: *Self-Blame* via the predictive principle of introjection). Instead of responding in these ways, a therapist may choose to employ an antithetical response of open, nondefensive disclosure that addresses what the patient is saying (2-2: *Disclose*) to help defuse the situation and invite understanding (1-2: **Affirm**). This position could then be used to engage in a more collaborative discussion of whatever problem had arisen and return focus to the patient (therapist, 1-2: **Affirm**; and patient, 2-2: *Disclose*).

In another example of antithesis, intrusive control (1-5: **Control**) by another might be diminished by clear assertion of limits, boundaries, and different views. In other words, the antidote response separation (2-1: *Separate*)

52 • *Basic Principles*

would pull for the other to complement it by emancipating (1-1: **Emancipate**). In each case, a tug-of-war may result between one behavior and its antithesis, with each behavior pulling for its own complement.

Of course, the logic of an antidote can apply to anywhere on the model. For example, a person's initial trust and reliance on another (2-4: Trust) can be shifted toward an opposite wall-off (2-8: Wall-Off) position if the other person is experienced as neglectful (1-8: **Ignore**).

## USING SASB TO DEFINE A HEALTHY BASELINE FOR BEHAVIOR

Normal, healthy relating has been operationalized in SASB theory (Benjamin, 2003, 2006) as having a specific behavioral profile associated with secure attachment as defined by Bowlby (1969). This profile involves a baseline of relating that involves moderate degrees of warmth, moderate degrees of differentiation, and flexible, contextually appropriate focus on the self and others. The baseline reflects what is expected to occur under expectably safe conditions for human primate evolution in groups. This definition reflects a well-attached, healthy pattern that converges with nonclinical norms reported for the SASB-based Intrex questionnaire (Figure 2.9; see Table 2.10 in Benjamin, 2000). The pattern has been replicated in additional samples (e.g., Benjamin, 2018; Conroy & Pincus, 2006; Knobloch-Fedders, Critchfield, & Staab, 2017; Pincus et al., 1999) as well as for patterns of relating between parents and children (Teti et al., 1995; Woehrle et al., 2023). As a result, the three clusters on the far right of the model are collectively referred to as the *attachment group* (AG), while the three clusters on the far left are referred to as the *disrupted attachment group* (DAG; Benjamin, 1995, 2003, 2006).

Context matters to the definition of healthy relating, of course. Even the friendly baseline described earlier can prove maladaptive if adhered to inflexibly in the wrong context (e.g., trusting someone without a relatively firm basis for that trust, or consistently responding to an abusive partner with warm acceptance). Some variations on this profile are expected based on factors such as cultural context. For example, some studies suggest that more authoritarian (i.e., controlling) parenting can be protective to children in high-risk, minoritized settings (Walker-Barnes & Mason, 2001). If divergences from the AG definition are substantial, however, then parallel behaviors, affects, and cognitions would be expected to follow (e.g., a greater sense of needing to control or constrain the self to stay safe).

**FIGURE 2.9. Normative Pattern for Three Relationship Types Measured by the Intrex Questionnaire (Long Form)**

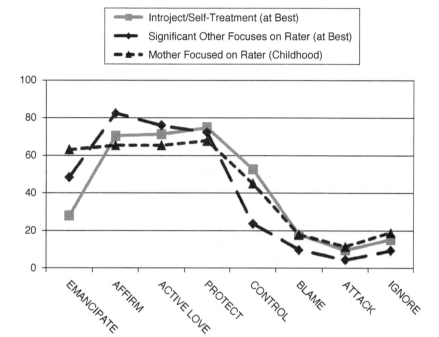

*Note.* Generated from norms reported in the Intrex Long Form Questionnaire manual (Benjamin, 2000).

As clarification, the AG baseline does not necessarily apply to domain-specific topics such as the resolution of a specific kind of conflict or developmental dilemma (Knobloch-Fedders et al., 2014; Smetana, 2017). For example, in a nonclinical, cross-cultural comparison of Tamang and Brahman families, Cole and colleagues (2006) reported an overall profile that was not within the AG. Use of parental protection was emphasized, with parent profiles of 1-4: **Protect**, 1-5: **Control**, and 1-6: **Blame**. The children's profiles were primarily 2-1: Separate, 2-4: Trust, and 2-6: Sulk. However, the study was narrowly focused on parental discipline in context of a child's experience of anger or shame. These findings can be understood as normative for this facet of parent–child relating but do not speak directly to the presence or absence of an overall AG pattern. Similarly, Knobloch-Fedders and colleagues (2014) presented SASB-based data showing normative departures for couples discussing a conflict, who otherwise tended to rate

54 • *Basic Principles*

one another on questionnaires as having a pattern falling in the AG region of secure attachment (Knobloch-Fedders, Critchfield, & Staab, 2017).

### Shaurette Principle: Shaping Interactions Over Time

As described by Benjamin (1993), the Shaurette principle proposes a use of SASB's structure to systematically alter the nature of interpersonal and intrapsychic behavior over time. This principle needs empirical testing but hypothesizes that small changes in SASB positions might be easier to accomplish than large jumps across the circumplex. The basic idea is that behaviors that are one step removed around the circumplex can be used in terms of their pull for complementarity to move a relationship pattern from one position to another. This might happen in a single conversation or in other contexts over time. For example, rather than trying to make the unlikely leap to a baseline of mutual warm affirmation (1-2: **Affirm** and 2-2: <u>Disclose</u>), a couple engaged in a regular pattern of hostile enmeshment (1-6: **Blame** and 2-6: <u>Sulk</u>) might be helped to move in steps around the circumplex, to neutrality, then to friendly enmeshment, followed by increasingly more differentiated, mutually affirming ways of relating until the relationship models the healthy, securely attached profile defined earlier.

### Copy Process: Predictive Principles Generalized Across Relationships

SASB's structure and predictive principles can also be used to track patterns of behavior across different relationships, times, or settings. Patterns that develop in formative attachment relationships and repeat in the present are of particular clinical interest, because their repetition suggests that they may have been internalized to become the basis for relating in other settings. The therapeutic implications of *copy process* are further described in Chapter 5. Briefly, the three primary copy processes are identification, recapitulation, and introjection.

*Identification* refers to similarity between an individual's behavior in the present and that of an earlier figure occurring in the present ("I act like the early other person"). *Recapitulation* involves a direct parallel with what was experienced in earlier relationships ("I act now as I did with the early others" or "I perceive that others now treat me the same way or ways I used to be treated"). *Introjection* as a copy process is the same as described earlier for the predictive principles, but with specific emphasis on the repetition of behavior directed toward the self by earlier figures ("I treat myself as I was once treated").

Copy process links between early adversity and adult problems are well represented in the empirical literature. For example, identification is consistent with studies showing links between early witnessing or experiencing of abuse and later abuse of both children and romantic partners (Carr & VanDeusen, 2002; Chermack & Walton, 1999; Heyman & Slep, 2002; Moe et al., 2004). Recapitulation is suggested by links between exposure to family-of-origin violence and later victimization by a romantic partner (Gladstone et al., 2004; Heyman & Slep, 2002) as well as in studies that have connected childhood sexual abuse with sexual (and physical) victimization as an adult (Arata, 2002; Desai et al., 2002; Noll et al., 2003; Schaaf & McCanne, 1998). Introjection (treating oneself as one was once treated) can be seen in correlations between remembered early psychological maltreatment and adult self-deprecation and self-blame (Brewin et al., 1993; Higgins & McCabe, 2000) as well as adult self-harm (Gladstone et al., 2004; Noll et al., 2003).

Empirical work using SASB suggests that copy process patterns are near ubiquitous, occurring in some form in nearly all clinical and normal cases (Critchfield & Benjamin, 2010). Normal cases are usually characterized by copying of a secure-base pattern of attachment. Clinical cases, by contrast, tend to show copying of patterns with greater hostility, less warmth, and/or extremes along the interdependence axis. For example, introjection of perceived parental hostility has been observed in individuals diagnosed with bulimia (Wonderlich et al., 1996) and in young adults with features of borderline personality disorder (Ruiz et al., 1999). Cushing (2003) studied the parenting behavior of populations with and without cocaine use disorder. In both groups, the author found copy process links to the remembered early mother–child relationship, especially among mothers without cocaine use disorder. Woehrle and colleagues (2023) studied mothers who had engaged in child maltreatment compared with a control group that had not. The group engaged in child-maltreatment showed a stronger tendency to recapitulate maladaptive patterns with their toddler, whereas the other group tended to introject maladaptive patterns when present in the prior generation.

There may be a slight tendency to copy hostility with greater potency than other behaviors, likely due to its salience as a cue to threat versus safety (Critchfield & Benjamin, 2008). However, patterns that do not involve hostility are also copied at high rates. For example, intergenerational transmission of perfectionistic self-control has been reported to occur by means of both parental modeling (identification) and psychological control of a child (introjection; Soenens et al., 2005).

**FIGURE 2.10. Fundamental Dimensions Spanning Affective, Behavioral, and Cognitive Models of Relating**

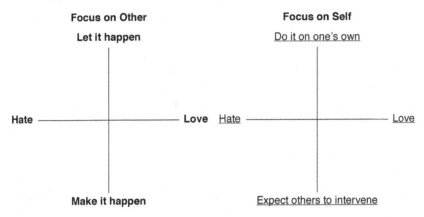

*Note.* Dimension labels and positions adapted from *Interpersonal Reconstructive Therapy: An Integrative Personality-Based Treatment for Complex Cases* (p. 149, Table 4A.1), by L. S. Benjamin, 2006, Guilford Press. Copyright 2006 by Guilford Press. Adapted with permission.

## PARALLEL STRUCTURAL ANALYSIS OF AFFECTIVE AND COGNITIVE BEHAVIOR MODELS

Dimensions underlying SASB are believed to extend to cognitions and affects. Benjamin (2003, 2006, 2018) articulated the underlying hypothesis in depth, arguing from a natural biological perspective that cognition, affect, and behavior have evolved in parallel and can be organized accordingly. Figure 2.10 presents the dimensions that organize all three domains.[6]

Figure 2.11 shows parallel language for the cluster model. One way to approach an understanding of the parallel cognitive and affective models is to ask these questions: "What cognitive style would typically accompany behavior X? What affect would go along with it?" Each model position is associated with the respective SASB behavior.

The parallel models can assist with understanding and predicting behavioral patterns. For example, in a recent therapy session, a patient began by asking whether medication adjustments might be needed. She reported being severely anxious and agitated. She was able to stay socially engaged

---

[6]To simplify presentation, introject is not included. Affects and cognitions associated with introjective focus follow the same logic as with relational behavior by following the focus-on-other descriptions and directing them toward the self (e.g., in the lower left: condemn self, scorn self).

**FIGURE 2.11. Cognitive and Affective Models**

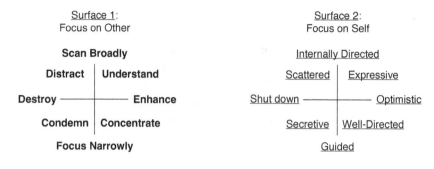

*Note.* Adapted from *Interpersonal Reconstructive Therapy: An Integrative Personality-Based Treatment for Complex Cases* (pp. 147-148), by L. S. Benjamin, 2006, Guilford Press. Copyright 2006 by Guilford Press. Adapted with permission.

but was having difficulty focusing on her work and had been damaging her skin. The patient had trouble reconstructing the week's events, saying she had been "in a fog." She also reported that nothing significant had changed from the prior week when she had been feeling good and all had been going well. After some exploration of when these feelings began, the patient recalled multiple interactions with peers that did not seem significant to her at the time, but involved others leading her to feel she was in the wrong and to blame for circumstances that were beyond her control. Her fearful and agitated affect, along with the sense of shutting down cognitively, suggested that she was behaviorally recoiling (2-7: Recoil), likely in response to a perceived threat. Exploration based on her affects helped the patient

58 • *Basic Principles*

reconstruct the events that led her to recoil. The patient was able to use her understanding of the pattern to calm the anxious response and find more adaptive coping strategies.

A questionnaire-based method, the Relational Cognitions and Affects Questionnaire (RCA-Q), has also been developed for assessing relational cognitions and affects based on the Structural Analysis of Cognitive Behavior (SACB) and the Structural Analysis of Affective Behavior (SAAB) models (Critchfield & Benjamin, 2016). Although the SASB model is the primary focus of this book, multiple clinical examples will emphasize the importance of tracking narratives and other cues in terms of expected parallels among cognition, affect, and behavioral domains.

## VALIDATION OF SASB'S STRUCTURE

Over roughly 50 years, SASB has undergone extensive empirical tests of its structure, item placement and wording, reliability, and validity. Comprehensive presentation of this work is available elsewhere (Benjamin, 1979, 2000; Benjamin, Rothweiler, & Critchfield, 2006) and includes the SASB-based Intrex manual (Benjamin, 2000), which includes data regarding internal consistency, split-half, and test-retest reliabilities. A summary of essential psychometric details for clinical use of the Intrex questionnaire is summarized in Chapter 3. The last part of this chapter focuses primarily on providing a brief overview of how SASB's dimensional structure was developed and tested, with major focus on its psychometric, structural, and validity properties.

### Developing and Refining Items via the Dimensional Ratings Approach

From inception, Benjamin wanted her map of relational behavior to directly reflect SASB's proposed underlying dimensions. The initial language to characterize each position on the model was first drafted as a set of descriptive items, and then research participants were asked to rate the degree to which each one reflected the intended degrees of affiliation and interdependence. An iterative process of tailoring the wording of each item and subjecting it to additional dimensional ratings was used until each one was judged to have its planned placement on the model. The final set of items would later be incorporated into the full model and organized for research and clinical use as the Intrex questionnaire (detailed in Chapter 3). In keeping with its initial approach to development, approved translations are required to also follow a dimensional ratings procedure in the new language, along with factor analytic reconstruction to be validated, rather than simple translation and backtranslation of each item. This approach carries forward the emphasis on underlying dimensions of relating, rather than language per se. This approach seeks to account for potential cultural differences in the perception of various degrees of affiliation and interdependence and, by not relying solely on linguistic cues, also reflects earliest uses of the model to describe nonverbal behavior in Harlow's studies of primate attachment (Benjamin, 1973). Benjamin (1974, 2000) confirmed the expected ordering and placement of items for each version of the SASB model. More recent, ongoing work has used the dimensional ratings method to develop the SACB and SAAB models (Critchfield, Pempek, et al., 2021; Park, 2005).

### Logic for Testing Circular Order of Concepts

A set of mathematical principles underlies any closed, circular ordering of concepts. Guttman (1954) coined the term *circumplex* based on a circular ordering of concepts in two dimensions. Although SASB is designed as a diamond, the behaviors on its perimeter nonetheless conform to the logic of overall circular ordering. The idealized correlation matrix for this situation, including its inherent geometry, is displayed in Figure 2.12 for the eight focus-on-other clusters. As can be seen, the (idealized) row entries for 1-1: **Emancipate** show a perfect correlation with itself (i.e., +1.0), followed by progressively reduced values for comparison with 1-2: **Affirm**, 1-3: **Active Love**, and 1-4: **Protect**, reaching a perfect negative correlation with 1-5: **Control**, and then increasing again by degrees for 1-6: **Blame**, 1-7: **Attack**, and 1-8: **Ignore**. The same circulant pattern can be observed for any row or column starting with comparison of one variable to itself on the main diagonal. To validate SASB's theory about the underlying structure of social behavior, corresponding data matrices would need to show that they conform to a similar kind of circulant pattern.

### Verifying Structure in Self-Reported Relational Patterns

Benjamin (1974, 2000) provided successful tests of SASB's structure and internal consistency using a variety of methods addressing the circular ordering of its concepts, including autocorrelation analysis to determine whether model points had the expected pattern on a within-subject basis (i.e., when raters applied the Intrex items to their own relationships). In the same reports, Benjamin also used between-subjects data to demonstrate circumplex structure in multiple samples as well as factor analytic reconstruction of underlying dimensions and their corresponding item placements.

60 • *Basic Principles*

**FIGURE 2.12. Geometry of Order Relations in an Idealized "Circulant" Matrix**

|  | Emancipate | Affirm | Love | Protect | Control | Blame | Attack | Ignore |
|---|---|---|---|---|---|---|---|---|
| Emancipate | 1.0 | 0.7 | 0.0 | -0.7 | -1.0 | -0.7 | 0.0 | 0.7 |
| Affirm | 0.7 | 1.0 | 0.7 | 0.0 | -0.7 | -1.0 | -0.7 | 0.0 |
| Love | 0.0 | 0.7 | 1.0 | 0.7 | 0.0 | -0.7 | -1.0 | -0.7 |
| Protect | -0.7 | 0.0 | 0.7 | 1.0 | 0.7 | 0.0 | -0.7 | -1.0 |
| Control | -1.0 | -0.7 | 0.0 | 0.7 | 1.0 | 0.7 | 0.0 | -0.7 |
| Blame | -0.7 | -1.0 | -0.7 | 0.0 | 0.7 | 1.0 | 0.7 | 0.0 |
| Attack | 0.0 | -0.7 | -1.0 | -0.7 | 0.0 | 0.7 | 1.0 | 0.7 |
| Ignore | 0.7 | 0.0 | -0.7 | -1.0 | -0.7 | 0.0 | 0.7 | 1.0 |

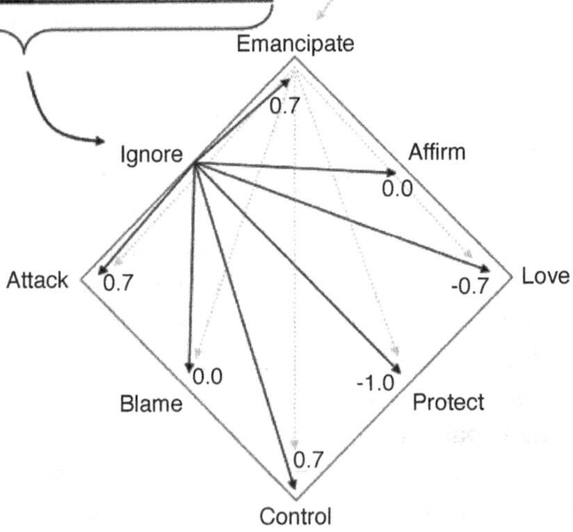

*Note.* Shading from light to dark follows the predicted pattern of similarities.

Other researchers have confirmed the structure and circular ordering of SASB items, including in other languages (e.g., Tscheulin & Glossner, 1993). The model's properties have been observed to vary somewhat based on the nature of the relationship rated, such as an individual's relationship with themselves when at worst versus the memory of their mother's behavior in childhood (Lorr & Strack, 1999). Pincus et al. (1998) used circumplex analysis applied to ratings made by nonclinical undergraduate students ($n = 376$) as well as clinical patients ($n = 187$) and confirmed a circular ordering of the items. They also found that the model conformed better to the shape of an ellipse that was stretched out along the affiliation axis, rather than a more symmetric shape. This finding is consistent with Benjamin's (1974, 2018) theory emphasizing the nonarbitrary nature of the underlying dimensions as well as the key role played by the affiliation axis in an evolutionary context.

The presumably later-evolved and more socialized or culturally shaped discernment of interdependence (including matters of power, hierarchy, and status) may be of secondary importance. In any case, both are deemed necessary to navigate relationships accurately. Additional research on the structural features of SASB is available from other sources (Benjamin, 2018; Benjamin, Rothweiler, & Critchfield, 2006). SASB-based research on specific applications (i.e., providing external, predictive, criterion, and construct validity) will be provided throughout this book in the context of topics discussed, as the primary focus remains on clinical application.

In Chapter 3, we turn to application of the SASB model in its questionnaire and observational coding system formats. Later in the book, we will return to more in-depth discussion and illustration of the in-session, direct clinical applications of the SASB model and its affective and cognitive parallels.

# 3 APPLICATION OF STRUCTURAL ANALYSIS OF SOCIAL BEHAVIOR TECHNOLOGY

There are two basic applications of the Structural Analysis of Social Behavior (SASB) model for clinical use.[1] The first is observational coding of interactions. SASB can be applied to the here-and-now process of an interaction as it unfolds (e.g., in-session relating between patient and therapist), or it can be used to clarify relationship patterns implicit in the patient's narratives about interactions with others (e.g., the content of patient narratives about relationships). The second basic application of SASB involves questionnaire-based assessments of the self and relationships with others. In this chapter, we first describe observational coding and then discuss questionnaire-based methods.

## OBSERVATIONAL CODING

### Basic Procedure

Table 3.1 presents the basic steps for coding any behavior with SASB. For coding purposes, behaviors are considered at the level of single actions,

---

[1] The clinical material used in this book is adequately disguised to protect patient confidentiality.

https://doi.org/10.1037/0000403-003
*Structural Analysis of Social Behavior (SASB): A Primer for Clinical Use*, by K. L. Critchfield and L. S. Benjamin
Copyright © 2024 by the American Psychological Association. All rights reserved.

64 • *Basic Principles*

**TABLE 3.1. Structural Analysis of Social Behavior (SASB) Coding Steps**

| No. | Step |
| --- | --- |
| 1 | Identify the referents |
| 2 | Determine the three dimensions: focus, affiliation, and interdependence |
| 3 | Locate the relevant cluster (or clusters) on the SASB model |
| 4 | Conduct the final clinical test |

sometimes referred to as *thought units* or *elements* of an interaction (Benjamin & Cushing, 2000). These elements are usually a single sentence, clause, or discrete nonverbal action that involves or implies a noun, verb, and direct or indirect object. For example, the statement "This is your fault" assigns 1-6: **Blame**, whereas an enthusiastic hug given in friendly greeting conveys 1-3: **Active Love**. Research coding usually involves statement-by-statement analysis of a transcript. This basic idea also applies in clinical practice, but without the need to follow the highly rigorous, detailed procedures recommended for research records.

Once a specific behavioral interaction is identified for coding, the first step is to identify who is interacting with whom. The *referents* of a behavior include (a) the actor (a person, persons, or entity enacting the behavior) and (b) the referent (a person, persons, or entity to whom the actor's behavior has reference). Sometimes a behavior has more than one referent, and the coder must make clear which aspect of a given behavior is being coded in relation to which interactant. For example, in group therapy, one member may "take sides" on an issue, simultaneously confronting one group member and allying with another (e.g., "You shouldn't give her such a hard time about her friends"). Even though only a single sentence is involved, it should be clear that a separate code is needed to track what is happening in each relationship: One person is being confronted, the other protected.

Once the referents are clearly identified and the interactions to be described are known, the next step is to determine the three underlying SASB dimensions for each relationship. First, the focus of a behavior is determined (focus on other, focus on self, or introject) followed by the degree of affiliation and interdependence, as defined in Chapter 2. Judgments regarding focus, affiliation, and interdependence determine the specific point (or points) on the SASB model used to describe a behavior.

The following example from a couple session illustrates the basic process, including the importance of specifying referents. The husband, in the presence of his wife, makes a case to the therapist that all the problems in their marital relationship trace back to his wife's refusal to provide him the nurturance and support he feels he needs: "Doc, this whole thing started

*Application of Structural Analysis of Social Behavior Technology* • 65

with how she stopped caring about my needs after the kids were born." In this example, several SASB codes are relevant simultaneously, with multiple referents. To simplify, one code applies to the process with the therapist as the husband provides his view of the marital situation. The husband is perceived as self-focused, friendly, and differentiated from the therapist as he tells the therapist his point of view (characterized as 2-2: <u>Disclose</u>).[2] Meanwhile, the same statement carries a different message in relation to his wife as the referent. He faults her for all their problems, including the sense of not having his own perceived needs met. In terms of underlying dimensions, he is moderately hostile, is strongly to moderately enmeshed, and invokes a focus that includes both his wife and himself (coded as 1-6: **Blame** plus 2-6: <u>Sulk</u>). The husband additionally reveals his view of his wife's past actions as neglecting him. From the husband's narrated point of view, his wife is other focused (i.e., on him) and blends hostility and distance in the sense of not attending to his needs (1-8: **Ignore**).

The appearance of at least four different SASB codes in our one-sentence example shows how relational communication can be complex, sophisticated, and multilayered. Even so, clinicians regularly consider the questions involved. The therapist hearing the husband's statement ("Doc, this whole thing started with how she stopped caring about my needs after the kids were born") may consider these questions: How is my patient relating with me right now? How is my patient relating with another person? How is my patient perceiving the actions of that other person? Each question invokes different referents and places them within a time frame and perspective.

The final clinical test is to determine whether the label given at the specified point on the SASB model fits well with or *captures* the behavior. If there is a poor fit, then the underlying dimensions must be reconsidered. For example, the coder can assign a complex code if a behavior has more than one component (e.g., simultaneously hostile and friendly, enmeshed and differentiated, or focused on other and self). For example, imagine that the husband expressed a different view of his wife. Instead of refusing to consider his needs, she became depressed and withdrew from the family after having children (e.g., "I know it was postpartum depression"). In this case, the label 1-8: **Ignore** does not capture his view precisely. This new description of the wife as withdrawing into depression shifts the attentional

---

[2]The nonverbal manner and timing of how something is said is part of determining the degrees of affiliation and interdependence. If the therapist had a strong sense that the husband was asking for a direct solution to this problem rather than simply stating his point of view, then the husband's statement might be coded as 2-4: <u>Trust</u> in relation to the therapist.

66 • *Basic Principles*

focus. The qualitative label for her then becomes 2-8: <u>Wall-Off</u>, which is a better fit for the revised example. A complex code could be applied if the husband's characterization conveyed that by withdrawing, his wife was also abandoning him (yielding 2-8: <u>Wall-Off</u> plus 1-8: **Ignore**).

To summarize, the coding steps are as follows:

1. Identify the referents.
2. Determine focus, affiliation, and interdependence.
3. Identify the appropriate point on the SASB model.
4. Compare the description on the SASB model with the actual behavior observed to determine whether the description is adequate.

In other words, does the description pass the final clinical test? If the description is inadequate, check the basic dimensions to consider the possibility of another code or consider a complex code. With deliberate practice, a clinician can eventually track behavior (observed as a here-and-now process or described in the content of speech) in a way that is relatively automatic and can be applied in real time.

More specific illustration of the coding process and its subtleties is given next and in multiple examples throughout this book. Before we turn to additional examples, we again emphasize the importance of clearly specifying who and what is being coded—that is, the referents. It is also crucial to note that the coding procedure is always anchored in the underlying dimensions of focus, affiliation, and interdependence. The emphasis on systematically identifying underlying dimensionality prevents system degradation, which can come from treating points on the model as if they are categorical and simply jumping to a SASB position based on the cluster or track label.

## Content Coding

A common and straightforward use of SASB in clinical practice is to identify and track patterns of behavior described in the content of a patient's narrative descriptions (as opposed to here-and-now observations of the in-session process, which are considered separately). Content coding involves simply translating what is reported into SASB language and then using the codes as an aid to summarize and distill core interpersonal themes. Predictions can then be made and interventions tailored to address the central interpersonal patterns.

An excerpt from a clinical interview is provided in Table 3.2, with each statement coded for interpersonal content. In this excerpt, only the narrative content of the patient, Steven, is coded; the here-and-now therapeutic

*Application of Structural Analysis of Social Behavior Technology* • 67

**TABLE 3.2. Illustration of Content Coding in Steven's Interview**

| Transcript | Coding of patient content |
|---|---|
| **THERAPIST:** Why don't we start with what you need? | |
| **PATIENT:** With what I need? | |
| **THERAPIST:** Yeah. | |
| **PATIENT:** I need to stop feeling like I want to die. | 3-7: *Self-Attack* implied |
| **THERAPIST:** Tell me about that. What is your feeling that you want to die? | |
| **PATIENT:** I just feel inadequate. I feel incomplete. I feel like everything that I've touched so far has turned to crap, I guess you'd say. It's just a rough feeling. | 3-6: *Self-Blame* |
| **THERAPIST:** I gather you came in this time because of an overdose. Is that correct? | |
| **PATIENT:** Yeah, I attempted suicide. | 3-7: *Self-Attack* |
| **THERAPIST:** Yeah. Can you tell me a little bit about what was going on and what you were thinking? | |
| **PATIENT:** Well, I haven't worked since June. | [Uncodable: not yet known why he has not worked] |
| **THERAPIST:** Why is that? | [Probes for clarity] |
| **PATIENT:** I lost my job because I was self-medicating with methamphetamines. | 3-8: *Self-Neglect* with naive attempt at 3-4: *Self-Protect* |
| **THERAPIST:** Okay. | |
| **PATIENT:** I was working about 90 hours a week and wasn't doing my counseling. I wasn't taking my medications properly. And so, when I get manic, I want to stay manic, and the only way to do that is to self-medicate. And they knew that I was doing it, but it was a convenience for them, you know? And then when it became a liability, then they let me go. | 3-8: *Self-Neglect* with 3-4: *Self-Protect*. Work benefitted from his use (2-4: <u>Trust</u> and 1-8: **Ignore**), then fired him for it (1-6: **Blame** plus 1-8: **Ignore**) |
| **THERAPIST:** They liked that they could get so much work out of you. | |
| **PATIENT:** Exactly. [Topic then shifts. Outside work, the patient describes enjoying physical fights and is proud when he puts others in the hospital for threatening him or loved ones] | 1-7: **Attack** (patient to others); 3-4: *Self-Protect*, 1-4: **Protect** (patient to loved ones) |

*(continues)*

68 • *Basic Principles*

**TABLE 3.2. Illustration of Content Coding in Steven's Interview (*Continued*)**

| Transcript | Coding of patient content |
|---|---|
| **THERAPIST:** But I'm still curious about you getting a job. Let's say you get a job, and now let's run the clock back to getting the moving company job. You get on it, and right away you stop taking your meds, and you start using, and you get in fights. Now how does that happen? Can you help me see how that works? | |
| **PATIENT:** Oh, it has a lot to do with the hours, because you know first, I start with 40 hours a week. And then, I'm not only a self-gratification person, but I'm a people-pleaser. And so, the boss needs this job done, and he needs this job done, and he needs this job done, so I have to stop taking my meds because they make me sleepy. And in order to work 90 hours a week, I have to self-medicate. | Patient submits (2-5: <u>Submit</u>) to perception of boss's demands (1-5: **Control** plus 1-8: **Ignore** from boss is implied) using a strategy that compromises his well-being (3-8: *Self-Neglect*) |

process is omitted. Unlike here-and-now processes, codable content is not present in every sentence and varies in degrees of clarity. As a result, inference is sometimes needed to assign a SASB code to describe content. If a clinician who is keeping SASB in mind during a session or interview notices that there is not enough information to identify a code, they may ask, "Could you please provide a specific example of that?" or "What did they [you] say?" Specificity is required for assigning accurate coding, developing accurate case formulations, and choosing and delivering effective interventions (Benjamin, 2018).

### Summarizing Codes in the Sample Clinical Narrative

If the coded details are extracted from Table 3.2 and reorganized to distinguish others' behavior from the patient's behavior, they tell the following story: Steven reports feeling overworked by his boss (likely 1-5: **Control**), who depends on Steven (2-4: <u>Trust</u>) and appears to exploit him by demanding unreasonable hours and knowingly allowing Steven to work while using street drugs (1-8: **Ignore**). Steven responds by trying to work long hours to give his boss what he wants (2-5: <u>Submit</u>) so he can stay employed (3-4: *Self-Protect*), but Steven does so by taking drugs, leaving counseling, and stopping his prescribed medications (3-8: *Self-Neglect*). Eventually, Steven's boss fires him for what had earlier been implicitly endorsed (complex 1-6: **Blame** plus 1-8: **Ignore**). Steven then criticizes himself harshly (3-6: *Self-Blame*) and wants to end his life (3-7: *Self-Attack*).

A SASB-based summary of the primary themes from Steven's overall clinical interview (not just the excerpts shown in Table 3.2) is presented in Figure 3.1 and is not far from the outline sketched earlier. When Steven is discussing problem areas in his life (the focus of the interview), he describes most others as being critical and sometimes neglecting as well. He also describes direct physical attacks. The SASB codes make it clear that Steven sees others as focusing on him in hostile ways, as shown on the left side of the model (1-6: **Blame**, 1-7: **Attack**, and 1-8: **Ignore**). His self-treatment

**FIGURE 3.1. Content Themes From Steven's Overall Interview**

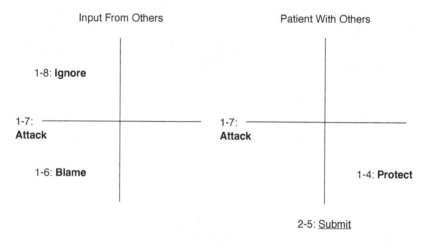

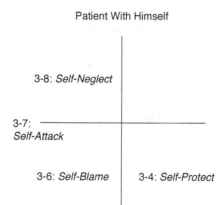

70 • *Basic Principles*

mirrors how he sees others treating him (3-6: *Self-Blame*, 3-7: *Self-Attack*, and 3-8: *Self-Neglect*). Steven's aggression (1-7: **Attack**) also mirrors his perception of others' behavior. Additional themes include caretaking (1-4: **Protect**), deferring to authority (2-5: <u>Submit</u>), and misguided attempts to take care of himself (3-4: *Self-Protect*) that have often resulted in further self-neglect.

SASB-codable interpersonal detail is nearly always present in a patient's narrative. Detail quality is enhanced when the interviewer asks for examples and descriptions. The SASB lens can clarify the story and bring it all together. For example, although only brief moments from a 90-minute interview with Steven are presented, the overall pattern of behavior can already be seen.

The tendency for relatively complete patterns to show up in even small segments of a narrative or an observed interaction has been called the *pond water theory*, and suggests that reliable patterning can often be found in small samples (Benjamin & Cushing, 2000). This notion is particularly relevant for understanding the predictability of themes contained in clinical narratives (i.e., content coding). It also has empirical support in observed processes with interactants who have established relationships, such as the stability of marital interactions (Knobloch-Fedders et al., 2014). However, context always matters. The pond water theory is less likely to hold for interactions that are in a process of formation or transition, which has been noted in studies of early therapeutic relationship formation (Ahmed et al., 2012; Wong & Pos, 2014). As the process changes or if the focus turns to a different part of the pond, the pond water may change accordingly.

## Process Coding

In addition to a focus on patient stories about relationships (*content coding*), SASB can be used to describe interactive processes in the here and now on a moment-by-moment basis. This is particularly relevant for therapists who value the therapeutic relationship (including aspects of the therapeutic alliance, transference, and countertransference) and wish to remain attuned to it. A review of the extensive empirical literature confirming the importance of the therapeutic relationship in determining therapy outcomes is beyond this chapter's scope; excellent summaries are provided by Norcross and Lambert (2019). SASB has been operationalized to detect the impact of interpersonal process codes on outcomes in early therapy sessions. Previous studies reported that the presence of even small amounts of hostility, often embedded in complex codes from either therapists or patients, is predictive of poorer outcomes in interpersonal and psychodynamic forms of therapy (Coady, 1991a, 1991b; Henry et al., 1986, 1990). A growing literature on

*Application of Structural Analysis of Social Behavior Technology* • 71

alliance ruptures and repairs (Safran et al., 2002) moves beyond the aggregate level of analysis to study sequential patterning of relationships. SASB provides an excellent tool for measuring these processes as they unfold in sessions (Muran et al., 2018). For clinicians who track patterns mentally, SASB can serve as an early warning system for identifying problems in the alliance and can also suggest possible reasons and remedies for alliance ruptures. Later chapters discuss strategies for using SASB codes to guide intervention in more detail. Next, we present a session using SASB codes to illustrate the basic process for a male patient named Arthur.

The following transcript uses brackets and a numbering system to identify each element to be coded. For research studies, careful transcription and segmenting are recommended for coding. As noted earlier, the same principles of coding apply in clinical practice, but such intense attention to every detail is impossible during the real-time flow of a session. Like learning any new language, the more practiced and fluent a clinician becomes, the easier it is to track the details of moment-by-moment relating and then intervene with awareness of their implications. The following transcript segment and patient material presented later are from an interview conducted as part of the APA Psychotherapy Videotape Series (Benjamin, 1997).[3] The transcript begins with a moment midway through an early therapy session between Arthur and his female therapist. Arthur, with some notable anxiety and hesitation (e.g., the stuttering apparent in the transcript), is describing difficulties at work:

PATIENT: [yeah,[91]] [um, the other day I came in a little bit late, traffic and stuff[92]] [and, and um, um, I got in late and I got busy doing something[93]] [and um I didn't change the flowers in the lobby[94]] [and the, the, the flowers need to be changed, they need to be fresh and stuff[95]] [and I didn't do it because you know I was busy because I had this other stuff to do bec-,[96]] [and um, um, and I didn't change the flowers.[97]] [And my boss came in and he saw the flowers that they were droopy[98]] [and he got mad at me for not changing them. Um, the flowers[99]] [and um, I tried to explain to him that, that, um, you know, that that, um you know, I, because I come in a little bit late that day um, that I had these other things to do with, with, you know, with making all the bills you know, getting all the bills together that came in you know that morning and, and so I didn't have a chance to change the

---

[3] See the Resource Library tab online (https://www.apa.org/pubs/books/structural-analysis-social-behavior) for Arthur's history, full session transcript, and related SASB codes.

72 • *Basic Principles*

flowers,[100] [but I was going to do it.[101]] [But he got really mad at me anyway.[102]] [And so I, you know, I, you know I'm doing what he tells me to do[103]] [and he gets mad at me anyway for not doing something else.[104]]

In the process coding of this passage, the goal is to describe the in-session, here-and-now relationship relative to the therapist using the steps outlined in Table 3.1. For the process with the therapist, units 91 through 104 all are coded as 2-2: Disclose. This is because, in relation to the therapist, Arthur is focused on his own experience (focus on self) and is friendly and open in relating it (upper-right portion of the SASB model, indicating he is comfortably "in his own separate space"). The label on the cluster model, 2-2: Disclose, seems to capture the patient's basic stance regarding the therapist. If the full model is consulted, specific tracks 214 (Clearly express) and 215 (Openly disclose, reveal) each seem to apply. Following Table 3.1, each step (referents, focus and dimensions, cluster assignment, and final clinical check) produces a clear result.

### Putting Process and Content Coding Together

Let us turn now to Arthur's narrative content about his boss. Arthur perceives his boss to exert hostile control, coded 1-6: **Blame** (units 99, 102, and 104). Arthur's description of his own behavior in relation to his boss includes 2-5: Submit (units 101 and 103) and a complex blend of 2-5: Submit plus 2-1: Separate (unit 100; i.e., he works hard to do what he was supposed to do but also arrives late and does not do part of the task).

Inference is used for some of these codes, such as coding the boss being "mad" at Arthur. In research, content coding is usually more inferential than process coding because it depends on the nature and adequacy of a patient's description of an event; process coding is of the here and now, as seen on the video (or in person). In clinical practice, if the details of an interaction are crucial to understand, then a therapist might ask for more specific information at the level of an interactional sequence. With Arthur, more detail could be sought to better understand his view (and render it more SASB codable) by asking, "What did he say or do that let you know he was mad?" Of course, follow-up questions can confirm an inference or move the clinician in a different direction: Arthur might have reported that his boss yelled at him, or he might have reported something more ambiguous that could lead the clinician to wonder if Arthur may be prone to "reading" anger in other uncertain interpersonal situations as well.

When tone of voice and nonverbal behaviors are available from the recorded interview, it becomes clear that Arthur is complaining in a manner consistent with hostile submission, coded 2-6: <u>Sulk</u> (especially units 103 and 104), in telling this story. However, these complaints involve a process implied in relation to Arthur's boss, not his therapist. Therapists sometimes may be uncertain about patient expressions of hostility and submission and wonder whether these expressions are in relation to the therapist, are enacted in relation to someone else, or represent a blend of both. This is an important distinction that involves the need to specify referents correctly. To preserve good collaboration in session, it may be important to appropriately reflect on what the patient is saying (in this case, regarding Arthur's relationship with his boss) and then clarify these possibilities by asking, "How are you feeling about our work together right now?"

Arthur's session transcript continues in Table 3.3, where we return to tracking the process via SASB codes. The research coding of Table 3.3 plus another approximately 5 minutes of interaction results in the profile presented in Figure 3.2. Like much interaction in psychotherapy sessions, the therapist in this example primarily focuses on the patient with a balance of friendly influence and friendly autonomy granting (1-2: **Affirm** and 1-4: **Protect**), while the patient focuses on himself in complementary ways (2-2: <u>Disclose</u> and 2-4: <u>Trust</u>). The overall similarity in profiles for both therapist and patient (Pearson's $r = .85$) suggests a high level of complementarity for the overall patterning of their relationship. The basic profile shape and the strong level of profile complementarity are not unusual for psychotherapy. However, the higher-than-usual level of patient sulkiness (2-6: <u>Sulk</u>) in this example is interesting, with approximately 13% of all codes for Arthur involving a detectable degree of hostile submission in relation to his therapist.

Although the descriptive profile of the interaction between Arthur and his therapist is informative its own right, it is further enriched by noting sequence and context. In our initial example, Arthur is coded as 2-6: <u>Sulk</u> in relation to a boss he perceives as being unfairly controlling. In Table 3.3, the same code appears in relation to Arthur's therapist only after she attempts to introduce more structure into their conversation. This occurs in unit 117 when the focus turns to what Arthur might do differently. The sequencing suggests that Arthur may have reacted with his therapist in a way that parallels the implied process with his boss; it also suggests that Arthur may have been a more sensitive coder of potential criticism than we were as coders.

### In-Session Process and Interface With Patient History

It is possible to analyze sequences of SASB-coded behavior to generate and test hypotheses about developmental history. We illustrate this in the case example of Arthur in Table 3.3. Based on the sequences with his boss and

**TABLE 3.3. Excerpt of Transcript With Structural Analysis of Social Behavior Process Codes Applied**

| Transcript | Process coding |
|---|---|
| **THERAPIST:** [I see[105]] | 1-2: **Affirm.** Therapist lets Arthur know she is tracking what he is saying about his own life. Full model tracks would be 114 (Show empathic understanding) and/or 115 (Friendly listen) |
| **PATIENT:** [and so I, that's, he got mad at me for that, and[106]] | 2-2: Disclose |
| **THERAPIST:** [So it sounds like he's asking for more than you can do.[107]] | 1-2: **Affirm** plus 1-4: **Protect.** Therapist listens, understands, and reflects consistent with cluster 2, but also provides additional interpretation seen in this case as influencing, consistent with cluster 4. Full model track for this added component would be 144 (Sensible analysis) |
| **PATIENT:** [Well I, I, you know, I I do the best I can[108]] [and and I do a good job[109]] [and I didn't change the flowers[110]] [and I was going to do it, I planned on doing it.[111]] | 2-2: Disclose (all units) |
| **THERAPIST:** [mm-hmm[112]] | 1-2: **Affirm** |
| **PATIENT:** [uh, but it just, but I didn't do it because I got in late[113]] [and I was late because of the traffic[114]] [and, and, you know how things get, it just, so[115]] | 2-2: Disclose (units 113 and 114) and 2-4: Trust (unit 115). Momentary shift in unit 115 suggests a more enmeshed stance with therapist |
| **THERAPIST:** [yeah[116]] [well, let's talk about what, if anything, you might have done differently there so that could have gone a little better.[117]] | 1-2: **Affirm** (unit 116) and 1-4: **Protect** (unit 117). If the phrase "if anything" were omitted, a case might be made to add complex 1-6: **Blame.** This possibility was "below threshold" for our sense of it |
| **PATIENT:** [(sigh) well, you know, I can't do anything about my leg, if it hurts it hurts,[118]] [but maybe I could have driven faster or something and gotten there not so late, you know,[119]] [hope I don't get a ticket[120]] [but you know get there a little earli-, faster and and maybe not be so late[121]] [and then maybe, you know, maybe he wouldn't be so mad at me.[122]] | Complex codes involving 2-6: Sulk (more obvious with voice tone) alongside 2-1: Separate (unit 118), 2-4: Trust (units 119, 121, and 122), and 2-2: Disclose (unit 120) |
| **THERAPIST:** [oh, I see,[123]] [dear, I, the idea of speeding sounds like more potential trouble, but[124]] | 1-2: **Affirm** (unit 123) and 1-4: **Protect** (unit 124) |

**FIGURE 3.2. Proportion of Structural Analysis of Social Behavior Codes Assigned to Arthur and His Therapist in Table 3.3**

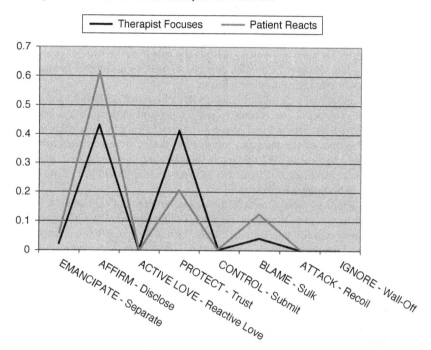

his therapist involving forms of control followed by sulking, we hypothesize that Arthur is potentially sensitive to forms of control (or criticism). This hypothesis-testing approach begins with the clinician attempting to observe how the patient interacts in the present and then attending to consistencies across settings and relationships that may represent recurrent themes.

We believe that recurrent themes can be identified if one attends to the patient's specific interpersonal learning history and views their behavior in the present with this information in mind, as discussed further in the context of the theory of Interpersonal Reconstructive Therapy (IRT) in Chapter 5. Next, we summarize early experiences reported by Arthur, our control/criticism-sensitive patient coded in Table 3.3. The interactions Arthur describes with his boss and his in-session relating with the therapist make sense—and are even predictable—considering his history:

> Arthur was born while his father was serving in the U.S. Army during World War II. His early childhood memories of his mother were of consistent caring and warmth. However, when Arthur was 3 years old, his father returned from the war and the family dynamics changed radically. According to Arthur, his

76 • *Basic Principles*

father was cold and rejecting of him, and interfered with his relationship with his mother by sending him away whenever he saw the two of them together. His father's discipline was harsh. For example, when Arthur did not obey his father immediately, his father would switch his legs with tree branches. At first his mother objected to his father's treatment of him. Arthur remembers her coming to his room and putting salve in the cuts from the switchings and comforting him. However, this soon changed as well, as his mother became pregnant 3 months after his father returned.

Arthur remembered that after his sister's birth, his father's behavior became even more antagonistic. He seemed to make a point of showing Arthur how much he loved his little girl and how this contrasted with this contempt for Arthur. Slaps across the face and humiliating taunts were commonplace. Arthur was given responsibilities for helping around the house that were beyond his capabilities and then was punished when he did not perform according to his father's expectations.

. . . When Arthur was a teenager, he was expected to not only do his own chores, but was also held responsible for his sibling's chores. When anyone failed to keep up with their responsibilities, Arthur was physically punished. Slaps often turned into pushing and shoving. Once when Arthur attempted to defend himself, his father hit him with his fists. After this incident, Arthur simply submitted to whatever punishment was meted out.

Still, Arthur harbored a secret wish to gain his father's approval. When Arthur was a senior in high school and doing poorly in all but his art class, he abruptly quit school. He impulsively joined the Army, hoping to win his father's approval. His father did briefly relent from harassing him, saying that Arthur may have made the right choice for the first time in his life.

During basic training, Arthur was hurt during a hazardous field exercise. His left leg was badly injured, incapacitating him from active service. He was given an honorable discharge and VA benefits. Returning home, Arthur found his father brutally critical of him, accusing him of deliberately getting injured because he was not fit for military life. Arthur fled his parent's home in Allentown, Pennsylvania, vowing never to return. (Benjamin, 1997, pp. 6–7)

In an overall distillation of Athur's early history with his father, we see that his father exerted unrealistic and unfair control (coded as complex 1-5: **Control** plus 1-8: **Ignore**), extreme criticism (1-6: **Blame**), and harsh punishments (1-7: **Attack**) whenever Arthur did not, or could not, comply. Over time, Arthur adjusted by simply submitting (2-5: Submit) and, when possible, by avoiding and escaping (2-8: Wall-Off).

Arthur's work history as an adult is marked by the same basic patterns. After leaving his parents' home, he took a job at an automobile factory:

Unfortunately, Arthur reported, his foreman had it in for him from the start. The foreman claimed that Arthur's work was slower than others on the line,

Application of Structural Analysis of Social Behavior Technology • 77

and he was issued several warnings. But Arthur felt the foreman was critical of him simply because he was not a local, or even from Ohio. Arthur felt he did not have a chance, and after 3 months, when he sensed he might be fired, he abruptly quit. "The foreman ran the show," he said, "I got tired of banging my head against the wall." (Benjamin, 1997, p. 7)

The basic pattern seen with his father was repeated on the job with his foreman, with Arthur experiencing the foreman as unfairly demanding performance and judging him (1-5: **Control** plus 1-8: **Ignore**, and 1-6: **Blame**). Meanwhile, Arthur deals with this by trying to comply for a time, apparently performing below standard, and then quitting (2-5: <u>Submit</u>, followed by 2-8: <u>Wall-Off</u>). He also reports other relationships, mostly with bosses and authority figures but also his wife, that follow the same pattern.

Given the pervasive sense of unfair punishment, rejection, and blame in his history, it would not be surprising if Arthur expected others, including his therapist, to also exert unfair control and/or lie in wait to blame him for any real or imagined problems. Although it has not emerged as a major theme in Arthur's story as presented earlier, the expected, complementary response to this perception of others would be to complain, defend, or warily comply. The code for these behaviors is 2-6: <u>Sulk</u>. If Arthur responds to a therapist's directive interventions, however benign or well intentioned, with sulking or walled-off behaviors, this may be a sign that he has perceived those interventions through the "filter" of his early history—one that is indirectly detectable through his behavior as a result. This appears to have occurred in lines 117 to 122 of the session transcript presented in Table 3.3. A therapist who is carefully tracking the process (or the content of stories in the present) and knows the basic pattern of the patient's history will have an idea of what to expect and why. The repetitions themselves suggest the presence of a copy process and have implications for understanding problems and planning interventions. This chapter aims to provide an initial, concrete demonstration of how SASB can be used to help a clinician track problem patterns and symptom-related themes that occur in sessions and across relationships. The following chapters provide more detail about how to recognize and use SASB-coded patterns to intervene optimally.

### Reliability and Validity of SASB Observational Coding

Well-trained raters can use SASB observational coding to reach high agreement at the moment-by-moment level. The SASB coding manual suggests that research raters can achieve good reliability for research with 30 to 50 hours

78 • *Basic Principles*

of training and practice with clinical materials (Benjamin & Cushing, 2000); however, basic fluency is possible even without a high level of training. For example, our trainees have been able to match SASB-based summaries of patient case formulations (with all other identifying information removed) with the clinical interview from which they were derived with no more than a minimal introduction to SASB and a chart of the cluster model (Critchfield et al., 2015). Sensitivity to interpersonal processes, as noted in Chapter 1, is typically acquired naturally through a combination of clinical training and life experiences. Accordingly, most people trained to use SASB discover that their own relationship histories have informed their perceptions. Nuanced judgments of affiliation and interdependence require the ability to rely on one's own perceptions, informed by one's embodied, culturally situated experience. Because we all have unique learning histories, this can include the experience of being differentially sensitive to some types of interactions. Training in groups, as is often the case in educational and research settings, helps reveal an individual's perceptual blind spots through the process of reviewing and resolving discrepancies and then calibrating with others and establishing reliability.[4] The most common blind spots observed in training include a tendency to perceive hostility whenever control is present (or vice versa) or to overlook complexity when it is present.

For individuals who successfully complete research training, coding reliability is quite good. For example, Critchfield (2002) demonstrated strong reliability for content coding in research using videotaped clinical interviews. In this context, Cohen's weighted $\kappa$ (Cohen, 1968) was estimated at an average of .70 for unit-by-unit agreement across all the various codes in the cluster model. Process coding involves direct observation of behavior (rather than only a person's report of it) and thus usually has higher reliability. For example, Critchfield et al. (2007) reported an average weighted $\kappa$ of .81 and .82 for process coding of therapy sessions using pairs of raters trained at two different sites.

More disagreements between raters tend to occur when higher levels of interpersonal complexity are present (Critchfield, 2002; Fromm, 1981, cited in Benjamin & Cushing, 2000). In the Fromm (1981) study reported in the SASB coding manual (Benjamin & Cushing, 2000), reliability differed between observations of clinical and normal groups. Ratings of a sample of people with anorexia showed a weighted $\kappa$ of .66, whereas it was .79 for a comparison sample. Differences in reliability were attributed to group-based differences in communication complexity. Similarly, studies of relational

---

[4]Formal training can be arranged via the IRT Institute (https://irtinstitute.com/).

processes for couples in which one member was depressed, and they found average weighted κ values between .62 and .65 (Knobloch-Fedders et al., 2014; Knobloch-Fedders, Critchfield, & Staab, 2017). They noted considerable variability between couples in terms of the ability for objective raters to agree on SASB codes (ranging from .43 to .86). Future research is needed to explore whether the ease with which a person can be consensually understood by others is itself a variable associated with pathology.

The various reliability estimates just reported are for consensus between two raters for each element of an interaction. This kind of agreement occurs at the microanalytic level, is very rigorous, and applies when the concern is to precisely understand sequences of behavior. Sometimes the pattern in aggregate is the main interest, and then agreement on each moment is not so crucial. When SASB-based profiles such as those shown in Figure 3.2 are generated by different raters, they may be correlated using Pearson $r$ or an intraclass correlation coefficient (ICC; Shrout & Fleiss, 1979) to gauge their similarity. Critchfield (2002) found strong reliability for profiles generated from patient content describing the self (ICC = .75) and others (ICC = .71). Reliability of SASB codes included in IRT case formulations showed a Pearson $r$ of .99 for behaviors that both teams agreed should be included in a case formulation, with $r = .77$ when profiles allowed unmatched pairings (i.e., when one team coded a behavior that the other did not). For the latter set, agreement differed based on whether transitive ($r = .99$) or intransitive behavior ($r = .66$) was profiled.

Profiles of process codes show even stronger agreement, with Pearson $r$ values frequently observed at .90 and greater (Benjamin & Cushing, 2000). Critchfield (2002) explored the reliability of each cluster on the SASB model and showed that between-rater variability is small for nearly all SASB clusters relative to the differences found between patient-reported relationships.

Evidence of convergent and predictive validity is found in the empirical literature. Observational coding has been used to generate and compare patient case formulations (Bennett & Parry, 1998; Schacht & Henry, 1994), predict psychotherapy outcomes (Coady, 1991a, 1991b; Critchfield, 2002; Critchfield et al., 2007; Henry et al., 1986, 1990; Jørgensen et al., 2000), and explore predicted links between interpersonal relating and measures of personality and psychopathology (Critchfield, 2002; Critchfield et al., 2015). In addition to the advantage of observer objectivity, SASB codes allow reliable unpacking of complex communications (Humphrey & Benjamin, 1986) and highly informative analyses of sequences (Benjamin, 1986; Karpiak & Benjamin, 2004). Overall, SASB data have been used to elucidate family processes, distinguish clinical groups, and predict outcomes and have been

80 • *Basic Principles*

shown to be meaningfully associated with relevant aspects of personality, symptom reports, and therapy outcomes.

## SASB INTREX QUESTIONNAIRE: ASSESSMENT VIA SELF-REPORT

The Intrex questionnaire is a self-report assessment methodology based on the SASB model (questionnaires and scoring software are available from https:// irtinstitute.com). Three versions of the questionnaire have been developed: long, medium, and short forms. The long form has a single item written to correspond to each point on the SASB full model. This results in four or five separate items assessed per cluster and a total of 36 items per SASB surface (focus on other, focus on self, and introject). The short and medium forms of the Intrex contain one and two items, respectively, for each position on the SASB cluster model. The Intrex long form is the most reliable of the three assessment methods, owing to the larger number of items. It also provides the richest data, allowing for a high degree of model specificity and (with special scoring methods not discussed here) the ability to analyze its separate tracks in addition to the usual scoring parameters. A typical administration asks about multiple relationships, including the contribution of the self and others in multiple psychological states, and can rapidly become very lengthy. The medium form is usually recommended as the best compromise between rich, reliable data and brevity, because it includes the minimum number of items sufficient to allow reliable inspection of cluster results. Unless otherwise noted, data from medium-form Intrex analyses are presented throughout this book.

### Importance of Perspective and Context: Rating Both Self and Other

Intrex allows for ratings of the self (*me* forms), others (*he, she, it,* or *they* forms), and self-treatment (introject). Using the separate forms, assessments can be tailored to a given patient, clinic, or research setting so that all important relationships and relevant states chosen by the assessor (e.g., best/worst, intoxicated/sober, normal/depressed, before/after trauma) are included.

The SASB model emphasizes interaction and views relational behavior as involving (a) traitlike processes that are stable in each individual, (b) the state or states they are in when interacting, and (c) the setting in which they are relating. As such, SASB embraces a trait-by state-by-situation model.

This model contrasts with other common methods to clinical interpersonal measurement that explicitly or implicitly assume consistency and approach relational behavior as an internal, stable, traitlike aspect of personality, such as the interpersonal circle tradition following Leary (1957) and Wiggins (1979). SASB measures and procedures can also be used to assess traitlike aspects of behavior simply by changing instructional sets to assess "yourself in general" and/or "others in general." For most settings, however, we do not endorse this approach. If an individual shows strong traitlike consistency across all relationships and settings, we believe it is better to assess relevant circumstances and let the data inform about consistency rather than make it an assumption of the rating system. We also find that enhanced understanding of the contingencies at work in a patient's life provides a better basis for connecting with patient experience and planning interventions.

The Intrex standard series asks individuals to rate their self-treatment when *at best* and again when *at worst*. The current (or recent) relationship with a significant other (usually a romantic partner but can be anyone salient in the present) is then rated, also at best and at worst. The significant other is typically rated first, followed by the self in relation to that person, repeated for each state. Ratings of the remembered relationship with mother and father in childhood are provided next (the parent and the self are both rated). If "mother" and "father" are not caregiving labels applicable to a person's experience, patients can complete these forms with relevant, identified other caregivers in mind. Finally, the remembered relationship between parental figures is assessed. Ratings of best and worst states are intended to draw out separate ratings for the (likely) idealized or socially desirable view of relationships versus more problematic states likely to be the focus of clinical attention.

As discussed in Chapter 2, the Intrex questionnaires perform well in terms of the predicted circular ordering of items, and they show good concurrent and predictive validity with a variety of data sets collected and analyzed by different investigators. Data regarding Intrex reliability are also good. Tests of internal consistency for the long form yield mean cluster $\alpha$ values of .74 for inpatients and .71 for nonclinical samples, based on ratings of introjective self-treatment at best and at worst, mother's transitive focus on the rater, and rater's reactions to mother (Benjamin, 2000). The average internal consistency for patterning across items can be measured with split-half correlations. These values are .82 for the medium form and .76 for the long form. Test-retest reliability of profile similarity is reported as .87, .84, and .79 for the long, medium, and short forms, respectively.

82 • *Basic Principles*

### Clusters, Dimensions, and Pattern Coefficients: Understanding the Basic Intrex Output

Evidence is strong for test-retest reliability for other parameters measuring the underlying SASB dimensions (Benjamin, 2000). As an example, Figure 3.3 shows part of the general report output from the SASBQuest scoring program for Intrex (specifically, the output file labeled "GeneralReport.txt"). The sample patient is Joe, a 52-year-old man recently released from the hospital after making his fifth lifetime suicide attempt by overdose of psychiatric medication and hanging. He filled out the Intrex as an outpatient. For present purposes, Figure 3.3 focuses only on one patient's introject ratings at best and at worst, to simplify presentation and help readers get oriented to the output and some of its implications. Chapter 6 provides additional clinical examples, including added discussion of methods for using Intrex output to provide feedback and enhance discussion directly with patients.

The Intrex output first presents the introjective surface, starting with "Emancipate Self" (cluster 3-1: *Self-Emancipate*) and then going clockwise around the cluster model until reaching "Neglect Self" (cluster 3-8: *Self-Neglect*). The number to the left of the cluster indicates the average score given to items in that cluster. Since the medium form was used, two items are averaged. These scores can range from 0 to 100, with a score of 50 or greater indicating that the cluster of behavior is characteristic of the patient (i.e., a "yes" response). A series of asterisks (*) provides a visual profile. When rating himself at his best, Joe endorsed 3-5: *Self-Control*, 3-3: *Active Self-Love*, and 3-4: *Self-Protect*, with 3-1: *Self-Emancipate* being the only other cluster scored at or greater than 50.

The ideal SASB interpersonal profile is S-shaped or sinusoidal in nature. That is, it tends to peak in one region and then falls away in an orderly pattern until it reaches the cluster on the opposite side of the SASB model. Such a pattern would hold if Joe's score on 3-1: *Self-Emancipate* were lower and 3-4: *Self-Protect* were the highest score. Obviously, not all patient ratings conform to an ideal curve. Some are instead bimodal or have other complex shapes. Under the heading "Summary and Estimate of Goodness of Fit," a label appears with the name of an idealized prototype profile that best matches Joe's ratings. Twenty-one prototypes[5] are defined and described in the *Intrex User's Manual* (Benjamin, 2000) to correspond to a range of interpersonal profiles, including those that center on each SASB cluster, as well as patterns that imply internal conflict or ambivalence (e.g., strong

---

[5] Interested readers may learn more about these prototypes and how they were developed in the Intrex manual (Benjamin, 2000).

Application of Structural Analysis of Social Behavior Technology • 83

**FIGURE 3.3. Joe's Intrex Output for Introject Ratings at Best and Worst**

```
My introject at best

Rater focuses inward

50.EMANCIPATE SELF ********************

40.AFFIRM SELF       ****************

65.LOVE SELF         **************************

60.PROTECT SELF      ************************

75.CONTROL SELF      ******************************

30.BLAME SELF        ************

15.ATTACK SELF       ******

 5.NEGLECT SELF      **

SUMMARY, AND ESTIMATE OF GOODNESS OF FIT.

Affirm, protect & control self. .86

PROFILE NUMBER: 11

ATTACK PATTERN = -.736 PROFILE 2

CONTROL PATTERN = .829 PROFILE 8

CONFLICT PATTERN = .371 PROFILE 18

WEIGHTED AFFILIATION, AUTONOMY SCORES

85.31 -49.69

INTERNAL CONSISTENCY = .77

CLUSTER SCORES 1 to 8

50. 40. 65. 60. 75. 30. 15. 5.

-------------------------------------------
```

*(continues)*

84 • *Basic Principles*

**FIGURE 3.3. Joe's Intrex Output for Introject Ratings at Best and Worst (*Continued*)**

My introject at worst

Rater focuses inward

50.EMANCIPATE SELF ********************

25.AFFIRM SELF      **********

25.LOVE SELF      **********

35.PROTECT SELF     **************

40.CONTROL SELF    ****************

60.BLAME SELF    ************************

50.ATTACK SELF    ********************

40.NEGLECT SELF    ***************

SUMMARY, AND ESTIMATE OF GOODNESS OF FIT.

Conflict: Self-attack vs. Let self go .86

PROFILE NUMBER: 17

ATTACK PATTERN = .814  PROFILE 2

CONTROL PATTERN = -.455  PROFILE 8

CONFLICT PATTERN = .204  PROFILE 9

WEIGHTED AFFILIATION, AUTONOMY SCORES

-46.88 -7.13

INTERNAL CONSISTENCY = .84

CLUSTER SCORES 1 to 8

50. 25. 25. 35. 40. 60. 50. 40.

endorsement of opposites like self-affirm and self-blame). As shown in Figure 3.3, the pattern with the best fit to Joe's ratings is relatively complex: "Affirm, Protect & Control self." The goodness of fit between this label and the actual ratings is based on a correlation coefficient (ranging from $-1.0$ to $+1.0$), which is .86 in this case. When this correlation is around .90 or greater, the pattern is a near perfect match and the label is likely to be a very good description of the patient's responses—one with a psychological meaning that should resonate with the patient's experience. Values below .70 (i.e., <50% of variance shared between ideal and real profiles) suggest a unique pattern of response that is not well described by any of the 21 prototypes.

In addition to a best-fit pattern, the Intrex questionnaire provides parameters based on affiliation and interdependence. The attack (ATK) and control (CON) pattern coefficients each indicate the degree of correlation with prototype profiles reflecting the extreme of interpersonal attack and control, respectively (for more detail on these scores and their properties, see Benjamin, 2000). ATK and CON values can be plotted together in the SASB model as $X$ and $Y$ Cartesian coordinates for interpretation.

Figure 3.4 shows the location for Joe's best and worst introject states using this approach. When Joe rates himself at his best, he falls into the region of 3-4: *Self-Protect*; at his worst, he is characterized by 3-8: *Self-Neglect*.

The next pattern coefficient listed is the *conflict pattern* or CFL. This number reflects the degree of simultaneous endorsement of opposites in the profile. For example, a conflict pattern of $-1.0$ is consistent with a pattern that peaks on both clusters 3 and 7 at each end of the horizontal dimension. Such a person is *conflicted*, in the sense of being both very loving and very attacking (or recoiling, if focus is on the self) in the same relationship and state. Conversely, a value of $+1.0$ reflects conflict on the vertical axis of the rated surface (e.g., both 2-5: <u>Submit</u> and 2-1: <u>Separate</u>, or both 1-5: **Control** and 1-1: **Emancipate**).

Weighted affiliation (AF) and autonomy (AU) provide an alternative method of computing the underlying dimensions. AF and AU differ from pattern coefficients in that they consist of a weighted linear combination of all the clusters.[6] The resulting values range from $+210$ to $-210$. For example, a maximum endorsement of all items involving friendliness and a minimum endorsement of all items involving hostility would yield AF = +210. Equal rates of endorsement of friendliness and hostility would produce AF = 0. Maximum endorsement of all hostile items and minimum endorsement of all

---

[6] Specific weights and formulae for computation are provided in the Intrex manual (Benjamin, 2000).

**FIGURE 3.4. Introject at Best and Worst for a Sample Patient Based on Attack and Control Pattern Coefficients**

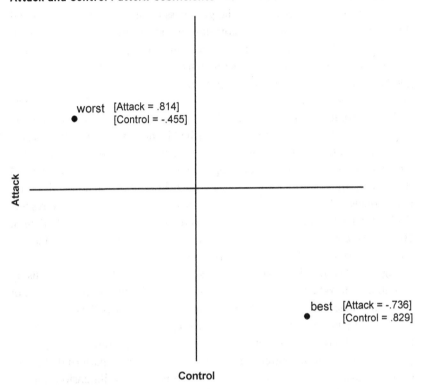

friendliness items would produce AF = –210. The same logic applies to the AU scores, except they are organized around endorsement of items involving degrees of independence (contributing to positive AU values) versus interdependence (contributing to negative AU scores). AF and AU scores tend to be normally distributed and thus tend to be used most in statistical analysis. Like ATK and CON, they may be graphed as Cartesian coordinates. For Joe, this results in a configuration that is like the graph shown in Figure 3.4, but with greater emphasis on affiliation differences between his best and worst states. His self-treatment at best would be located by AF = 85 (horizontal, X-axis), AU = –50 (vertical, Y-axis; i.e., lower-right quadrant, but projecting relatively more along the horizontal). His self-treatment at worst would be located at AF = –47, AU = –7 (i.e., extending to the left, very close to the horizontal axis). This method of summarizing again shows that Joe has an overall self-protective profile at best. He has a more self-attacking profile at worst, but one that does not extend as far out into hostile territory as is shown in Figure 3.4. Differences between plotted points based on ATK/CON versus AF/AU are sometimes meaningful. In a technical sense, they result from differences between a computational strategy emphasizing the overall profile shape (ATK/CON) versus one that emphasizes the absolute degree of endorsement of each item (AF/AU). The primary way to arrive at an interpretation is to inspect the cluster-level scores, because both approaches to a dimensional summary derive directly from them.

Internal consistency reflects the degree to which similar items (i.e., from the same SASB cluster) are endorsed to the same degree. It is computed as a correlation coefficient across clusters for matched halves of the data (and so is not available for the Intrex short form). It may range from +1.0 to –1.0. When a patient is motivated to receive feedback and is attending to all items, variations in internal consistency usually have psychological meaning. Lower values can suggest ambivalence or inconsistency in how the relationship is viewed. If low internal consistency is pervasive across all relationships and situations of an entire assessment, it may indicate an invalid administration.

The next rated surface is then presented in Figure 3.3 (in this case, "My Introject at Worst"). For Joe, the only items endorsed here as generally true (scores of ≥50) are 3-6: *Self-Blame*, 3-7: *Self-Attack*, and 3-1: *Self-Emancipate*. This pattern is best matched to a profile labeled "Conflict: Self-attack vs. Let self go." The profile shape indicating conflict (i.e., endorsement of opposites on the model) is not a simple product of ambivalence, since there is a high level of internal consistency to Joe's ratings (.84).

Joe's Intrex profile fits what is known about him clinically. As described earlier, he was referred for treatment because of his history of suicide attempts. Each had been very self-damaging and appeared impulsive and reckless. Comparison of Joe's at-best and at-worst profiles shows that at best, he is a generally self-controlled individual who cares for himself; at worst, he can be unrestrained in his self-attack in ways that have led to disfigurement, multiple surgeries, and chronic pain. Interestingly, the single-point summary in Figure 3.4 does not suggest the intensity and severity of Joe's self-attacks. The alternative approach using AF/AU suggests self-attack when at worst, but not with the intensity seen in Joe's known behavior. However, inspection of specific cluster values suggests that when at worst, Joe's 3-6: *Self-Blame* and 3-7: *Self-Attack* occur in the context of little self-restraint, 3-1: *Self-Emancipate*.

## Summary Report

The degree of detail provided in the general report can be overwhelming when expanded to include all relationships, focuses, and states. A summary

88 • *Basic Principles*

report is also available that simply lists the pattern names for the best fit to each Intrex surface rated. Figure 3.5 provides the complete summary report for all of Joe's rated relationships.

A quick scan of the output reveals that Joe and his wife are both very loving to one another when at their best. When the relationship is at its worst, the dynamic becomes more distant. In terms of their focus on each other, Joe perceives both he and his wife to be affirming overall. He responds to his wife with conflict between loving versus walling off. The relatively low goodness-of-fit value of .64 suggests that the label "separate" does not fully capture his wife's reaction to him, so the cluster-level data should be consulted to obtain better understanding.

Summary relationship patterns with each of Joe's parents are then presented. These patterns show that Joe had a very loving relationship with his father, but he experienced his mother as blaming and distant. Joe focused on his mother by loving her and giving her space. His reaction to her is labeled "trusting," but the goodness of fit of only .65 again suggests a more complex response that could be understood better at the level of individual clusters. Joe saw his father as being loving toward his mother, but that she was neglectful and distant ("very separate") in that relationship.

Even at this level of abstraction, the output can be used to generate hypotheses for clinical work and areas for further exploration. For example, there may be possible links between Joe's self-concept, especially his 3-6: *Self-Blame* at worst and 1-6: **Blame** he perceived in childhood from his mother. Relational distance and lack of warmth and caring seen in Joe's self-treatment (e.g., 3-1: *Self-Emancipate* when at his worst) may have been further modeled by her separateness from him. Implicitly, the connection may be, "She didn't stick up for me when I needed her, so what happens to me when things get bad?"

Joe's Intrex data map closely to his report in the clinical interview with his therapist (conducted without knowledge of the Intrex results). Joe recalled his mother looking the other way despite knowing that he was being sexually humiliated by adult associates of his father when they would visit the house. He reports struggling as an adult to take care of himself in basic ways, leading to repeated feelings of humiliation and embarrassment when personal, financial, and health problems ensue.

Even closer connections between Joe's self-concept and his mother's behavior are apparent when cluster-level details are compared. Figure 3.6 shows a strong overlap between Joe's self-treatment and the way his mother used to treat his father. These data suggest areas that may be worth further exploring with Joe, including (a) the impact of early input from his mother on his current self-concept and (b) the possibility that he has internalized and

## FIGURE 3.5. Joe's Summary Report

My Introject at Best
Rater focuses inward
Affirm, Protect & Control self     .86

----------------

My Introject at Worst
Rater focuses inward
Conflict: Self-attack vs. Let self go     .86

----------------

My (female) significant other person at best (she is rated)
Me with my (female) significant other person at best (I am rated)
The other person focuses on the rater
Loving     .89
Rater reacts to the other person
Loving     .89
Rater focuses on the other person
Affirming     .87
The other person reacts to the rater
Loving     .86

----------------

My (female) significant other person at worst (she is rated)
Me with my (female) significant other person at worst (I am rated)
The other person focuses on the rater
Affirming     .86
Rater reacts to the other person
Conflict: Loving vs. Walling Off     .90
Rater focuses on the other person
Affirming     .92
The other person reacts to the rater
Separate     .64

*(continues)*

90 • *Basic Principles*

**FIGURE 3.5. Joe's Summary Report (*Continued*)**

My mother when I was aged 5–10

Me with my mother when I was aged 5–10

The other person focuses on the rater

Blaming .92

Rater reacts to the other person

Trusting .65

Rater focuses on the other person

Loving but Freeing .91

The other person reacts to the rater

Very separate .85

----------------

My father when I was aged 5–10

Me with my father when I was aged 5–10

The other person focuses on the rater

Loving .93

Rater reacts to the other person

Loving .90

Rater focuses on the other person

Loving but Freeing .93

The other person reacts to the rater

Loving .92

----------------

My mother (person 1) with my father (person 2) when I was aged 5–10

My father with my mother when I was aged 5–10

Rater sees person 1 focus on person 2

Neglectful .78

Rater sees person 2 react to person 1

Loving .96

Rater sees person 2 focus on person 1

Loving .90

Rater sees person 1 react to person 2

Very separate .75

**FIGURE 3.6. Similarity Observed Between Patient's Self-Treatment and Mother's Focus on Father (Raw Scores)**

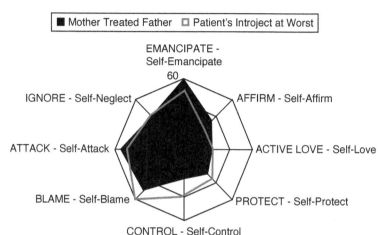

identified with aspects of his father based on the way Joe saw his mother treating them both. In the clinical interview (again, without clinician knowledge of the Intrex results), Joe reported that he had great affection for his now deceased father, had always identified strongly with him, and had followed in his footsteps in significant ways, including empathizing with how his father had been mistreated by his mother. This example further suggests the validity of the Intrex as a way to elicit clinically relevant data about patterns.

## REPEATING THEMES ACROSS RELATIONSHIPS (EXPLORING WITHIN-SUBJECT CORRELATIONS)

Intrex scoring software provides correlation coefficients and can be used to create the radial and line graphs presented in this section. Providing clinical feedback to patients using graphical representations of rated relationships is often useful for helping them recognize and then explore the meaning of repeating themes across important relationships. To supplement and help interpret visual profiles, a measure of similarity from +1.0 (perfect match) to –1.0 (perfect opposite) can be constructed using Pearson $r$ for the eight points on a SASB surface. For example, Figure 3.7 shows Joe's rated relationship with his wife when they are at their best. The match between profiles shows a high degree of complementarity in every area except that he does not separate (2-1: <u>Separate</u>) even though she emancipates (1-1: **Emancipate**) him. The similarity between profiles is $r = .73$.

**FIGURE 3.7. Strong Complementarity Rated for Significant Other at Best (r = .73)**

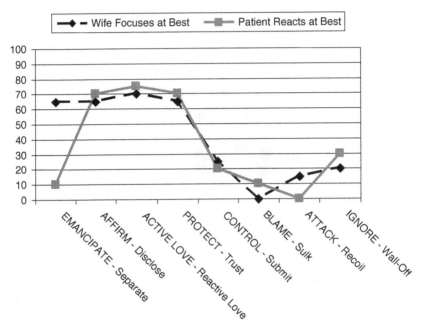

Other comparisons can be made between past and present relationships to explore for potential copy process patterns (described in Chapter 2). Joe reports that his wife, when the relationship is at its best, treats him nearly the exact opposite of how his mother treated him as a child (Figure 3.8). When Joe's marital relationship is at its best, it appears he has chosen a partner unlikely to recapitulate his mother's behavior. The correlation between the two profiles is −.90. Despite differences in Joe's perception of his wife and his mother when the relationship is at its best, the story is different when Joe's relationship with his wife is at its worst (Figure 3.9). In the worst state, he reports focusing on his wife in nearly the same way he focused on his mother (copy process of recapitulation). In both instances, he rates himself as giving space and affirmation to the other (1-1: **Emancipate** and 1-2: **Affirm**). This correlation is .92.

### Comparing Patient Responses to Normative Base Rates of Behavior

The preceding profiles and examples are based on raw-score patterns, which we recommend for clinical use of the Intrex questionnaire in general. Raw scores characterize relationships in absolute terms around the SASB model

Application of Structural Analysis of Social Behavior Technology • 93

FIGURE 3.8. Opposite Profiles Observed for Mother's Focus (Remembered From Childhood) and Wife (in Present) as Rated by Joe (r = −.90)

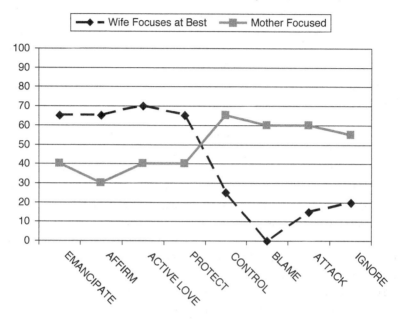

FIGURE 3.9. Recapitulation With Wife of the Maternal Relationship When Rated "At Worst" (Raw-Score Profiles, r = .92)

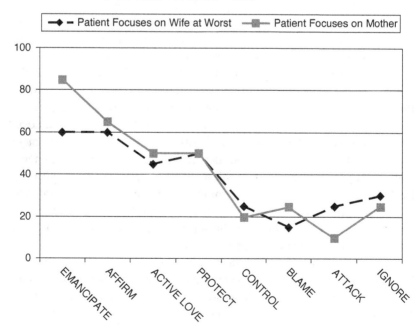

94 • *Basic Principles*

and have the advantage of offering direct interpretability about degrees of hostility, friendliness, control, and so on. Normed data, by contrast, must be interpreted as deviations from what is typically the case in other people's lives. For example, a significant other may be seen as friendly in an absolute sense (i.e., rated in friendly space to the right of the SASB model) but still be less friendly than the *average* significant other. Presentation of norm-referenced results can complicate clinical processes by requiring patients to compare their lives with the "average" lives of others. This kind of awareness can be useful sometimes but can be distracting or demoralizing at other times, and it should only be pursued with some sensitivity to this fact. With that caveat in mind, norms are available for each of the Intrex standard series administrations (short, medium, and long forms) and can be used to contextualize relational behavior when this may be useful. The approach is offered here with some caution about the nature of available norms for the Intrex. They were collected at various points by the authors from research studies that involved the Intrex in some way and have not had the kind of support to allow pursuit of a sample constructed to match community demographics. As described in the Intrex manual, norms were gathered "under collaborative conditions in which research subjects were offered the Intrex report as a self-enhancing, growth experience" (Benjamin, 2000, p. 15), which suggests valid responding by motivated participants. However, the available norms do not reflect a wide range of cultural diversity and have largely been developed from dominant culture settings in the United States.

Keeping the limitations of this approach in mind, a norm-based lens can sometimes reveal patterns that have potential to inform clinical conceptualization. For example, when Joe's at-best ratings of his wife and his mother (Figure 3.8) were rescored relative to normative data, they produced the profile shown in Figure 3.10. In this view, their patterns are similar rather than opposite. Compared with available norms for mothers and significant others, they are both less warm (i.e., lower 1-2: **Affirm**, 1-3: **Active Love**, and 1-4: **Protect**) and more hostile (1-7: **Attack** and 1-8: **Ignore**). Although the pattern for Joe's wife does not depart significantly from norms, never going outside 1 *SD* from the mean, his mother's pattern departs significantly. Despite this, the two patterns of norm-referenced deviation show moderate to strong correlation, $r = .77$. This correspondence between Joe's views of both his wife and his mother may have psychological relevance that could also be explored further in therapy.

Another use of normative data is to identify relationship disturbance. Benjamin, Wamboldt, and Critchfield (2006) proposed a method to identify relational disorders as part of a revised *Diagnostic and Statistical Manual of Mental Disorders*. The procedure is simple. Intrex scores on each surface and

Application of Structural Analysis of Social Behavior Technology • 95

**FIGURE 3.10. Normed Profiles for Wife (at Best) and Mother, Focusing on Patient Reveal Subtle Similarities (r = .77) Despite Raw-Score Profiles Suggesting They Are Opposites**

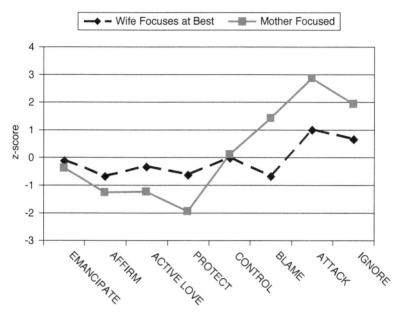

dimension for each member of a couple are inspected to determine whether they fall more than 2 *SD* away from normative patterns. If so, a relational disorder is identified. This method could provide a theoretically informed and empirically grounded way to define relational disorders, especially if more representative norms can be pursed in work that remains to be done for the Intrex method. In Joe's case, it is interesting to note that even though he experiences significant psychiatric symptoms and personality pathology, his at-best and at-worst ratings for current relationships remain within the boundaries of available norms.

PART **II**
USING STRUCTURAL
ANALYSIS OF SOCIAL
BEHAVIOR TO PUT
CLINICAL THEORY
INTO CLINICAL
PRACTICE:
AN OVERVIEW

# 4 STRUCTURAL ANALYSIS OF SOCIAL BEHAVIOR AS PRECISE DESCRIPTION

*Applications in Diverse Theoretical Frameworks*

Structural Analysis of Social Behavior (SASB) can be applied across theoretical perspectives whenever interpersonal aspects of functioning are pertinent.[1] Clinicians and researchers from a variety of theoretical orientations have used SASB in diverse ways to inform their work. This chapter shows how SASB can be—and has been—used to understand and track a variety of clinically relevant processes, from articulation of theory to case conceptualization and to elucidation of nuanced clinical process details. It is beyond the scope of this chapter to present all uses of the SASB model in detail. This chapter instead illustrates ways in which SASB has been used in cognitive behavior therapy, psychodynamic, and humanistic or existential settings. In each case, SASB is used to translate concepts from diverse theoretical orientations into a transtheoretical framework focused on relational patterns. The translation process offers opportunities for theoretical and empirical comparison and suggests potential avenues for integration and/or theory testing. The translation process also provides additional opportunities to practice applying SASB's dimensions to diverse clinical material.

---

[1]The clinical material used in this book is adequately disguised to protect patient confidentiality.

https://doi.org/10.1037/0000403-004
*Structural Analysis of Social Behavior (SASB): A Primer for Clinical Use*, by
K. L. Critchfield and L. S. Benjamin
Copyright © 2024 by the American Psychological Association. All rights reserved.

## ELICITING NARRATIVE DETAIL IN SESSION

Regardless of theoretical orientation, SASB can be used to guide clinician choices about when follow up might be needed to understand a patient's narrative. To determine the availability of the minimum level of detail about the referents, along with focus, affiliation, and interdependence, a clinician might ask themselves, "Can I code this?" For example, a female patient said the following about her significant other in an angry but dejected tone: "He doesn't care about me. Everything is about him. I feel completely unsupported and invalidated and it's too much!" The patient's here-and-now process with the therapist is clear enough and involves 2-2: <u>Disclose</u>. It is also clear that 1-6: **Blame** and 2-6: <u>Sulk</u> are directed toward the partner (an implied process to him, since he is not physically present). It is also clear that the patient codes her partner as doing something that qualifies for 1-8: **Ignore**. Yet what the significant other did or said is unclear, and this information might provide the therapist additional clarity. In other words, the content about the partner is unclear: There is little to no information about the significant other's behavior sufficient to judge his focus, affiliation, or interdependence relative to the patient.

Lack of ability to understand what happened via SASB is almost always a therapeutic cue to become curious. For example, the clinician may ask the patient, "What happened that led you to feel this way?" or "Can you tell me what he did or said?" Some responses the patient might give, along with SASB-based characterization of the content of her narrative description of her partner, are presented next as a thought experiment about a range of possibilities.

Consider this alternate patient response:

> Yesterday, he came home from work and yelled at me for what seemed like forever because dinner wasn't ready for him. He said I was lazy, that it's obvious I don't care for him, and a lot worse than that. Then finally he stormed out and came home late, drunk. He wouldn't even talk to me until noon today even though I needed his help getting rides for the kids. He knew that I had a doctor's appointment and wouldn't even be home to start dinner until just before he arrived. I just don't get it.

In this version of the story, the significant other's behavior followed a sequence beginning with 1-6: **Blame** and perhaps 1-7: **Attack** depending on what exactly was said, which is an area to potentially explore for more detail. As he storms out, gets drunk, returns late, and refuses to help with the kids, his behavior turns to 2-8: <u>Wall-Off</u>, 1-8: **Ignore**, and perhaps even 3-8: *Self-Neglect* (i.e., becoming drunk, and potentially other suggestions of self-sabotage by acting this way). The patient's role is sketched out in more detail as well. She notes self-care via a doctor's appointment, communication with her partner about schedules, and a request for help with transporting their children, suggesting potential codes from the friendly side of the model (3-4: *Self-Protect*, 2-2: <u>Disclose</u>, and 2-4: <u>Trust</u>) that might be relevant to understand clinically as well.

A different patient response could be imagined, with very different codes for each partner:

> Yesterday, I came home from work and the house was a complete disaster. I was pissed because I told him to clean it up while I was gone and he didn't do it. It's not like he does anything all day long. He said he was sorry and made some excuse about "I forgot" and being busy and all—and you know even though he finally cleaned the place up, it takes me standing over him to do it. I just feel like he doesn't listen to me at all. He doesn't respect me. He doesn't consider any of my needs. I work hard. I don't think I deserve this!

In this example, description of the significant other's behavior follows a very different sequence starting with what may be 2-1: <u>Separate</u> or 2-8: <u>Wall-Off</u> to reflect him being busy doing something else, followed by 2-5: <u>Submit</u> and perhaps 2-6: <u>Sulk</u> as he then apologizes and works to do as she wishes. We also learn that the patient's behavior is critical and controlling (1-6: **Blame** and then 1-5: **Control** as she stands over him). The level of detail provided here still only gives an approximate view of each partner's behavior, but the clinician's understanding is dramatically enhanced beyond the patient's initial statement about being "invalidated." The picture in this variation suggests the patient's view that if her partner does not submit to her, then he must not care about or respect her.

Here is yet another possible patient response:

> Yesterday, I came home from work and he wasn't there. We had plans to go out last night but he didn't even return my calls until it was way too late. He gets so wrapped up and stressed about his work, and it seems like he's just disappearing into all that stuff ever since his mother passed away. I worry about what's going on with him. But it's been a long time since she died, and I just feel so alone in the relationship now. He doesn't see me, and it's like I don't have a partner. I'm on my own all over again.

In this example, the partner's behavior is described as predominantly 2-8: <u>Wall-Off</u> in each sentence about him. The context appears to be one of complicated bereavement. There may even be 3-8: *Self-Neglect* on her partner's part if he is burying himself in work to avoid acknowledging his grief. In this case, the patient's behavior remains unclear, but her sense of being left alone and what that means to her is clearly important for improved understanding in the context of her other relationships, especially given her last phrase "all over again."

Each example provides a potential follow-up to the same initial description. The point here is that SASB can help the therapist (a) know when there is enough detail to obtain sufficient understanding of what a patient is communicating and (b) know that an initial impression of an interpersonal circumstance may or may not prove to have been an adequate guess once a narrative is unpacked. Because not all interactions are equally important to clarify, it is up to clinicians to decide how and when to elicit or follow up with relevant detail, guided by their clinical theory and formulation of patient needs.

## STRUCTURAL ANALYSIS OF SOCIAL BEHAVIOR AND COGNITIVE BEHAVIOR THERAPY: TRACKING INTERPERSONALLY RELEVANT BELIEFS AND COGNITIONS IN COGNITIVE BEHAVIOR WORK

Most clinical theories invoke interpersonal circumstances in relation to the self or others, making these aspects amenable for interpersonal translation. For example, Ellis (1994) summarized three main irrational beliefs believed to be common contributors to depression and other problems:

- I must be outstandingly competent, or I am worthless.
- Others must treat me considerately, or they are absolutely rotten.
- The world should always give me happiness, or I will die. (as cited in Zahn et al., 2010, p. 239)

Each of these beliefs involves an expectation about interpersonal behavior in one form or another. Interestingly, each statement seems to follow the SASB focus distinction. The first statement allows for only two ways of dealing with the self: 3-2: *Self-Affirmation* or 3-6: *Self-Blame*. Ellis's second irrational belief prototype implies a parallel view of others whose behavior is judged as acceptable (i.e., they are considerate and may therefore be affirmed [1-2: **Affirm**]), or they are judged harshly (i.e., they are blamed [1-6: **Blame**]). The third belief could be coded on the SASB model's intransitive, focus-on-self surface. The self is seen as experiencing either 2-3: <u>Reactive Love</u> relative to "the world" or else must experience the opposite extreme, suggesting 2-7: <u>Recoil</u>.

Ellis's (1994) expectation that depression and similar problems are associated with these cognitions is also consistent with the idea of a parallelism between interpersonal and affective behaviors. Descriptors on the Structural Analysis of Affective Behavior (SAAB) interpersonal model (described in Chapter 2) predict that if the beliefs are not upheld, there will be affects of scorn and agitation in relation to the self ("I must be outstandingly competent, or I am worthless") or in relation to others ("Others must treat me considerately, or they are absolutely rotten"). A feeling of being terrified is predicted to accompany "or I will die." Parallel cognitive styles on the SAAB model are also suggested. This involves condemnation directed toward the self and others and a cognitive style of shutting down in relation to the world. Overall, for patients holding Ellis's or other similar beliefs, translating them into SASB terms sketches out a rich phenomenology consistent with depression.

Articulating theory in interpersonal terms opens the door for further application of the SASB model to follow up on theoretical predictions using an interpersonal route. For example, the predicted relationship patterns associated with each belief could be assessed and tested using the Intrex questionnaire. The SASB model could also be used as part of an intervention strategy to help develop more rational (for the cognitive behavior therapy [CBT] practitioner) or workable (for the acceptance and commitment therapy practitioner) alternative beliefs about the self and others by considering, or behaviorally experimenting with, a wider and more flexible range of options for relating.

In another example from the CBT literature, Beck and Freeman (1990) posited that specific irrational beliefs organize various forms of personality disorder. Many of the most important beliefs listed by Beck concern relationships between the self and others. As an illustration, Beck's initial overview of dysfunctional beliefs characteristic of paranoid personality disorder is presented in Table 4.1, with hypothesized SASB translations for each associated belief. Compared with standards typically used for observational coding, some inference is required to translate the beliefs. Even so, the SASB-based summary of Beck's list of beliefs for paranoid personality disorder is coherent and precise: The primary themes involve expectation of hostility and manipulation by others (1-6: **Blame** or 1-7: **Attack**). The individual then reacts, with a need to defensively control themselves (3-5: *Self-Control*) and wall-off from others (2-8: Wall-Off). Some beliefs imply further that the patient feels that others must be controlled (1-5: **Control**) or blamed (1-6: **Blame**) to prevent their exploitation of the patient.

In terms of clinical practice, patient narratives can be inspected for prototypic interpersonal positions to aid in diagnostic decision making. To establish an evidence base across diverse theoretical perspectives, SASB provides a shared language that facilitates comparison and testing. For example, Benjamin (1996) developed interpersonal descriptions for each personality disorder in the fourth edition of the *Diagnostic and Statistical Manual of*

104 • *Using Structural Analysis of Social Behavior*

**TABLE 4.1. SASB-Based Summary of Beck's Beliefs for Paranoid Personality Disorder**

| Beck's prototypic beliefs for PAR | SASB-based analysis |
| --- | --- |
| 1. People are potential adversaries. | Hostile engagement with others is expected but the referents and focus are not specified. Most likely codes for both others and self are 1-6: **Blame**, 1-7: **Attack** |
| 2. I cannot trust other people. | Suggests the opposite of 2-4: <u>Trust</u>, which is 2-8: <u>Wall-Off</u> |
| 3. Other people have hidden motives. | Suspicion and criticism of others implies a position of 1-6: **Blame**. "Hidden motives" suggests expectation of the same code (i.e., hostile control) from others, and that others will 2-8: <u>Wall-Off</u> to avoid having their true intentions discovered |
| 4. I have to be on guard at all times. | Unclear what "on guard" consists of behaviorally, possibly a mixture of 2-7: <u>Recoil</u> or 2-8: <u>Wall-Off</u> plus 3-5: *Self-Control*. Also implied is expectation of intrusive hostility from others in the form of 1-7: **Attack** or 1-6: **Blame** |
| 5. It isn't safe to confide in other people. | 2-2: <u>Disclose</u> and 2-4: <u>Trust</u> are avoided. Implies that 2-8: <u>Wall-Off</u> is likely, as is strict 3-5: *Self-Control* |
| 6. People will take advantage of me if I give them the chance. | Expects others to 1-6: **Blame** or 1-7: **Attack.** Implies the individual will 2-8: <u>Wall-Off</u> and 3-5: *Self-Control* when around those others |
| 7. Other people will deliberately try to demean me. | Expects others to 1-6: **Blame** |
| 8. I will be in serious trouble if I let other people think they can get away with mistreating me. | Likely codes again reflect expectation of mistreatment from others (1-6: **Blame**, 1-7: **Attack**) and need to control others, perhaps in a hostile manner (1-5: **Control**, 1-6: **Blame**), and potentially also to maintain control over the self (3-5: *Self-Control*) |
| 9. If other people find out things about me, they will use them against me | Expects 1-6: **Blame** from others; implies that 2-8: <u>Wall-Off</u> may be employed to avoid it |

*Note.* Beck's beliefs are from Beck & Freeman (1990). PAR = paranoid personality disorder; SASB = Structural Analysis of Social Behavior.

*Mental Disorders* (American Psychiatric Association, 1994). The following description is for paranoid personality disorder (PAR):

> There is a fear that others will attack to hurt or blame. The wish is that others will affirm and understand. If affirmation fails, the hope is that others will either leave the PAR alone or submit. The baseline position is to wall-off, stay separate, and tightly control the self. If threatened, the [person with PAR] will recoil in a hostile way or attack to counter-control or gain distance. (Benjamin, 1996, p. 404)

This summary appears to align well with the view of Beck and Freeman (1990), but with a more interactive emphasis in terms of the relational patterning.

### Early Interpersonal Schema and Structural Analysis of Social Behavior

Young et al. (2003) defined 18 prototype schemas consisting of beliefs and expectations about the self and others thought to contribute to psychopathology, especially personality pathology. A method for addressing these schemas, *schema-focused therapy*, has been applied widely and received empirical support (Giesen-Bloo et al., 2006). In Young et al.'s (2003) formulation, different individuals develop problems as a result of application of maladaptive schemas. Most, if not all, contain interpersonal components codable with SASB. To illustrate how SASB can be used to specify theory in ways that further articulate degrees of similarity, overlap, complexity, and so on, a few of Young et al.'s schemas and their hypothesized SASB translations are presented in Figure 4.1 and described next:

- *Mistrust/abuse:* The expectation that others will hurt, abuse, humiliate, cheat, lie, manipulate, or take advantage. Usually involves the perception that the harm is intentional or the result of unjustified and extreme negligence. May include the sense that one always ends up being cheated relative to others or "getting the short end of the stick."

- *Social isolation/alienation:* The feeling that one is isolated from the rest of the world, different from other people, and/or not part of any group or community.

- *Failure:* The belief that one has failed, will inevitably fail, or is fundamentally inadequate relative to one's peers, in areas of achievement (school, career, sports, etc.). Often involves beliefs that one is stupid, inept, untalented, lower in status, less successful than others, and so forth.

- *Self-sacrifice:* Excessive focus on voluntarily meeting the needs of others in daily situations, at the expense of one's own gratification. The most

106 • *Using Structural Analysis of Social Behavior*

**FIGURE 4.1. Structural Analysis of Social Behavior Codes for Sample Young et al.'s Maladaptive Schemas**

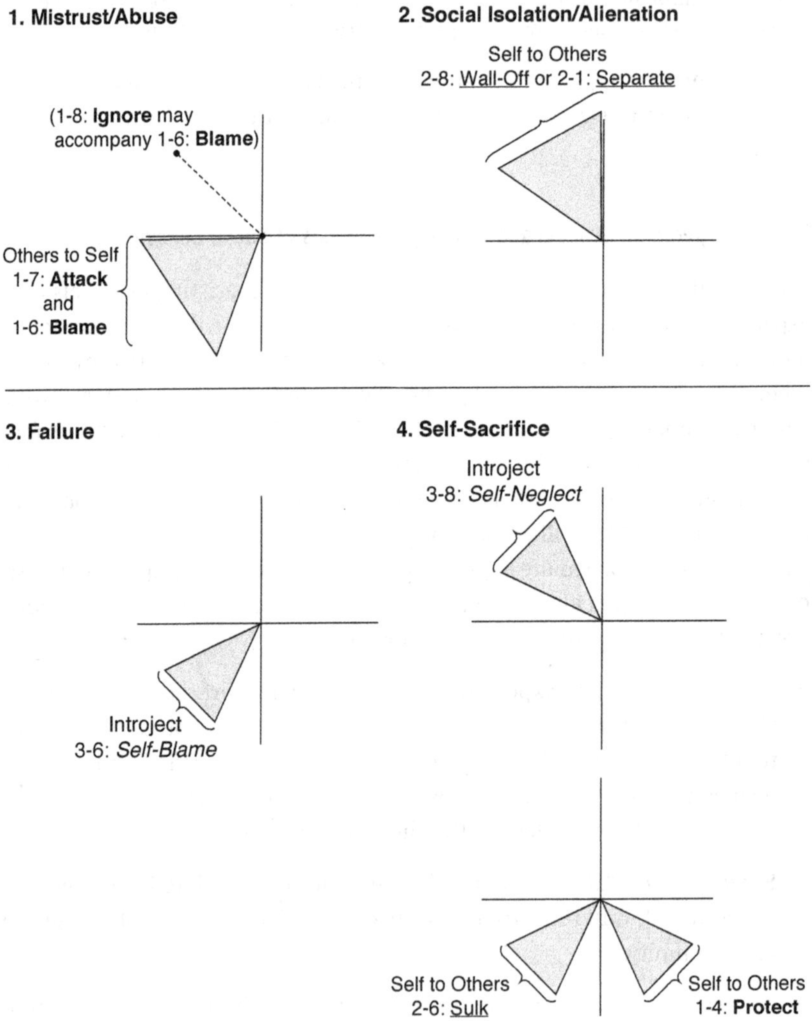

**1. Mistrust/Abuse**

(1-8: **Ignore** may accompany 1-6: **Blame**)

Others to Self
1-7: **Attack**
and
1-6: **Blame**

**2. Social Isolation/Alienation**

Self to Others
2-8: Wall-Off or 2-1: Separate

**3. Failure**

Introject
3-6: *Self-Blame*

**4. Self-Sacrifice**

Introject
3-8: *Self-Neglect*

Self to Others
2-6: Sulk

Self to Others
1-4: **Protect**

*Note.* The maladaptive schemas are described in Young et al. (2003).

common reasons are: to prevent causing pain to others; to avoid guilt from feeling selfish; or to maintain the connection with others perceived as needy. Often results from an acute sensitivity to the pain of others. Sometimes leads to a sense that one's own needs are not being adequately met and to resentment of those who are taken care of. (Young et al., 2003, pp. 14–17)

In addition to depicting the interpersonal aspects of schema in a shared framework, the SASB model suggests additional complementary positions of others or self. For example, the mistrust/abuse schema is likely associated with 2-6: Sulk and 2-7: Recoil as a common stance relative to others, based on what they expect to receive as input.

## Dialectical Behavior Therapy

Research in dialectical behavior therapy (DBT; Linehan, 1993) has used SASB to specify and test theory about optimal therapist interventions. Shearin and Linehan (1992) used Intrex ratings to assess outcomes relative to using a recommended therapist stance that balances acceptance and change. This stance was conceptualized as the therapist's emancipation (1-1: **Emancipate**) coupled with protection (1-4: **Protect**) and control (1-5: **Control**). Patients rated their therapist. Reductions in nonsuicidal self injury (NSSI) for patients with borderline personality disorder (BPD) were associated with this theory-predicted profile. Bedics and colleagues (2012a, 2012b) then used the SASB model to further test DBT theory about optimal therapy relating and to explore DBT mechanisms of change involving the therapeutic relationship. This work validated the theory by observing that patients receiving DBT had significant improvements, over and above a control condition, in the direction of self-affirmation, self-love, and self-protection (3-2: *Self-Affirmation*, 3-3: *Active Self-Love*, and 3-4: *Self-Protect*, respectively). They also showed greater reductions in 3-7: *Self-Attack*. The authors noted that this use of SASB allowed definitive demonstration that DBT affects intrapsychic and personality functioning in addition to reducing symptoms such as NSSI. In other words, DBT works actively to improve self-concepts evident in more affiliative self-treatment, such as improved self-esteem and sense of social competence "best characterized as a tendency to work hard in order to take care of oneself" (Bedics et al., 2012a, p. 74).

Bedics et al. (2012a, 2012b) also demonstrated the central importance of the therapeutic relationship in DBT. In a first set of analyses, patients were observed to introject their DBT therapist's perceived degree of 1-2: **Affirm** and 1-3: **Active Love** in the next week as greater 3-2: *Self-Affirm*

108 • *Using Structural Analysis of Social Behavior*

and 3-3: *Active Self-Love*. The opposite effect was observed for a control group receiving other forms of community-based treatment from experts. This between-group difference in relational impact suggests that the timing, context, and targets of therapist validation (especially 1-2: **Affirm**) matter greatly to outcomes. Bedics et al. concluded that DBT therapists worked to systematically validate positive self-views for their patients. Therapists in the control condition may have used a similar stance but were either less precise or validated other topics that may have unintentionally reinforced hostile views of the self. This finding is consistent with work by Karpiak and Benjamin (2004), among others, who noted differential impacts of therapist affirmation.[2]

In the studies by Bedics et al. (2012a, 2012b), the relational aspects of DBT also had numerous other positive effects, such as links between therapist and patient warmth to one another, and improved outcomes, including more friendly self-treatment and reduced NSSI. There was also a caveat: Bedics et al. (2012b) found that therapists who flexibly or selectively applied the recommended dialectical relational stance for DBT (defined using its SASB profile) had improved outcomes in terms of patient self-treatment in the following week. The opposite effect appeared to occur among a subset of therapists who used the same stance rigidly with all their patients, again suggesting that context and timing matter for effective use of relational processes in treatment. Indeed, as reviewed further in Chapter 8, one advantage of the SASB lens is being able to discern when to use validation and affirmation and when to use more structure and influence. Chapter 8 returns to these issues in the context of optimizing treatment processes relative to an individual patient's SASB-based case conceptualization.

## PSYCHODYNAMICS: INTERPERSONAL MEASUREMENT OF TRANSFERENCE, COUNTERTRANSFERENCE, AND DEFENSES

Transference-focused psychotherapy (TFP; Clarkin et al., 1999) is a psychoanalytic approach to treating BPD. Like DBT and Young et al.'s (2003) schema-focused approach, TFP has been the subject of significant research attention and demonstrated efficacy in long-term treatment of BPD in two separate randomized clinical trials (Clarkin et al., 2007; Giesen-Bloo et al., 2006). In TFP, the internal configuration of representations of the self and

---

[2] Therapeutic effects associated with different SASB clusters, in different contexts, will be reviewed further in Chapter 8.

others (i.e., internal object relations) is a key element for understanding BPD and the affective and relational disturbances that accompany it. Views of the self and other are typically polarized in BPD, with good and bad components split from each other rather than integrated into a more adaptive view of the self and others as having many qualities (Clarkin et al., 1999; Kernberg, 1984). Although some theorists posit that high levels of constitutional aggression or negative affect contribute, the primary emphasis is on early relationships as forming templates for adult relating (Gurvits et al., 2000; Kernberg, 1984; Levy et al., 2006). This framework is used to understand *transference* as the transferring of expectations, thoughts, feelings, and motives from object-relational templates to current interactions with a therapist. Transference usually involves a distortion of reality as some aspects of the current relationship are downplayed, heightened, or overlooked. Accordingly, interventions in TFP maintain a primary focus on the therapeutic relationship to detect use of object-relational templates and then work to modify them. Because the primary focus in TFP is on real and imagined relationship patterns, SASB may represent a useful tool to track patterns in its transtheoretical measurement framework.

Clarkin and colleagues (1999) described therapeutic use of transference as follows:

> A useful way of making sense of the overt behaviors is to consider the interchanges as scenes in a drama, with different actors playing different roles. . . . By imagining the role that the patient is playing at the moment and the role into which the therapist has been cast, the therapist may gain a vivid sense of the patient's internal representational world. For example, in one case, the roles involved were a strict, disgusted parent and a filthy, bad infant; and, alternatively, a loving, tolerant parent and a spontaneous, uninhibited child. (p. 33)

Clarkin et al. (1999) also provided a listed of common roles, as shown in Table 4.2. These illustrative role pairs suggest a variety of mostly complementary positions on the SASB model. To the degree that they reflect early relationships, the pairings additionally suggest the copy processes of recapitulation (behaving as if still with an important other) and identification (behaving in the same way as an important other).

Clarkin and colleagues (1999) described the process by which dyadic roles are understood and formulated in TFP as follows:

> The therapist gathers these data by encouraging the patient to describe precisely the experience of interacting with the therapist in the here-and-now. This process, part of the work of clarification, involves actively inquiring about the patient's immediate experience and presenting the therapist's view of the interaction for the patient to correct and refine. (p. 34)

110 • *Using Structural Analysis of Social Behavior*

**TABLE 4.2. Sample Object-Relational Pairings**

| Illustrative role pairs for patient and therapist | |
|---|---|
| Destructive, bad infant | Punitive, sadistic parent |
| Controlled, enraged child | Controlling parent |
| Unwanted child | Uncaring, self-involved parent |
| Defective, worthless child | Contemptuous parent |
| Abused victim | Sadistic attacker |
| Sexually assaulted prey | Attacker, rapist |
| Deprived child | Selfish parent |
| Out-of-control, angry child | Impotent parent |
| Naughty, sexually excited child | Castrating parent |
| Dependent, gratified child | Doting, admiring parent |

*Note.* From *Psychotherapy for Borderline Personality* (p. 34), by J. F. Clarkin, F. E. Yeomans, and O. F. Kernberg, 1999, John Wiley & Sons. Copyright 1999 by John Wiley & Sons. Reprinted with permission.

In other words, a TFP therapist attends to both the process of the ongoing interaction as well as content elicited regarding the patient's experience of the therapist.

In the following example, Clarkin and colleagues (1999) described some of the initial process of clarifying a patient's perception of the transference relationship. This is done essentially by making observations regarding the therapy relationship, summarizing and reflecting patient statements about the process, and checking to determine the degree to which the characterization is accurate and/or the patient's responds somehow to the characterization.

> Ever since the session began today you have been somewhat secretive and evasive, as though you see me as dangerous. Am I right in this? The patient's comment might correct the statement and add important refinements: Why should I talk to you? You never answer my questions but just rephrase what I have already told you. The therapist might then amend the original hypothesis: So your secretiveness is a reaction to your perception of me as a withholding person. Would that be more correct? (p. 34)

Translated into SASB terms, the exchange contains these elements:

**THERAPIST:**   [Ever since the session began today, you have been somewhat secretive and evasive, as though you see me as dangerous.]

Content codes can be used to track (a) the therapist's expressed view of the patient and (b) the therapist's hypothesis about the patient's view. The terms *secretive* and *evasive* suggest hostile withdrawal consistent with patient 2-8: <u>Wall-Off</u>. The word *dangerous* is not easily codable. However, it

## FIGURE 4.2. Therapist's Initial Characterization of the Patient

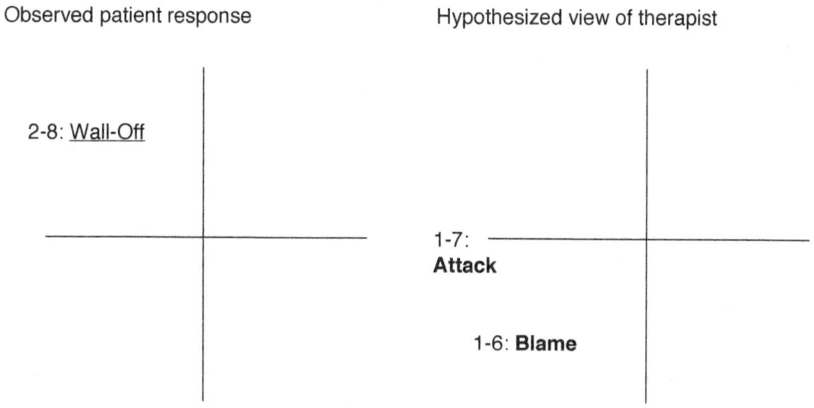

Observed patient response             Hypothesized view of therapist

2-8: <u>Wall-Off</u>

1-7: **Attack**

1-6: **Blame**

most likely refers to hostility directed toward the patient, likely in the form of 1-6: **Blame** or 1-7: **Attack**. This formulation of the therapist's comments is shown in Figure 4.2. Using the predictive principle of complementarity, another view of the therapist is also suggested as 1-8: **Ignore**—that is, the therapist might be seen as uncaring, neglectful, or uninterested, rather than dangerous in more direct or threatening ways.

Let us look at the therapist's process. If the therapist's statement seems to fit the context and is reasonable and warm in delivery, it likely could be coded as 1-2: **Affirm**. The somewhat pejorative terms *secretive* and *evasive* could suggest subtle criticism, especially if the tone is not entirely warm. In that case, complex addition of subtle blame (1-6: **Blame**) may be needed to fully capture the process.

THERAPIST:   [Am I right in this?]

Checking in with the patient in this manner places the therapist in the role of friendly reliance on the patient's judgment, consistent with 2-4: <u>Trust</u> as the process code that applies to the here-and-now relationship observable via the transcript.

PATIENT:   [Why should I talk to you?] [You never answer my questions but just rephrase what I have already told you.]

The patient's response ("Why should I talk to you?") involves the processes of hostile separation (2-8: <u>Wall-Off</u>) coupled with a criticism of the therapist (1-6: **Blame**). The content about how the therapist was perceived is captured by 1-8: **Ignore**, consistent with the predictive principle of complementarity just mentioned.

THERAPIST: [So your secretiveness is a reaction to your perception of me as a withholding person.] [Would that be more correct?]

The therapist here reflects a summary of the patient's content and offers an updated view of the patient's perception, as shown in Figure 4.3.

In terms of process codes, the therapist seems to be expressing a desire to understand accurately (coded 1-2: **Affirm**) in the first sentence and relies on the patient for input as to accuracy (2-4: Trust) in the second sentence. This set of codes appears to characterize the baseline interpersonal process recommended by Clarkin and colleagues (1999) for engaging in *clarification*, developing an in-depth understanding of object-relational patterns in the transference. Ulberg and colleagues (2014) described in-depth use of SASB to track the process and content of transference discussions. They presented a single case vignette that involved only limited therapeutic progress. SASB coding suggested that the limited progress was linked to an unmarked disconnect between the ways in which the therapist and the patient each characterized their relationship. Aspects of their interpersonal process together, including how their disconnect was handled, appeared to replay problematic aspects of the patient's relationship with her father in childhood.

SASB has also been used to operationalize defense mechanisms in interpersonal terms. For example, interpersonal defense theory (Westerman, 2005) views interpersonal behavior in terms of its likelihood of eliciting wished-for versus feared responses from another person. A series of studies used SASB to analyze transcripts for predicted patterns consistent with wish-fear conflicts, for example, to understand alliance processes (Westerman & Muran,

**FIGURE 4.3. Therapist's Updated Characterization of the Patient**

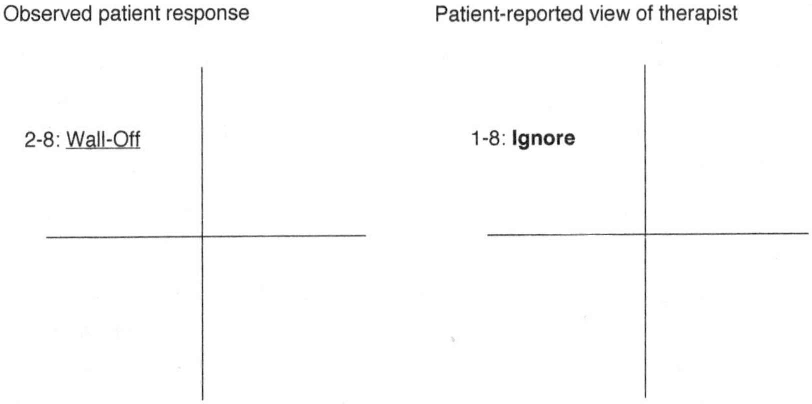

Observed patient response                Patient-reported view of therapist

2-8: Wall-Off                                      1-8: **Ignore**

2017) and to formulate characteristic patterns associated with individuals (Westerman, 2021). Benjamin (1995, 2003, 2006) also described interpersonal behavior as serving defense functions but framed them as preserving connection to internalized figures. Use of SASB as a common metric for analysis raises the possibility of testing competing hypotheses about the meaning, context, and patterning of relational processes (Messer, 2021).

## STRUCTURAL ANALYSIS OF SOCIAL BEHAVIOR AND PROCESS-EXPERIENTIAL APPLICATIONS

Emotion-focused therapy (EFT) builds on process-experiential, humanistic, and existential traditions. This approach incorporates modern theories of emotion and cognition to carefully track and work with a patient's affective experience across treatment (L. S. Greenberg, 2017). SASB has been used in the EFT tradition to assist with study of the dyadic process in treatment (Wong & Pos, 2014) and in the process of couples therapy, use of the two-chair technique, and the process of resolving unfinished business (L. S. Greenberg, 1979; L. S. Greenberg & Foerster, 1996; L. S. Greenberg et al., 1993; L. S. Greenberg & Malcolm, 2002; Paivio & Greenberg, 1995).

### Operationalizing Treatment Goals

Goldman and Greenberg (1997) described the EFT approach to therapy as follows:

> facilitating conscious choice and reasoned action based on increased access to and awareness of inner experience and feeling . . . [Process-experiential] therapy stresses the importance of self-acceptance and the ability to integrate various disowned aspects of the self as well as the need for restructuring maladaptive emotional responses as a means of overcoming psychological dysfunction. (pp. 402–403)

Translating this description into SASB terms, the goals involve increased access to and awareness of one's own experience and greater self-understanding, consistent with 3-2: *Self-Affirm*. Problems involving "disowned" aspects of the self would typically be evident in 3-8: *Self-Neglect* as well as 3-6: *Self-Blame* and 3-7: *Self-Attack*. Accordingly, outcomes research in this area using the Intrex has shown statistically significant increases in self-directed affiliation from pretreatment to posttreatment (L. S. Greenberg & Malcolm, 2002; Paivio & Nieuwenhuis, 2001). The Intrex introject surface has proven

114 • *Using Structural Analysis of Social Behavior*

to be a sensitive indicator of change in outcomes research involving a range of approaches (Constantino, 2000; Hara et al., 2022; Vittengl et al., 2004).

## Process-Experiential Formulation in Interpersonal Terms

SASB has been used in the psychodynamic and interpersonal traditions to study methods of individual case formulation. For example, SASB has been used as part of the core-conflictual relationship theme method (Luborsky, 1976; Luborsky & Crits-Christoph, 1998) to elaborate on Strupp's cyclic maladaptive pattern (Henry, 1997; Schacht & Henry, 1994) and to validate the formulation method used in Ryle's cognitive-analytic therapy approach (Bennett & Parry, 1998). This section focuses on Goldman and Greenberg's (1997) illustration of process-experiential case formulation in EFT as another potential use of SASB to build bridges across theoretical perspectives. The process-experiential approach to formulation is unlike most other approaches in that it emphasizes the patient's moment-by-moment experiencing of emotions, including the meaning made of them. EFT therapists use a moment-by-moment approach to formulation that allows for monitoring of a patient's emotional state as expressed, for example, through vocal tone and other indicators. Goldman and Greenberg (1997) emphasized that formulation themes should emerge from the narrative rather than be determined in advance. Interventions are then tailored based on the moment-by-moment assessments.

As illustrated in the following case example, emotions and meaning often involve relatedness with the self or important others. Goldman and Greenberg (1997) described Jan, a patient aged 44 years who sought help with depression:

> Currently involved in her second marriage, she felt that the communication had broken down and the marriage was "on the rocks." She had left home at the age of 16. Home was a place where she remembered feeling overburdened with responsibility, underappreciated, and emotionally neglected. She soon entered her first marriage, in which she was emotionally and physically abused. After 6 years Jan left this marriage, leaving behind her two sons. She feared that taking them with her might put all of them into danger. Jan carried a great deal of grief over her decision to leave her sons with their father, in spite of presently being on good terms with them. (p. 419)

A SASB-based sketch of this summary is provided in Figure 4.4. As reported by Goldman and Greenberg, the following eventually became the thematic treatment focus: (a) a need to be perfect, (b) difficulty legitimizing feelings, and (c) an unmet need for approval and acceptance from her mother. The summary provided by Goldman and Greenberg (1997) for each of these

**FIGURE 4.4. Sketch of Jan's Interpersonal History**

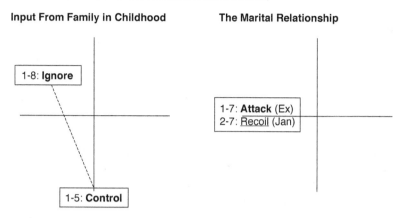

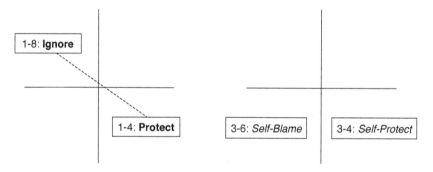

*Note.* A dashed line indicates a complex code.

themes is described next, along with a SASB-based translation that incorporates material beyond that shown in Figure 4.4.

Regarding the need to be perfect, Goldman and Greenberg (1997) stated the following:

> Jan felt that she had to be perfect in every respect in order to be lovable. Being perfect meant being independent and strong in her capacity as daughter, wife, sister, and friend. She felt bad about herself if she did not live up to these standards. (p. 423)

The phrase "need to be perfect" often suggests 3-5: *Self-Control*. When taken to problematic extremes, it usually also involves 3-8: *Self-Neglect*. In this case, the patient sought perfection in the hope of receiving love from others, most likely a simple code of 1-3: **Active Love**. Jan felt that she must be perfect by being "independent," which seems to mean avoiding any sense of needing help from others (2-4: Trust), rather than being assertive about her own views or perspectives. By implication, she did the opposite (2-8: Wall-Off) by not revealing her needs or vulnerabilities to others. Additional quotes about Jan's desires for herself help the coding task: "to be able to do everything, hold down a full-time job, do the cleaning, cook gourmet meals, do all the housework, drive my family around, be there for them when they need me" (Goldman & Greenberg, p. 420). Her description indicates that the desire to be strong primarily means taking care of others, 1-4: **Protect**. Jan feeling bad about herself for not living up to her standards would be coded 3-6: *Self-Blame*. If the standards are unreasonable or impossible, as suggested by "to do everything," this could also involve 3-8: *Self-Neglect*. A summary is shown in Figure 4.5.

Goldman and Greenberg (1997) described Jan's difficulty legitimizing feelings this way: "Jan did not value her own feelings and needs, and constantly put others before herself. She believed that feelings of vulnerability were signs of weakness and must be controlled. She had trouble disclosing her feelings and asserting her needs" (p. 423). Codes of this theme parallel those in Figure 4.4. Jan engaged in both 3-5: *Self-Control* and 3-8: *Self-Neglect* when she controlled her feelings, denying and disowning her own needs. "Putting others before herself" seems to again imply her caretaking of others, 1-4: **Protect**, while likely also submitting to their perceived needs, 2-5: Submit (this last code may be clarified by exploring specific examples). Trouble disclosing to others and asserting her needs indicates that healthy, well-attached behaviors of 2-2: Disclose and 2-4: Trust were not part of her

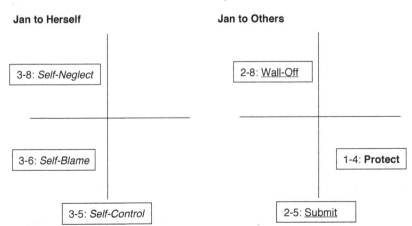

**FIGURE 4.5. Sketch of Jan's Current Interpersonal Circumstances**

repertoire now but they, alongside their self-focused parallels, may be important therapeutic goals to pursue. Codes from the first two themes fit together into a coherent picture. Jan's story involves submitting to the perceived demand that she should provide others with support and caregiving, in part by exerting tight control over herself to the point of devaluing and neglecting her own needs.

The final theme described by Goldman and Greenberg (1997) was Jan's "unmet need for approval and acceptance from her mother" (p. 423). Jan saw loyalty and obedience to her mother's rules and values (2-5: Submit) as the best way to try and receive wished-for love and acceptance. Jan's obedience to her mother's values seemed to be the precondition, or price to be paid, to feel her mother's love and was likely being recapitulated with others Jan tried to serve and please by putting their needs before her own.

Goldman and Greenberg (1997) also described Jan's therapy. Jan explored her feelings about her mother by using a two-chair technique to speak to her directly and come to terms with that relationship. Her overwhelm, self-negation, and depression all seemed to trace back to continued attempts to apply her mother's rules to current relationships—all in an attempt to feel love from the internalized version of her mother. This focus seemed highly relevant, given the strong parallels between Jan's current SASB profile and the configuration sketched for her early family history. As described in more detail in Chapter 5, the desire for love and acceptance, especially from important attachment figures like parents and siblings, is key to Benjamin's Interpersonal Reconstructive Therapy approach (Benjamin, 2003, 2006, 2018).

# 5 INTERPERSONAL RECONSTRUCTIVE THERAPY

Research and clinical use of Structural Analysis of Social Behavior (SASB) confirm that individuals tend to repeat relational patterns that mirror those available in their learning history with close others, even when those patterns are maladaptive and linked to clinical problems (Conroy & Pincus, 2006; Critchfield & Benjamin, 2008, 2010; Critchfield et al., 2015; Woehrle et al., 2023).[1] The theory of Interpersonal Reconstructive Therapy (IRT; Benjamin, 2003, 2006, 2018) addresses how and why we tend to repeat relationship patterns in this way. IRT also offers an individually tailored approach to blocking problem patterns and learning new, more adaptive responses based on each patient's learning history of close relationships. The theory articulates a set of interpersonal mechanisms that support psychopathology and hold the keys to transformative change. This chapter provides a brief outline of the approach sufficient to give context to the detailed clinical uses of SASB described in the chapters that follow. For greater detail on IRT methods, readers are encouraged to read the original work in Benjamin (2003, 2006)

---

[1] The clinical material used in this book is adequately disguised to protect patient confidentiality.

https://doi.org/10.1037/0000403-005

*Structural Analysis of Social Behavior (SASB): A Primer for Clinical Use*, by K. L. Critchfield and L. S. Benjamin

Copyright © 2024 by the American Psychological Association. All rights reserved.

and the deeper articulation of these methods relative to the underlying neurobiology of attachment in Benjamin (2018). Although the examples in this book are largely confined to a focus on outpatient psychotherapy with individuals, IRT principles have application in work with groups, couples, families, and more.

## OVERVIEW OF MAJOR CONCEPTS

IRT brings together existing clinical wisdom from across therapy schools in such a way as to make underlying principles of psychopathology and change clear and amenable to testing, including at the individual patient level. The object-relations, interpersonal, family systems, and attachment literatures all have direct relevance to the case formulation procedure, as does learning theory. Aspects of cognitive behavior, humanistic, and existential techniques and perspectives are also incorporated in IRT's view of the optimal change process. As noted in Chapter 1, SASB was developed with the initial goal to describe primate social interactions and was later extended to a range of human developmental settings, including the content and process of psychotherapy (Benjamin, 1973, 1979). Key observations with SASB were built on the work of both Harlow (1958) and Bowlby (1969), especially to track how relational experiences in close, early attachment relationships had an impact on and were precisely repeated in patterns of social relating in later developmental phases (Benjamin, 2003, 2006). In psychotherapy, these patterns typically accompany and make sense of presenting concerns, symptoms, and diagnoses. In IRT, SASB is used to track and understand symptoms in light of their interpersonal context and meaning.

### Linking Symptoms to Interpersonal Patterns

Benjamin (2003, 2006, 2018) described how interpersonal context can help make sense of presenting symptoms. Benjamin's early work with D. T. Graham (Graham et al., 1962) regarding the *specificity hypothesis* informed her thinking about copy process. Graham's specificity hypothesis states that specific interpersonal patterns tend to be associated with specific chronic physical problems. Subsequent research using interpersonal models supports this line of reasoning. For example, T. W. Smith, Baron, and Grove (2014) linked relationship processes to heart disease, and Gunn et al. (2017) explored an interpersonal model of sleep. Literature differentiating mental health symptoms by their associated interpersonal patterns also exists and is summarized elsewhere (e.g., Horowitz, 2004; Kiesler, 1996).

Understanding the links between symptom states and relational patterns on a patient-by-patient basis is essential to IRT treatment planning. Benjamin (2003, 2006, 2018) provided interpersonal prototypes for depression, anxiety, and anger. As she framed it, depression is an evolutionarily understandable response of shutting down in the face of perceived overwhelm, loss, and/or relentless self-blame. Anxiety can be understood in similar terms but with a response tendency that involves the felt need to mobilize and face perceived challenges or threats (without adequate resources or expectation of success). Anger also involves mobilization to neutralize perceived threats through a strategy of quickly exerting control over circumstances so that others involved will submit or move away. Case formulation in IRT is even more precise, following the logic of the specificity hypothesis. As Benjamin put it, "for every symptom there are reasons" (Benjamin, 1993, p. 385), and relationships with important others can "encourage expression of the symptoms and contribute to their shape" (Benjamin, 2006, p. 62).

### Learning, Loyalty, and Love for Internalized Figures: Red and Green Parts of the Self

In IRT, interpersonal patterns help make sense of current problems. They are in turn derived from prior relationships in which the patterns were first learned. These key relationships are referred to as *important persons or their internalized representations* (IPIRs). They are also referred to more plainly as the *family in the head* (Benjamin, 2018). Both terms will be used interchangeably in this book. IRT theory suggests that people repeat problematic patterns, and even resist efforts to change them, because of their ongoing desire to feel close to and approved of by IPIRs in the present: This desire leads people to continue attempting to implement the rules and values of their IPIRs even to the point of dysfunction. In other words, an active process of attachment to representations of the internalized family serves to keep patterns stable, even when the environment no longer reinforces those patterns or even when the original family members have changed or are no longer around. For example, Sarah (described in Chapters 1 and 2) used strategies in the workplace that were originally effective in minimizing rejection and bringing hoped-for approval from her father during her childhood. She persisted with the old strategies as an adult in the workplace, despite substantial costs to her mental and physical health, time away from her family, and so on.

Figure 5.1 presents three levels for working with and thinking about pattern repetition. At the surface is the idea that patterns may repeat simply because they were learned at critical moments in development ("you know

122 • *Using Structural Analysis of Social Behavior*

**FIGURE 5.1. Two Selves and Motivational Depth of Description**

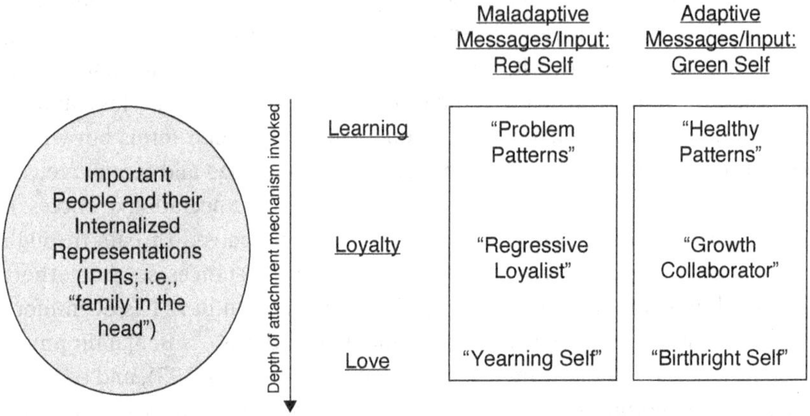

| | | Maladaptive Messages/Input: Red Self | Adaptive Messages/Input: Green Self |
|---|---|---|---|
| | Learning | "Problem Patterns" | "Healthy Patterns" |
| Important People and their Internalized Representations (IPIRs; i.e., "family in the head") | Loyalty | "Regressive Loyalist" | "Growth Collaborator" |
| | Love | "Yearning Self" | "Birthright Self" |

*(Vertical axis label: Depth of attachment mechanism invoked)*

what you know"). When this is the only process holding a pattern in place, it is likely to change easily through provision of alternatives and an opportunity to practice them in the context of a positive therapeutic alliance. However, different considerations come into play when patterns are also maintained by an individual's sense of loyalty to loved ones and constitutes a central part of their shared identity, as shown at the vertical midline of Figure 5.1. Enabling a patient's will to change is harder when it is motivated at this level. Change attempts often prompt patients to ask themselves (and their therapist) questions like these: "If I am not this, then what am I? How can I be so selfish [as to dare assert, or to change for the better]?" Or patients may say, "It's a betrayal [of internalized family] to do things differently." The bottom of Figure 5.1 invokes what is termed the *gift of love* (GOL). This is the idea that pattern repetition can also be fueled by yearnings for the love and acceptance of IPIRs as key attachment figures. At this level, when a patient repeats old patterns, it expresses messages to internalized family: "Everything I do is a testament to you, now please love me." Each layer of motivation to learn and repeat the ways and values of loved ones has everything to do with the evolutionarily supported need for close attachment figures to lay developmental groundwork for how to seek safety and to understand and respond to threat, as described in detail by Benjamin (2018). A key observation of IRT work is that problem patterns are often linked to the GOL. This is especially evident with patients whose prior treatment attempts have not addressed the issue adequately, and problems persist.

As also shown in Figure 5.1, IRT focuses on two parts of the self that are necessary to keep in mind for accurate formulation and treatment planning.

For all of us, one part of the self responds to perceived threat and seeks safety by repeating old ways and values that we have learned and internalized. When those ways are maladaptive and miscued relative to a fair assessment of safety and threat in the environment, this part of the self is referred to as *red*. The red part has also been described as the *regressive loyalist* and the *yearning self* (Benjamin, 2018). The other part of the self that we all have is referred to as *green*. The green part seeks healthy adaptation based on realistic appraisals of the present. From a therapeutic point of view, this is the *growth collaborator* and was also termed the *birthright self* by Benjamin (2018). Our birthright self is the version of us that came or would have come about naturally if our caregivers had consistently offered the evolutionary-shaped, normative conditions for secure attachment. The range of terms in Figure 5.1 vary in their depth and power to evoke (or diffuse) affect. Although each level has a place in the IRT process, the GOL has primary emphasis and is considered the key to change. When pattern repetition is driven consciously or unconsciously by a part of the patient that is yearning for love, approval, acceptance, and/or protection from key attachment figures, the change process requires substantial revision and even letting go of that wish so the patient can wrest internal permission to make changes at other levels.

The severity of clinical problems can be thought of in terms of a patient's relative strength, or the degree of presence of the red and green parts. Figure 5.2 is reproduced from Benjamin (2006) and illustrates a patient's relative balance of red and green, along with five steps of adherent intervention in IRT (described in the "Five Therapy Steps" section). When lessons learned from attachment figures are consistent with adaptive functioning and secure attachment relating, including nurturance of a healthy self, then life problems are expected to occur in a clear and meaningful context and are unlikely to result in clinical disorder. But for many clinical patients, especially those with more long-standing or severe problems, green is smaller than red at the beginning of treatment. One way to think of IRT treatment goals is to help nurture a patient's green to become strong enough to oppose red messages from IPIRs. Beyond blocking red, the therapist's goal is to assist the individual in growing their green birthright self until they can truly thrive.

### Using SASB to Identify IPIRs and Define How Red Patterns Link to Symptoms

*Copy process* is the language used in IRT to describe the repetition of old patterns linked to IPIRs. The primary copy processes are *identification* ("Be like them"), *recapitulation* ("Act as if they are still there and in charge"),

124 • *Using Structural Analysis of Social Behavior*

**FIGURE 5.2. Green and Red in Relation to the Five Steps of Interpersonal Reconstructive Therapy**

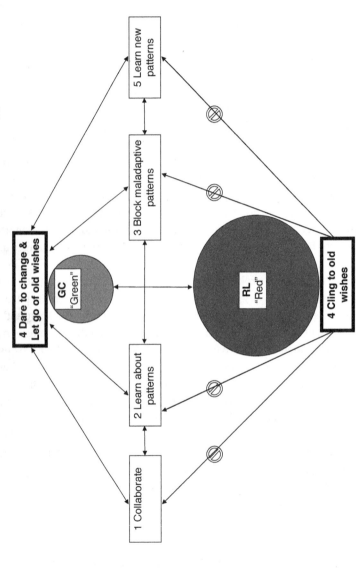

*Note.* Minor changes to labels have been made to enhance clarity in present context. Adapted from *Interpersonal Reconstructive Therapy: An Integrative Personality-Based Treatment for Complex Cases* (p. 23), by L. S. Benjamin, 2006, Guilford Press. Copyright 2006 by Guilford Press. Adapted with permission.

and *introjection* ("Treat yourself as you were treated"). Consider this example: If a male patient recalls being substantially neglected in childhood by his parents (1-8: **Ignore**), then introjection of those relationships would be suggested if he now also neglects his own needs or feelings as an adult—for example, by behaving recklessly, failing to protect himself, or spacing out and not really knowing himself (3-8: *Self-Neglect*). Identification would be present if the patient acts like his parents by neglecting the feelings or needs of others in his important relationships (1-8: **Ignore**). If he experiences others as repeatedly letting him down, "ghosting" him, or being uninterested in his needs, then this suggests recapitulation of the relationship with his parents (i.e., others 1-8: **Ignore**).

Copy processes are not mutually exclusive, can involve behaviors from anywhere on the SASB model, and can include multiple IPIRs. Opposite copying can also occur and is precisely defined as repeating behaviors that are 180° opposite of those experienced with a past loved one. For example, a parent who was harshly disciplined and criticized as a child (1-5: **Control** and 1-6: **Blame**) now allows their child to do whatever they want and validates the child's behavior (1-1: **Emancipate** and 1-2: **Affirm**), persisting in this approach even when structure, discipline, or critique would be more appropriate for the context. In clinical samples, opposite copying may accompany the other copy processes in approximately 10% of cases (Critchfield et al., 2015). Research to evaluate copy process patterns in IRT interviews shows that patients can be reliably distinguished from one another based on unique patterns of symptom-linked copy process (Critchfield et al., 2015). As a result, copy process patterns provide a unique and recognizable signature that makes it possible to tailor treatment and recognize red patterns when they appear in the process or content of therapy.

The logic of an IRT case formulation is straightforward: A person's symptom-linked way of being is often seen to repeat patterns they learned in prior relationships, especially those with their close attachment figures. A person's repeated patterns suggest the possibility that the other with whom they first learned those patterns is an IPIR. Table 5.1 returns to Sarah's case in more detail to show the logic and evidence for patterns of recapitulation and introjection that link her current problems (depression, anxiety, and suicidality) to early learning with her father.

### Copy Process as a GOL to Internalized Versions of Attachment Figures

Humans do not come into the world biologically preprogrammed to adapt directly to specific environments. Instead, like all primates and herd animals,

**TABLE 5.1. Clinical Case Example of Sarah, Illustrating Copy Processes With SASB Codes Applied**

| Sample early pattern | Copy process | Patterns consistent with copy process |
|---|---|---|
| In clinical interview Sarah described her father as having been very controlling of her and her siblings, providing compelling examples of extreme demands for performance exceeding what might be reasonable to ask of a child. Father enforced compliance with harsh physical discipline followed by long silences if his children deviated and was generally emotionally distant. Unlike her siblings, Sarah reports being successful at avoiding punishments by anticipating and complying with father's demands. As a result, she was able to spend more time with her father, something she desired very much. She was called "Daddy's favorite" by siblings. | Recapitulation (acts as if the other is still present and in charge) → | Sarah reports anxiety and depression as she tries to comply with considerable demands from her boss at work. On the few occasions when she asks for relief in the form of a lessened workload, better pay, or for other help, her boss acknowledged the problems but did little to change things. She reports continuing to attempt the overwhelming tasks.

*Interpersonal summary*: Complies (2-5: <u>Submit</u>) with demands of an authority figure perceived as both controlling and neglectful (1-5: **Control**, 1-8: **Ignore**). |
| | Introjection (treats self the way she was treated) → | Sarah reports responding to pressure to perform at work (and at home) by pushing herself harder. She appears to have done this to her own detriment in significant ways, e.g., working on written projects despite carpal tunnel pains, foregoing social opportunities, not receiving benefits or good pay relative to others in the office. When she fails to perform well, even with unreasonable tasks, she is self-critical and resolves to work still harder. |
| Interpersonal summary: Father described as exerting high levels of control (1-5: **Control**) ignoring the child's limitations (1-8: **Ignore**). Sarah reports compliance (2-5: <u>Submit</u>) in attempt to gain father's acceptance and avoid punishment (1-6: **Blame** and 1-7: **Attack**, followed by 1-8: **Ignore**). | | *Interpersonal summary*: Self-control is combined with self-neglect (3-5: Self-Control, 3-8: Self-Neglect), failures result in self-criticism (3-6: Self-Blame). |
| | Identification (acts like the other) → | Identification was not clearly in evidence for Sarah. However, patterns consistent with Identification could have included interpersonal behavior reported as paralleling father (i.e., controlling and distant, 1-5: **Control**, 1-8: **Ignore**). This might have been found in relation to her children, her spouse, people under her charge at work, etc. |

*Note.* For clarity, Sarah's name inserted where the original version reads "patient." SASB = Structural Analysis of Social Behavior. Adapted from "Internalized Representations of Early Interpersonal Experience and Adult Relationships: A Test of Copy Process Theory in Clinical and Non-Clinical Settings," by K. L. Critchfield and L. S. Benjamin, 2008, *Psychiatry: Interpersonal and Biological Processes, 71*(1), p. 76 (https://doi.org/10.1521/psyc.2008.71.1.71). Copyright 2008 by Guilford Press. Adapted with permission.

we learn about safety and threat (among other things) by bonding with, attending to, and taking cues from the other creatures who are our proximal caregivers. This usually refers to a mother and a father; when these caregivers are not present, infants and young children simply seek to attach to whomever or whatever with which they might engage to fulfill the evolutionary need to be safe through connectedness. The nervous system and the attachment system are intertwined in this developmental process, which calibrates affect, cognition, and behavior in ways that are rehearsed and essentially automated by the nervous system over time (Benjamin, 2018).

As described in preceding chapters, the SASB lens allows for specificity in the tracking of patterns, including across past and present attachment relationships. The close parallels seen in copy process are expected in light of IRT theory regarding the role of attachment relationships in learning how to recognize and respond to threat and to seek or maintain safety. The basic idea is that evolution provides that we do not forget or disobey rules from attachment figures regarding threat and safety (Benjamin, 2018). When those rules are maladaptive, then enacting the old scripts is referred to as a red GOL. Repeating the ways of their close others brings people a sense of psychological proximity and the hope of finally receiving the yearned-for love, acceptance, approval, and protection from the internalized family in the head, in exchange for adhering faithfully to their rules and ways.

Rules learned early on with caregivers about survival powerfully regulate affect and deploy the behavioral sequences that are detectable as copy process. This is why an individual's characteristic responses to perceived safety and threat are often linked to learning in close attachment relationships. Copy process patterns are what evolution and attachment together indicate "should" be adaptive (Benjamin, 2018). When normative, secure-base conditions have been provided by attachment figures, then the learning process that results in copy process is expected to be highly adaptive. Such green patterns support development of a healthy birthright self that is well prepared to function and thrive in the world. Accordingly, via the same mechanisms, maladaptive messages lead to problems. For example, a strict message such as, "If you violate our rules and values, we will have nothing to do with you," can lead to a child who calmly complies, but to an adult who feels severe distress when autonomy-taking is needed. If this message has been delivered and was rehearsed with few exceptions, then defiance of the family's rules and values would result in self-criticism and self-rejection, accompanied by a sense of loss and possible dysfunction. Affects consistent with depression, anxiety, and anger could all be expectable results, depending on the specific context.

## Summary

In IRT, people's symptoms and problems are understood through the lens of copy process, which are often in turn motivated by the GOL. Symptoms are often the natural consequence of our attempts to adapt using maladaptive strategies that in turn lead to overwhelm, grief, burnout, and more. Problems can also directly reflect copy process, such as a person shutting down and becoming depressed just as their mother did. Seeking safety through felt proximity to loved ones is a normative response. Repeating the old patterns often "feels right" to patients, even when maladaptive, because it is not only familiar but also involves a sense of psychic proximity—or closeness, solidarity, love, protection, agreement, or the familiar pattern of striving for any of these with loved ones. When problems are organized in this way, a major treatment implication is to help patients get distance, to differentiate from problematic aspects of internalized loved ones, and/or to supersede their messages by enhancing healthier attachments and healthier ways of being in the present. The first step in constructing such a treatment is to identify the key internalized attachment figures and motives to persist with the problematic ways and values learned with them.

## DEVELOPING A COPY PROCESS FORMULATION

A clinician usually begins an IRT formulation by learning about the distressing symptoms, problems, and experiences that motivate someone to seek treatment. The formulation starts with listing the symptoms and problems that need to be understood. The next step is to put those problems into their interpersonal context from the patient's point of view and to use that to understand how the patient's experience might make sense, given their learning history.

### Interview Process

The case formulation interview, described in detail in Benjamin (2003, 2006), is guided by the goal of understanding presenting symptoms and problems in terms of their interpersonal origins and motivation to persist in the present. This can be accomplished in a safe, inpatient setting in a single interview (e.g., 90 minutes). In the outpatient context, the process often unfolds across the first few sessions. The process begins with the question, "What do you need help with?" From there, the interviewer seeks to create a collaborative interview process that offers empathy and prioritizes experiences that have strong or salient affect. Overall, the therapist has the following goals in mind to complete the case formulation:

1. Clarify the interpersonal context of presenting problems.
2. Describe links to learning history with key figures.
3. Where copy process is found, articulate hypotheses about GOL motivation.
4. Identify needed new learning, including implications for the family in the head and expected changes if the treatment is successful.

These four goals are described next. To be adherent to IRT, the process must be collaborative. This includes the idea that the formulation is only valid if the patient agrees that it is. Exhibit 5.1 presents the major headings in an IRT formulation template.

---

**EXHIBIT 5.1. Interpersonal Reconstructive Therapy Case Formulation Outline**

### Section 1: Pattern in the present

Presenting problems

Current stresses

Responses to stresses

Conscious self-concept

Current figures

Summary of current pattern(s) in terms of Input > Response > Impact on self

### Section 2: Diagnostic and contextual factors

Family history of mental disorder

Current diagnoses

Diagnostic criteria for personality disorder

Treatment history

### Section 3: Copy processes and gifts of love

List of key figures

Separate descriptions of interactions with and attributes of each key figure

List of copy processes for each key figure

Links between key figures and each symptom

Gift of love hypothesis (and associated evidence) linking presenting problems and key figures

### Section 4: Treatment implications and recommendations

Short-term goals, needs, and resources

Long-term therapy goals

*Note.* From "Formulating Key Psychosocial Mechanisms of Psychopathology and Change in Interpersonal Reconstructive Therapy," by K. L Critchfield, M. T. Panizo, and L. S. Benjamin, in U. Kramer (Ed.), *Case Formulation for Personality Disorders: Tailoring Psychotherapy to the Individual Client* (p. 188, Table 10.1), 2019, Elsevier Academic Press (https://doi.org/10.1016/B978-0-12-813521-1.00010-2). Copyright 2019 by Elsevier. Reprinted with permission.

130 • *Using Structural Analysis of Social Behavior*

## Case Formulation Step 1: Linking Symptoms and Interpersonal Patterns in the Present

For initial formulation and then throughout treatment, symptom-linked relationship narratives are organized as inputs from others, responses of the patient to others, and impacts on the self (i.e., effects on self-concept and self-treatment or that activate an internalized rule or conclusion). A schematic for these narratives is shown in Figure 5.3.

It may be necessary to ask a patient about each domain if SASB-codable details do not emerge naturally in the flow of the interview. Figure 5.3 can be used to help cue awareness of the basic elements. For example, if the patient describes the actions of others but mostly omits their own, the clinician may spotlight this by asking, "How did you respond to that?" If the interactive elements are clear but the impact on the patient is not known, a clinician might express curiosity about that domain and instead ask, "What impact did that have on you?" or "Did this affect how you saw yourself?" If the actions of others have not been described, the therapist might steer the discussion in that direction at an appropriate time: "So, what was happening right before all this started?" or "How did they respond?" The goal is to understand each domain sufficient to crystallize an overall theme at a level of detail similar to that described for Sarah in Table 5.1. Chapter 7 focuses on making a case formulation by applying SASB codes to interview content.

## Case Formulation Step 2: Characterizing the Learning History to Detect Copy Process

Once the relationship patterns that link to symptoms are sketched, the interviewer explores for copy process parallels with important figures in the patient's life. These figures are often parents and close family members, but they can include teachers, coaches, romantic partners, religious leaders, and others as well. The exploration often begins with the therapist reflecting the pattern to the patient and asking if it sounds like any other relationship the patient has been in before. Language from SASB can be useful for reflecting patterns in a way that might suggest links.

The *copy process speech* provides a template for how to approach the topic collaboratively:

> I believe that everything makes sense. Usually problem patterns we have in adulthood reflect things we learned as children. The connections often are quite direct. What we do as adults often copies early patterns that we learned from mother or father or other important people in our lives. There are three ways to do it: "Be like him or her," "Act as if he or she is still there," "Treat yourself as he or she treated you." For example, I notice that you say you are [a perfectionist] and you have been talking about how your [father] also [was a perfectionist]. . . . Do you see other connections? . . . Here are some that I see, although they will need further checking. (Benjamin, 2006, p. 47)

Interpersonal Reconstructive Therapy • 131

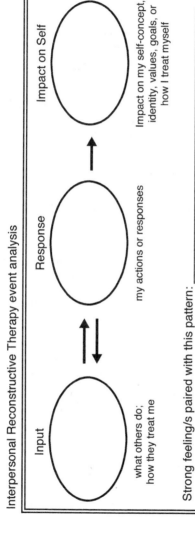

FIGURE 5.3. Analysis of Interpersonal Narratives (Worksheet Version)

132 • *Using Structural Analysis of Social Behavior*

It is also possible to ask about the patient's early history separate from discussion of current patterns, and then work to make the links clear at a later point. In Chapters 6 and 7, the use of SASB to detect copy process patterns in clinical data is explored in detail using the Intrex questionnaire and the clinical interview method, respectively.

### Case Formulation Step 3: Formulating the GOL Hypothesis

Maladaptive patterns copied from close attachment relationships tend to persist despite negative consequences. As mentioned in the earlier discussion of IRT theory, when problem patterns are motivated by a desire for love and acceptance from internalized attachments, they are said to be a GOL to those loved ones. The regressive loyalist, red part of the self seeks to stay connected to internalized loved ones by adhering to their rules and ways. When maladaptive patterns have been internalized, this part is necessarily in conflict with the growth collaborator, green part of the self that is interested in healthy adaptation in the present. The following statements, each made by a separate patient, reflect how unhealthy behavior can suggest desires for love, support, and alignment with family in the head:

> If I am happy, I make my family sad. Being different is murderous. I lose if I take care of myself. If I fall apart, then they will love me. I am more at home with situations that are not working. It doesn't feel good, but it feels normal. If you are strong, you cannot be nice. (Benjamin, 2008, p. 417)

When the GOL fuels problem behavior, it needs to be understood and addressed so that red ways can truly be let go in favor of adaptive alternatives. For example, the motivation behind Sarah's willingness to take on too many tasks and then criticize herself if she could not complete them was a GOL to her father. Sarah's motivation in childhood was made clear in her initial interview when she explained, "I tried to get Dad to love me by doing all that he said." The core of the recommended treatment approach for Sarah is to help her give up this continued quest in her adult life. The IRT GOL speech provides a model for how to introduce and explore the GOL hypothesis with patients like Sarah:

> So you see that in many ways, you are being faithful to the rules and values that you learned when you were little. The question remains: Why do we do that? Why do we keep on following those old ideas, especially when they don't work so well anymore? Well, often it is because without realizing it, we are trying to "get it right" with [Dad, Mom, brother, etc.]. It is like we do it the way they seemed to want it, in hopes that they will approve and be pleased. It is as if we hope that maybe things could be better after all. Does that make any sense? (Benjamin, 2006, p. 49)

When a GOL hypothesis is detected, it should be explored sensitively but straightforwardly with the patient, as modeled in the language used in the examples just described. The GOL hypothesis must never be imposed or delivered in a manner that is confrontational or blames the patient or others. It should be supported by behavioral data from copy process and verified collaboratively. Memories and implications associated with a GOL can be very painful and difficult to hold, and they often entail grief over a wished-for "past that never was." A confrontational approach, even if accurate in its observations, could be iatrogenic and profoundly disorganizing for some patients, given the sensitive nature of the topic.

### Case Formulation Step 4: Outlining Treatment Implications—Therapy Goals Using SASB

Figure 5.4 presents the therapy goal in IRT, which is to have a baseline of healthy green relating in normative social contexts and with the self. Consistent with the definitions of normality and secure attachment in Chapter 2, the SASB-based position involves friendliness, moderate enmeshment, moderate differentiation, and a reciprocal balance of focus on the self and others. These behaviors, all located on the right of the SASB model, should be present in normal relational contexts in which there is reasonable expectation for safety and reciprocity.

By contrast, psychopathology is associated with forms of hostility, extremes of enmeshment, extremes of differentiation, or an imbalance of focus. Patterns in the case formulation that link to symptoms usually involve these other SASB codes. The therapy goal region can be used to chart a course from red to green. These definitions of health versus maladaptation are supported by empirical data applying SASB-based measures among nonclinical and clinical samples (Benjamin, 2000; Benjamin, Rothweiler, & Critchfield, 2006).

Goals of IRT can be explained to patients in terms of not only behavioral patterns but also ways of thinking and feeling via language in the parallel cognitive and affective models (Structural Analysis of Cognitive Behavior and Structural Analysis of Affective Behavior) presented in Chapter 2. A sample *goal speech*, similar to the following, is one way to approach it:

> The goal of this therapy is to help you learn to relate to yourself and others in friendly and balanced ways that are neither too controlling nor too compliant nor too disconnected. Examples of goal behaviors are: Affirm others and yourself. Disclose honestly to yourself and loved ones. Love others and accept love from them. Love yourself too. Protect loved ones and yourself. Trust. The goal ways of relating tend to be associated with feeling that you can: accept, love and nurture. You can be: centered delighted and hopeful.

134 • *Using Structural Analysis of Social Behavior*

**FIGURE 5.4. Behavioral Definition of Treatment Goals**

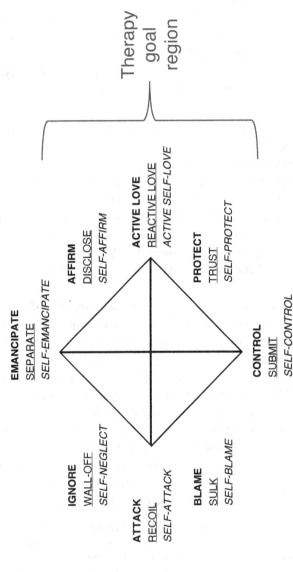

*Note.* Figure adapted from the original to specify the therapy goal region consistent with a pattern of secure attachment relating. Adapted from *Interpersonal Diagnosis and Treatment of Personality Disorders* (2nd ed., p. 55), by L. S. Benjamin, 1996, Guilford Press. Copyright 1996 by Guilford Press. Adapted with permission.

The goal ways of relating tend to be associated with thinking that you can: understand, enhance, and concentrate. You can be: expressive, optimistic, and well-directed. (Benjamin, 2006, p. 162)

The goal is that the following behaviors, if present, should become less likely: Ignoring the interests and well-being of others or self; walling off from others; attacking others or self; recoiling from others; blaming others or self; sulking; extreme tendencies to control, to submit or to distance from others. To the extent that these behaviors change, associated feelings should diminish: These include tendencies to: disregard, hate, or scorn others. To be: alienated, terrified, or agitated. To the extent that these behaviors change, associated ways of thinking should diminish. These include tendency to: distract, destroy, or condemn others. To be: scattered, shut down, or secretive. (Benjamin, 2006, p. 163)

To set therapy goals, it may be helpful to provide the patient with a copy of the SASB model and discuss both the current patterns and those in the therapy goal region. The level of detail provided by the full model is particularly helpful for this task. A final step in the case formulation is to summarize both the red patterns and specific implications for therapy goals that fit the patient's particular history, patterns, circumstances, and learning needs. The case formulation can be updated as needed to increase its accuracy, precision, and comprehensiveness as additional information is learned across therapy.

## IRT Goals and the Spectrum of Severity

Deep reconstructive personality change at the GOL level is not always necessary to achieve therapy goals involving symptom management and enhancement of self-treatment. In many standard outpatient settings, the green part of a patient is sufficiently strong and resilient to make use of strategies offered by many standard approaches to treatment. However, when standard methods appear blocked, it can be helpful to briefly invoke elements of the case formulation to get things back on track. For example, a patient seen in a health setting was unable to stick with her sleep hygiene procedures. Her clinician, with sensitivity, asked her to describe what happened each night and whether her thoughts and feelings reminded her of any prior time in her life. The patient then reported details from her childhood that were not already known: She needed to remain vigilant and stay awake in case she needed to protect her mother and sisters when her father arrived home late after he had been drinking. She was the only one who could pacify his rages and ensure safety due to her "favorite child" status in his eyes. Once this patient saw the link, she was able to use it each night and separate

136 • *Using Structural Analysis of Social Behavior*

past from present enough to let herself be okay to "stand down" and finally allow sleep. In her case, a basic knowledge of her patterns and motivations allowed for a healthier adjustment relative to treatment for insomnia.

Deeper reconstructive change involving the GOL often occurs when other approaches have not been enough to allow green to develop fully, such as when gains are limited or when a sense of thriving as a result of therapy is lacking. IRT is especially well suited to address mental health problems that are chronic, severe, or complex, such as with personality disorder, complex trauma, or substantial psychiatric comorbidity.

Most IRT research to date has been conducted with patient samples characterized as CORDS, based on a profile of having *comorbid* diagnoses, being *often rehospitalized, dysfunctional* (high levels of symptoms and impairment), and *suicidal* (Critchfield et al., 2015). In the remainder of this book, case examples drawing from patients seen in this setting will be used to illustrate clinical application of SASB and IRT. Reconstructive change with such cases is a longer-term process. As outlined earlier, it involves patients learning about their patterns, where they come from, and what they are for in a way that allows them to give up red yearnings and practice green goals.

Whatever the level of severity involved, a key mechanism of change in IRT involves people gaining psychological distance from problematic internalized figures sufficient to set aside the maladaptive patterns learned with them and practice a more adaptive way of being. In SASB terms, this means pursuit of a baseline toward the top of the model in relation to maladaptive members of the family in the head. The prototype is 2-1: <u>Separate</u> and involves the ability to assert and choose separately for oneself, in contrast to remaining enmeshed, loyal, or dependent (2-4: <u>Trust</u> and 2-5: <u>Submit</u>) out of a sense of yearning for old attachment needs to be met by close others according to their rules and ways.

It can be profoundly difficult for people to differentiate, let go, and move on from their old quest to be loved and accepted by close others with a particular set of rules. The reconstructive change process can involve considerable grief and loss. However, once a patient has wrested internal permission to change and separate from the early patterns, standard treatment approaches can have profound beneficial effects.

## PURSUING CHANGE

The optimal treatment process follows directly from the individual case formulation and involves both the process and content of sessions. Exhibit 5.2 presents the rules of engagement to guide the tailoring of IRT.

*Interpersonal Reconstructive Therapy* • 137

**EXHIBIT 5.2. Interpersonal Reconstructive Therapy Rules of Engagement**

### Rules of engagement for IRT process skills (core algorithm)

1. Work from a baseline of accurate empathy.
2. Support green more than red.
3. Relate every intervention to the case formulation.
4. Seek concrete illustrative details about input, response, and impact on self.
5. Explore in terms of the three domains of affect, behavior, and cognition.
6. Relate interventions to at least one of the five therapy steps.

### Five therapy steps

1. Collaborate toward green goals.
2. Learn about patterns.
3. Block maladaptive patterns.
4. Enable the will to change.
5. Learn new patterns.

*Note.* IRT = Interpersonal Reconstructive Therapy.

## Therapist Rules of Engagement and Steps in the Change Process

The *core algorithm* (Benjamin, 2003, 2006), also known as the *process skills* of IRT (Benjamin, 2018), specifies what a therapist should do in each session. The first rule is to work from a baseline of empathy. Specifically, empathy should be directed systematically to support a patient's strengths and well-being. Empathy is most often expressed in SASB terms as 1-2: **Affirm** and especially applies to the patient's green self. Relatedly, the second rule of IRT is that more support should be offered for green than for red in any given session. As with empathy, all interventions should be geared toward greater support of positive adaptation than continued use of maladaptive copy processes. Sometimes this requires "cozying up to red" to press for change later—for example, by acknowledging and understanding outrage, shame, and fear that is disproportionate to the circumstances, without endorsing them as the only viable responses. To do this authentically, the therapist should remember that red represents a part of the self that seeks safety in the face of perceived threat. This part developed as an attempt to adapt to or survive a prior experience and is typically organized by desires for loving connection with key attachment figures. Rule 3 is that every intervention should relate to the case formulation. To assist in this process, rule 4 asks the therapist to elicit details about relationships that are SASB codable and interactive in the sense of including input, response, and impact on the self. Rule 5 ensures a balanced focus on affects, behaviors, and cognitions. Rules 4 and 5 ask for a level of specificity that facilitates current pattern recognition relative to patterns in the case formulation itself.

138 • *Using Structural Analysis of Social Behavior*

## Five Therapy Steps

The sixth and final rule is for the therapist to use interventions that relate to and facilitate at least one of IRT's five therapy steps. The steps outline a rough sequence of tasks typically addressed across treatment. The five steps are not intended to be a strict stage model of change: They outline areas of emphasis expected to unfold, and to be returned to as needed, across the change process. The first step is to establish collaboration, specifically in pursuit of green goals. The second step reflects a view of therapy as being a process of "learning to recognize your patterns, where they come from, and what they are for" (Benjamin, 2006, p. 51). As awareness of these patterns grows, possibilities for blocking maladaptive patterns increase (step 3), as does the ability to pursue new and healthy ways that reflect therapy goals (step 5).

Perhaps most crucial to the change process is step 4, enabling the will to or motivation for change. It is rarely simple to relinquish long-held loyalties and yearnings to be loved, accepted, or protected by specific loved ones in specific ways. The process can be stormy and can at times require a sense of deep support and trust in the therapy relationship. A clear sense of therapeutic goals, often crystallized in terms of a *healing image* of the green, birthright self, can also be sustaining for patients. Optimally, a healing image involves an embodied, interactive process that includes choices that are not currently present; it includes individually tailored, valued ways of being that involve the freedom to choose how to experience oneself, interact with others, and invest in oneself. The healing image would be SASB codable and fall into the therapy goal region.

A wide range of techniques can be used to work at each step, so long as they fit with the patient case formulation, address current concerns, and move toward the therapy goal way of being. Figure 5.5 organizes useful interventions at each step based on those that emphasize either self-discovery or self-management. Self-discovery interventions primarily derive from psychodynamic and humanistic schools. The self-management side is more action oriented and draws primarily from cognitive behavior therapy techniques.

## Example of High Adherence: Miriam

The following example demonstrates high adherence in terms of the therapist's in-session process and tracking. The case formulation for this patient, Miriam, is presented in more detail in Chapter 6. Briefly, Miriam exhibits a pattern of blaming herself and taking responsibility for the behavior of a series of chaotic and violent men who have harmed her. This pattern

Interpersonal Reconstructive Therapy • 139

FIGURE 5.5. Techniques Associated With Each of the Five Steps of Interpersonal Reconstructive Therapy

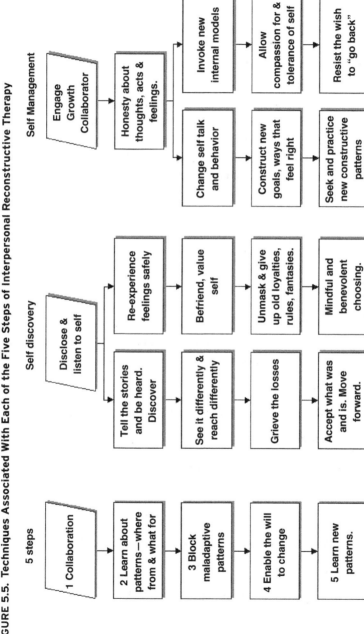

Note. From *Interpersonal Reconstructive Therapy: An Integrative, Personality-Based Treatment for Complex Cases* (p. 88), by L. S. Benjamin, 2006, Guilford Press. Copyright 2006 by Guilford Press. Reprinted with permission.

140 • *Using Structural Analysis of Social Behavior*

replicates history with a violent, adopted older male cousin who her mother supported and defended. Miriam's assignment was to "be the peacemaker," in other words to manage the cousin's emotions, protect her sisters, and take responsibility when the cousin was enraged. Early in therapy, the (male) therapist attends to aspects of their relationship process while also trying to track patterns that make sense of new symptoms in light of Miriam's formulation, as developed and discussed in prior sessions:

PATIENT: Well, I just, I had to work at 5 this morning, so got up at 4, and I hadn't slept in two nights, not on purpose, just I can't get control of it. So anyway, so I went to work until 10 and I left work, and then tried to go to bed but I can't sleep. But I didn't want to get out of bed because I would do something stupid. [*laughs*] So I stayed in bed. So that's my day. Not a good day.

THERAPIST: Do you know what got it kicked off? What was happening?

PATIENT: I don't know. [*starts to cry*] I'm trying to think of things. [*grabs a tissue*]

THERAPIST: Maybe I'm not on the same page as you right now, as to where you're at.

PATIENT: I don't know. [*wipes tears*]

THERAPIST: You said you didn't want to get out of bed or you would do something stupid?

PATIENT: Mm-hm.

THERAPIST: What was the something stupid?

PATIENT: Cutting.

THERAPIST: You wanted to cut yourself?

PATIENT: Mm-hm.

THERAPIST: But you stayed in bed, and you didn't.

PATIENT: Mm-hm. But I didn't sleep either. I wish I could do that.

THERAPIST: What happens when you try?

PATIENT: Just, my thoughts are racing. I can't sleep.

THERAPIST: Okay, your thoughts are racing. You catch any of them as they went by?

Interpersonal Reconstructive Therapy • 141

PATIENT: Um. I don't know. I just, got really angry. I was on my dinner break at work and I went over to Walmart, and these two guys in a truck pulled up really close to me and they were like, making like obscene gestures with like their tongues and their hands and stuff and asking me to, like, come in the truck; and I pulled out my phone, and I think they thought I was calling the cops cause then they drove off as soon as I got my phone. . . . A lot of people in the Walmart parking lot, why'd they pick me? . . . It's different if it's like [*laughs*], I don't know. [*grabs tissue, wipes eyes*] I don't know. And I got really mad. And I got madder because I said I was going to do my hair that day and, and wear makeup because I went out on another date. And, um, and then I decided that maybe they picked me because I was wearing makeup, but that doesn't make any sense because I've been picked before when I'm not wearing makeup.

THERAPIST: So you were feeling good about yourself before that?

PATIENT: Mm-hm. [*nods*]

THERAPIST: And it was okay to be pretty again?

PATIENT: Yeah. But right now it's not. [*sniffles*]

THERAPIST: And now when you try to sleep, you're angry.

PATIENT: Mm-hm. [*nods*]

THERAPIST: So it feels like you're a target?

PATIENT: [*nods*]

THERAPIST: Makes sense to be panicked and anxious if you're a target.

PATIENT: Yeah. [*sighs, sniffles*]

THERAPIST: Can you help me understand how that turns to wanting to cut yourself?

### Reconstructive Change: Recuing Rules for Safety and Threat

Benjamin (2008, 2018) compared the self and identity to the immune system. When correctly cued, the immune system promotes health by correctly identifying nonself cells and destroying them. In an autoimmune disorder, the same system identifies healthy parts of the organism as nonself cells.

In much the same way, the red self seeks adaptation in the face of perceived threat, but it is miscued based on the learning history with key attachment figures. Red can respond powerfully to say that truly adaptive ways of being are dangerous or wrong, a betrayal, or a sign that love and acceptance from the family in the head will never come. For example, Miriam and her therapist discussed how she was mad at herself for the men in the truck, linking it to having hope and engaging in self-care recently.

PATIENT: I don't know, I got really mad. And I got madder because I said I was going to do my hair that day and, and, more makeup because I went out on another date and then I decided maybe they picked me because I was wearing makeup, but that doesn't make any sense because I've been picked before when I'm not wearing makeup so, that doesn't make any sense or when my hair's just in a ponytail for some reason doesn't make any difference if I dress up or not. Just always picked on by all those people.

THERAPIST: So you were feeling good about yourself before that.

PATIENT: Uh-huh.

THERAPIST: And it was okay to be pretty then.

PATIENT: And now it's not.

As demonstrated in Chapter 6, Miriam's logic (blaming herself for the actions of abusive men) parallels her mother's input about past abusers. Mirriam's application of her mother's logic to herself in the form of self-blame and cutting is an example of introjection. It also suggests a GOL to her mother, an implication explored in later sessions (a theme that will be revisited in discussions of Miriam across Chapters 6, 8, 9, and 10).

Correct cuing should involve an adaptive match between input from reality and a patient's reactions to it, including associated self-concepts. The *recuing* process involves two parts: (a) getting psychological distance from problematic figures and their rules; and (b) envisioning, and then practicing, adaptive ways of seeing the self and of being in the world. Each aspect of this process can be defined using SASB terms and is a focus of intervention-based Chapter 8. Grief and a temporary return of symptoms can occur in advanced stages of therapy as patients choose to truly let go of wishes for love and acceptance and to take stock of what has been lost or sacrificed along the way.

### Anticipating Response to Change by Family in the Head

It can be difficult to get internal permission to have a self that can choose to be separate from the (maladaptive) rules and values of loved ones. One reason is the existential problem of letting go of old ways or old self-concepts that have seemed to provide security: "If I am not this, who would I be?" This process takes sustained courage and faith in the belief that new ways are possible, along with concrete and accessible examples and a green healing image of what the therapy goals might look like when practiced in the individual's life. For example, Sarah might hold on to the healing image of being able to relax and play guilt-free with her children at the end of the workday. Sarah might elaborate on or crystallize this healing image in the form of a person she likes and can name, or even one modeled after a historical figure or character in a movie or book. For Miriam, a healing image might be one of spreading her wings and exploring her talents as she saw a favorite aunt do, without fear of being judged and oppressed as in the past because she has become self-possessed and empowered enough to assert her boundaries, know the true scope of her responsibility, and trust feeling safe in the world. A therapist who can credibly stimulate hope that green goals are attainable with practice and time is often key in supporting the process of change through difficult periods. Periodic review of the evidence that progress is being made toward green goals, even if it is nonlinear, can help sustain motivation and resist setbacks across treatment.

A second expectable reason for difficulty pursuing change is *revenge of the red*, or the idea that implementation of new ways can result in significant backlash from the family in the head. This is often detectable as a return of copy process. They typically serve to bring the family in the head closer and suggest that the attachment system has been activated to defend against perceived threats. For example, one patient thought of herself as "weak" and "wrong" whenever she disclosed about childhood events in therapy. On her drive home after sessions, the patient felt as if her deceased parents were in the car, telling her how ashamed she should be; this often undid whatever peace or centeredness she had achieved. In more severe examples, suicidal ideation, self-harm, or significant self-sabotage may occur after progress is made. The likelihood of these more dangerous forms of backlash may be greater when the case formulation suggests that forms of autonomy (of having a separate self) have been reliably punished or forbidden. This pattern seems to follow the developmental research of Skowron and colleagues (2011), suggesting that "parenting which stifles preschoolers' friendly autonomous actions may have adverse physiological implications in the form of underdeveloped regulatory capacity" (p. 671). Predictable backlash can often be mitigated by the patient and the therapist anticipating it together: "If you try this new idea, what do you think your family would have to say about it? How would you like to respond to them?" In the example just given, the patient and the therapist worked out a creative solution that involved putting the patient's parents in the trunk or threatening to do so if they were not quiet. This image was effective for the patient during that phase of work to allow some distance and respite on the way home.

Lasting change can require patience, persistence, and practice involving many repetitions of recognizing red responses and shifting to green ones. Multiple repetitions of moving from red to green help rewire associative networks and recue old response patterns that typically have a biological basis, being oriented toward threat and safety and supported by a history of attachment-based learning. Therapists working in this way should help their patients anticipate and manage powerful responses from internalized figures. Benjamin (2003, 2006) devoted a chapter to issues of dynamic crisis management by direct use of the underlying GOL and red attachment figures.

IRT case formulation has been explored using the Intrex questionnaire as well as clinical interviews. For the latter, raters can distinguish reliably between patients based on the SASB-defined copy process patterns of their case formulations. These findings confirm that the case formulation provides the basis for individually tailored treatment as opposed to a one-size-fits-all picture of internalized attachment relationships (Critchfield et al., 2015). Chapters 6 and 7 focus on case formulation using SASB and copy process theory. Chapter 6 emphasizes use of the Intrex questionnaire, whereas Chapter 7 focuses on the clinical interview method. Later chapters focus on implementation and progress monitoring using SASB in IRT settings.

PART **III** OBSERVING, ASSESSING, AND FORMULATING PATIENT PATTERNS

# 6 FORMULATION USING STRUCTURAL ANALYSIS OF SOCIAL BEHAVIOR INTREX QUESTIONNAIRES

This chapter focuses on the administration, organization, and interpretation of results from the Structural Analysis of Social Behavior (SASB)–based Intrex questionnaires for individual case formulation.[1] The interview method for developing a formulation is described in Chapter 7. One advantage of using a self-report questionnaire is that it prompts for comprehensive assessment of all relevant relationships included in the administration. As demonstrated in this chapter, the information provided (i.e., relationship profiles, comparisons among relationships, and their qualitative labeling using SASB) can assist therapists and patients in exploring links between relationship processes and their presenting concerns. Review of Intrex profiles can also be used to articulate and clarify treatment goals relative to the self and others.

Intrex questionnaires are designed to assess relational patterns in any user-specified context. Each form of the questionnaire (long, medium, or short) is structured so that for each rated relationship, there are parallel items for both the rater (*I* or *me* forms) and for another person, entity, or group

---

[1]The clinical material used in this book is adequately disguised to protect patient confidentiality.

https://doi.org/10.1037/0000403-006
*Structural Analysis of Social Behavior (SASB): A Primer for Clinical Use*, by
K. L. Critchfield and L. S. Benjamin
Copyright © 2024 by the American Psychological Association. All rights reserved.

(*he, she, it,* or *them* forms). Specific contexts or states can also be included in the instruction set. For example, the standard series requests ratings when relationships are "at best" or "at worst." Clinicians are free to tailor the series for administration by choosing other contrasts, such as "when sober" or "when intoxicated."

Item content is transparent, so validity is enhanced when the Intrex is administered to a person motivated to learn about their own experience and perspective on their relationships. Ideally, the purpose of the assessment should be made clear to patients, including that they will receive feedback designed to increase self-knowledge and inform therapy. Respondents are asked to recall and focus precisely on the nature of present and past relationships. Therefore, rating with the Intrex can be difficult for some people, especially those who have experienced major loss, trauma, or other difficult relational experiences. For these patients, we recommend administering the Intrex in the context of a therapeutic collaboration that allows for additional discussion and/or discontinuation when needed.

## NAVIGATING THE OUTPUT TO CONSTRUCT A FORMULATION: TWO CASE EXAMPLES

To illustrate the use and interpretation of Intrex data, this chapter presents ratings from two clinical patients: Tomas and Miriam. Both patients rated the medium form (16 items per surface) toward the beginning of treatment with Interpersonal Reconstructive Therapy (IRT). Procedures for processing raw data files and graphing output are described in the SASBQuest program manual and are not reviewed here.

Intrex output can be interpreted at multiple levels of analysis, including (a) individual profiles, (b) dyadic patterns in the present, and (c) dyadic patterns spanning the past and present. The interpretive process starts with a review of the summary report described in Chapter 3, which provides a general overview in terms of the best-fitting prototype profile for each SASB surface. Greater detail about cluster profiles, SASB dimensions, and internal consistency of ratings can be inspected in the general report ("GeneralReport.txt"). Finally, within-subject correlations provided by the Intrex software are used to identify relationship parallels, suggest predictive principles, and detect copy processes. Space limitations prohibit presentation of all Intrex output generated for Tomas and Miriam, so this chapter highlights essential features to illustrate how Intrex pattern data can be translated into clinical understanding.

## Clinical Case 1: Tomas

Tomas is a 23-year-old gay, single, White man who works in retail sales and as a club DJ. He was recently hospitalized for suicidal ideation, major depression, and paranoid ideation in the context of substance abuse. He reports a long history of depression and anxiety spanning the past 15 years, including multiple psychiatric treatments and four previous suicide attempts. Tomas says that after a recent argument with his mother, "I could feel myself slip. I lost control. . . . I became angry at the drop of a hat." He reports recent daily marijuana use and frequent drinking. He began having paranoid beliefs that several friends were trying to hurt him after his cocaine and MDMA (3,4-methyl?enedioxy?methamphetamine) abuse prior to the recent hospitalization. His medical chart lists diagnoses of major depression, dysthymia, generalized anxiety disorder, and cannabis and polysubstance abuse. Early in treatment, Tomas's therapist asked him to rate the Intrex standard series, which consists of Tomas's relationships with himself at best and at worst, a significant other at best and at worst, his mother during childhood, his most significant father figure from childhood (a stepfather), and the parental relationship between his mother and the father figure. Tomas reported few long-term romantic relationships despite having had many sexual partners, which have typically been brief encounters with older men. He identified a recent lover to rate for the significant other portion of the Intrex.

### Tomas's Summary Report

Tomas's summary report is presented in Table 6.1. Correlation between each rated pattern and the best-fitting prototype is shown under the heading "Fit." These values are all at or above .80, suggesting that the labels are likely to be psychologically accurate and resonate with Tomas's experience. Many of the patterns are loving profiles, especially those rated at best and with his mother. These profiles are defined as having a peak on cluster 3 and reducing systematically from there around a given SASB surface. When this profile characterizes both partners for focus on other and focus on self, it fits the prototype of normative, well-attached relating and falls into the therapy goal region. Disturbed forms of relating are seen in Tomas's introjective self-treatment at worst, in his behavior with his lover at worst, in his relationship with his stepfather, and in the parental relationship. Maladaptive copy processes of introjection and identification with Tomas's stepfather are suggested, based on repetition of the 1-7: **Attack** label across his stepfather's behavior, Tomas's self-treatment, and Tomas's own behavior with his lover at worst. A walling-off pattern (2-8: <u>Wall-Off</u>) also repeats between his stepfather and Tomas's behavior with his lover at worst.

150 • *Observing, Assessing, and Formulating Patient Patterns*

**TABLE 6.1. Intrex Summary Report for Tomas (Standard Series)**

| Rated relationship | Label | Fit |
|---|---|---|
| Self-treatment | | |
| Introject at best | Love self | .88 |
| Introject at worst | Attack self | .89 |
| Lover with me at best | | |
| The other person focuses on the rater | Loving | .89 |
| Rater reacts to the other person | Loving | .89 |
| Rater focuses on the other person | Loving | .93 |
| The other person reacts to the rater | Independent but loving | .88 |
| Lover with me at worst | | |
| The other person focuses on the rater | Loving but freeing | .86 |
| Rater reacts to the other person | Walling off | .87 |
| Rater focuses on the other person | Attacking | .82 |
| The other person reacts to the rater | Disclosing | .96 |
| Mother with me when I was age 5 to 10 | | |
| The other person focuses on the rater | Loving | .96 |
| Rater reacts to the other person | Loving | .94 |
| Rater focuses on the other person | Loving | .98 |
| The other person reacts to the rater | Loving | .99 |
| Father with me when I was age 5 to 10 | | |
| The other person focuses on the rater | Attacking | .82 |
| Rater reacts to the other person | Trusting | .81 |
| Rater focuses on the other person | Loving but freeing | .92 |
| The other person reacts to the rater | Walling off | .86 |
| Mother and father when I was age 5 to 10 | | |
| Rater sees mother focus on father | Loving but freeing | .90 |
| Rater sees father react to mother | Very separate | .91 |
| Rater sees father focus on mother | Attacking and rejecting | .89 |
| Rater sees mother react to father | Conflict: love and trust vs. recoil | .80 |

*Note.* For brevity in descriptions of rated relationships, *focuses* indicates focus on other and *reacts* indicates focus on self.

Tomas reports a very loving relationship with his mother that appears consistent with normative attachment in childhood. However, the parental relationship appears complex. Tomas's mother responded to his stepfather's hostility and distance with a complex profile that includes both loving and recoiling from him. Since Tomas and his mother are close and were treated similarly by his stepfather, two sets of copy process hypotheses are suggested.

## Formulation Using SASB Intrex Questionnaires • 151

**TABLE 6.2. Tomas's Medium-Form Intrex Data Compared With Normative Means for At-Worst Ratings**

| Rated relationship | SASB cluster | | | | | | | | Dimension | |
|---|---|---|---|---|---|---|---|---|---|---|
| | 1 | 2 | 3 | 4 | 5 | 6 | 7 | 8 | AF | AU |
| Introject at worst | | | | | | | | | | |
| Tomas treats self | 30 | **0** | **0** | **0** | **0** | 80 | 70 | **95** | **−167** | 38 |
| Relationship at worst | | | | | | | | | | |
| Tomas focus on other | 40 | 20 | **0** | **5** | 95 | 55 | **90** | **70** | **−144** | **−37** |
| Tomas focus on self | 95 | **10** | **5** | **5** | 0 | 0 | **95** | **85** | **−127** | **143** |
| Lover focus on other | 70 | 55 | 80 | 60 | 0 | 5 | 0 | 0 | 140 | 63 |
| Lover focus on self | 90 | **95** | **100** | 55 | 0 | 15 | 20 | 35 | 134 | 122 |

*Note.* SASB clusters are indicated by the final digit on the cluster model. Values in bold are more than 1.5 *SD* away from normative means, with underlined values indicating values that are below norms by that amount. AF = Affiliation (SASB horizontal dimension); AU = Autonomy (SASB vertical dimension); SASB = Structural Analysis of Social Behavior.

As already noted, Tomas's stepfather may have been directly internalized as an important person or their internalized representation (IPIR). A second possibility is that Tomas's adult profiles are linked to how he saw his mother and stepfather relate when he was a child. Key areas to explore further involve details of Tomas's thoughts, feelings, and memories about the relationships both he and his mother had with his stepfather. A clinician might start by introducing the descriptive labels of the summary report and then seeking more detail to better understand apparent links between these early relationships and Tomas's adult relationships and self-concept.

### Greater Detail for Tomas: The General Report

Additional detail can be gained by inspecting profiles in the general report, both for their absolute patterning and comparing them to norms available in the *Intrex User's Manual* (Benjamin, 2000). Select profiles are presented in Table 6.2. Tomas's introject at worst is more than 1.5 *SD* different from the available normative sample in the Intrex manual[2] in the direction of hostility (affiliation [AF] = −167). Cluster values show that self-directed friendly

---

[2]Limitations of the available norms are noted in Chapter 3. Briefly, they involve small samples that do not necessarily reflect a wide range of cultural diversity, having been developed largely from dominant culture settings in the United States. Appeal to normative data can still be informative but must be interpreted in light of the relation of a given individual to this comparison group. It is hoped that with future funding support, we will be able to enhance existing norms.

152 • *Observing, Assessing, and Formulating Patient Patterns*

behavior or self-control is lacking (clusters 2, 3, 4, and 5 in the top row of Table 6.2) and self-neglect is elevated (cluster 8). Tomas's profile also shows substantial 3-6: *Self-Blame* and 3-7: *Self-Attack*. Although these are not outside the norms for introject profiles rated at worst, they are not balanced by any form of friendliness toward the self. Tomas also shows little self-constraint (3-5: *Self-Control*), which suggests that he is not likely to stop his own reckless or self-destructive actions when in this state. This finding indicates the need for safety planning, especially given the patient's history of suicidality.

Profile graphs for Tomas's relationship with his lover at worst are shown in Figure 6.1 to supplement interpretation of the values in the bottom four rows of Table 6.2. Both data displays show that Tomas's lover is perceived as predominantly friendly, even when rated for the relationship at worst. Meanwhile, Tomas is hostile and controlling (top graph in Figure 6.1) to the point of being the near antitheses of his partner (within-subject $r = -.82$). Meanwhile, in the bottom graph, Tomas's response of 2-7: Recoil and 2-8: Wall-Off despite perceiving his partner as loving and autonomy granting is suggestive of the "paranoia" reported about Tomas's views of his friends prior to his recent hospitalization.

High degrees of relational hostility have been linked to various forms of distress and psychopathology (Benjamin, 2018; Benjamin, Wamboldt, & Critchfield, 2006). Relevant for Tomas is that low levels of 1-2: **Affirm**, 1-4: **Protect**, 2-1: Separate, 2-2: Disclose, and 2-3: Reactive Love have all been linked to depression. Anger has been associated with high levels of interpersonal hostility (especially 1-8: **Ignore** and 2-7: Recoil) and anxiety is associated with 2-7: Recoil. Consistent with his interpersonal profile, Tomas's clinical presentation involves all three types of distress.

### Links to Tomas's Early Learning

In line with similarities noted in the summary report, analysis of profiles and within-subject correlations show striking similarities between Tomas's behavior and that of his stepfather. Figure 6.2 shows almost exact parallels, with $r = .92$ for focus on other and $r = 1.0$ for focus on self. The ratings show how strikingly Tomas becomes like his stepfather in relation to his lover when at worst, a clear example of identification. Follow-up in therapy discussion could explore these links further to obtain specifics about narrative details, such as (a) what Tomas says and does when at worst and (b) whether these words and actions are similar to what his stepfather said or did to either Tomas or his mother. Awareness of the connection could be used to help Tomas consider whether he wishes to explore alternatives to continuing in his stepfather's footsteps.

Formulation Using SASB Intrex Questionnaires • 153

**FIGURE 6.1. Tomas and His Lover at Worst**

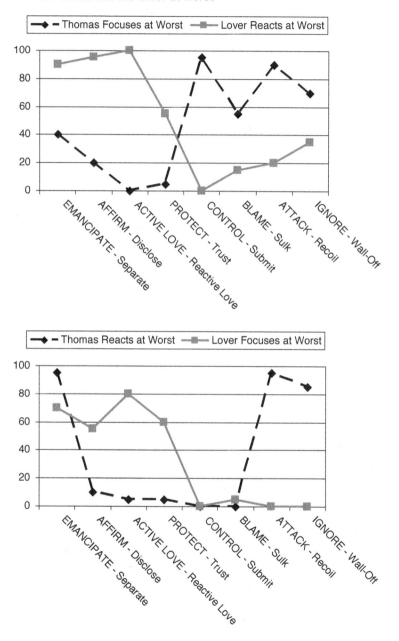

**FIGURE 6.2. Tomas and His Lover at Worst Compared With Tomas's Stepfather in Childhood**

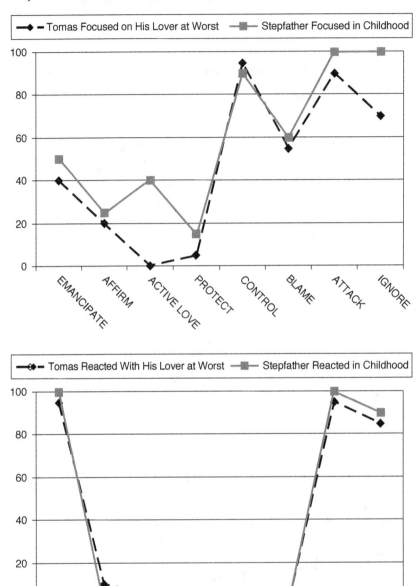

*Note.* Tomas's name replaces "patient" from the original source, while "lover" replaces "SO" from the original. Adapted from "Assessment of Repeated Relational Patterns for Individual Cases Using the SASB-Based Intrex Questionnaire," by K. L. Critchfield and L. S. Benjamin, 2010, *Journal of Personality Assessment, 92*(6), p. 484 (https://doi.org/10.1080/00223891.2010.513286). Copyright 2010 by Taylor & Francis/Informa UK Ltd. Adapted with permission.

An additional link to the past is shown in Figure 6.3. Tomas's lover focuses on him in much the same way his mother treated his stepfather. Exploration in therapy might focus on what responses Tomas hopes to elicit when he is hostile, controlling, or distant with his partner. If Tomas wishes to receive caregiving, understanding, and nurturance (as his mother provided to his stepfather, according to the summary report), then needed learning involves awareness of complementarity outside of what he learned in the parental relationship: that he will eventually burn out kind partners, or he will invite others to join him in abuse, hostility, fear, and so on. He may want to consider choosing between (a) re-creating in his adult life the relationship he saw his mother and stepfather have or (b) working to find more adaptive ways to connect with romantic partners.

### Comparing Tomas's Results With Interview Data

Tomas provided the following description of the history with his stepfather:

> The men she [his mother] brought into our life for me hurt both of us. He sexually abused me to hurt mother. It was never rough or violent . . . I wouldn't let him adopt me, but all my life I wanted a father. I am attached to him.

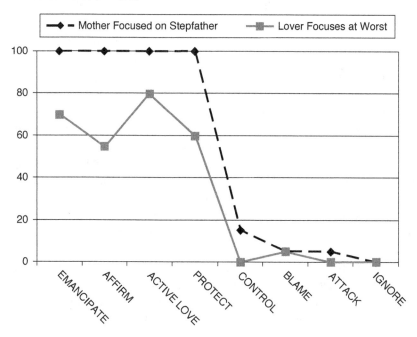

**FIGURE 6.3. Mother's Focus on Tomas's Stepfather and Lover's Focus on Tomas at Worst ($r = .97$)**

Tomas also described his stepfather and his mother as having frequent and dramatic arguments. His mother eventually had enough. Tomas described what his stepfather did next:

> After she kicked him out, he would stalk us. When I was alone at home, he would come down and try to get in. I felt helpless. I think his idea was to hurt her by hurting me. I thought he would kill me. I hid.

Tomas never told his mother that this happened, so as not to upset her and also because "he was my last chance at something I needed" (i.e., a father). He reported that his mother brought various men into the household who eventually "walked out on" and disappointed him. He continues to hunger for a father figure, he says. It is not hard to imagine Tomas learning to feel anxiety and paranoia, given his early experiences of being stalked and keeping it secret, as well as depression related to the loss of relationships with a sequence of potential father figures. The additional details may relate to Tomas's multiple sexual relationships with older men, and his sense that he is looking for a father in those relationships even now. Although there is evidence that Tomas has internalized the pattern with his stepfather, it is also possible that he repeats his mother's pattern in the serial search for a partner. IRT work with Tomas may need to address both internalized relationships in order for him to truly change his current patterns.

The close relationship Tomas rated with his mother on the Intrex was described in the interview in these terms: "We were inseparable. I was her lapdog. I loved it until I hit puberty." He reported attempts to pull away from his mother and, as he put it, to "divorce" her just before recent exacerbations of problems and symptoms began, suggesting that they are linked to his attempts to differentiate from her. Figure 6.4 shows a pattern consistent with an unusual degree of closeness that Tomas shares with his mother. The dark shaded areas show both Tomas and his mother as having more than the average amount of warmth in their relationship. He rated them at approximately 1 *SD* above norms (in some cases, the maximum possible rating) for clusters on the affiliative side of the model. In addition, he reported an unusually high degree of control (1-5: **Control**) over his mother in childhood and an unusual degree of submission (2-5: <u>Submit</u>) by his mother (both values near 1.5 *SD* from the mean). This pattern suggests a reversal of the usual roles for parents and children, with Tomas likely being a "parentified" child. As noted by Barnett and Parker (1998), this situation may have had both positive and adverse effects on Tomas's development. In any case, this pattern enhances the likelihood that Tomas's mother is a key member of his family in the head, and clinical work will likely need to contend with her input on his identity, values, and understanding of safety and threat in relationships.

**FIGURE 6.4. Tomas's Focus on His Mother and Her Reaction in Childhood, Compared With Normative Data**

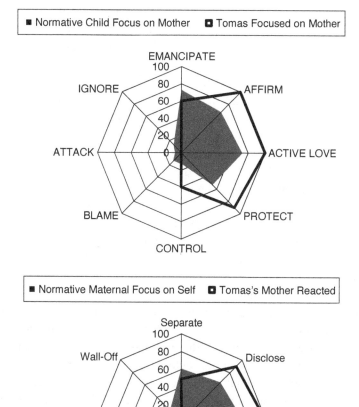

## Clinical Case 2: Miriam

Miriam is a 29-year-old single White woman with no children who has worked in a variety of roles in the film industry. When Miriam was referred to the IRT clinic, she had been hospitalized for a serious suicide attempt, the fifth in her lifetime. Test results showed her depression and anxiety at 3 *SD* above normative means, and she had diagnoses of posttraumatic stress

158 • *Observing, Assessing, and Formulating Patient Patterns*

disorder (PTSD) and major depression. The fifth suicide attempt occurred 2 days after a manager made harassing comments about Miriam's appearance and asked her to have sex with him. She responded with intense anger and fled from work, ruminating in her bed until deciding to attempt suicide. Her suicide attempt incorporated some of the same methods that a rapist used against her 10 years earlier.

In the earlier incident, Miriam was brutally beaten, raped, and nearly murdered by a peer-aged male individual she had known and been friendly with for some time through a religious social group. He invited her to have dinner with mutual friends but then took her to his home instead. In addition to being brutal, the rape included harsh and demeaning verbal messages about her worth and continued for hours. Miriam survived that awful evening but was warned that she would be murdered if she told anyone about it. A close friend of Miriam's learned of the attack and called the police, against Miriam's wishes. The rapist posted bail and subsequently made repeated threats on Miriam's life during the course of legal proceedings that took more than a year. Miriam first attempted suicide during that period, in direct response to his threats. The rapist was finally put in prison, but only after Miriam endured hearing defense attorneys repeatedly blame her for his actions. Since then, she has had frequent nightmares that replay various details of the rape, the fear she felt during the trial, and the rapist's threats for after he is released. She has made other suicide attempts in the intervening years. Six months before referral, Miriam made a suicide attempt after faulting herself for breaking up with her ex-fiancé, described as sexually jealous, critical, and controlling, because she was "unable to get into sexuality."

From an IRT perspective, repeated abuse, control, and intrusion by men and Miriam's suicidal reactions that replay the rape, persistent feelings of shame, and belief that she will never be a good partner all suggest copy processes linked to the rapist. In addition, the length and extent of their seeming friendship before the rape is consistent with Miriam having developed an attachment to him. Copy processes for Miriam include introjection (i.e., she treats herself as she was once treated) and recapitulation (i.e., she feels and responds as if the rapist is still present and in charge).

Exploration of Miriam's family history revealed that victimization, helplessness, and shame were not new to her life at the time she was raped. She is the oldest of three girls who are all close in age. Her childhood memories include being singled out and held responsible for chronic aggression and misbehavior of an older male cousin. Miriam's mother was highly supportive of this fourth "sibling" who had lived with the family since before Miriam's birth due to "problems at home." Miriam recalled locking herself and her sisters in her room to get away from this cousin who would burst in and "beat us around for a while." Her parents responded to the violence by focusing more time and attention on the cousin and asking Miriam, "What did you do to provoke him? Why didn't you manage him better?" The rape at age 19 was one in a long string of events that for Miriam seemed to confirm that abuse from out-of-control men is inevitable and that she is always responsible for it.

**Miriam's Intrex Results: Self-Treatment**
Miriam completed the standard series of the Intrex questionnaire with additions for the relationship with the rapist 10 years ago and also her cousin in childhood (both rated at best and at worst). She discussed the process of filling out the questionnaire with her therapist as needed and was interested in having the feedback.

Results of Miriam's full summary report are shown in Table 6.3. Paradoxically, Miriam's introject at best received a label that is even more self-hostile than at worst. During follow-up, Miriam explained, without irony, that she took the term *at best* to mean the times when she agreed with her mother that Miriam was at fault for her problems and deserved whatever happens to her. Seeing herself in friendly ways was "rebellious" and therefore chosen by her as the *at-worst* state. In Miriam's case, her devotion to her mother's values and views was so strong that it reversed the usual understanding of best and worst states. It also became clear that green therapy goals would require "rebellion" against the red patterns endorsed for Miriam by the mother in her head.

Miriam's ratings show problem patterns involving hostility and other departures from a loving, secure profile for most of her rated relationships. The more affiliative part of Miriam's introject, the component she rated as at worst, received the same label as her father's treatment of her in childhood: affirming, protective, and controlling. Her father's input may have contributed to her friendlier, rebellious self-concept. The relationship between her mother and father in childhood as remembered by Miriam, shown at the bottom of Table 6.3, suggests that her parents were not on the same page and that her mother may also have seen her father as rebellious. Meanwhile, the profile label for the rapist at worst, "Blaming," parallels ratings of her self-concept at best.

**Miriam's Interpersonal Relationships in Adulthood**
In Table 6.3, male figures in Miriam's adult life (ex-fiancé, rapist) show dramatic differences between affiliative labels at best and pervasive hostility

160 • *Observing, Assessing, and Formulating Patient Patterns*

**TABLE 6.3. Intrex Summary Report for Miriam**

| Rated relationship | Label | Fit |
|---|---|---|
| Self-treatment | | |
| Introject at best | Blame self | .92 |
| Introject at worst | Affirm, protect, and control self | .75 |
| Ex-fiancé with me at best | | |
| The other person focuses on the rater | Protective | .88 |
| Rater reacts to the other person | Loving | .77 |
| Rater focuses on the other person | Loving | .89 |
| The other person reacts to the rater | Disclosing | .93 |
| Ex-fiancé with me at worst | | |
| The other person focuses on the rater | Attacking and rejecting | .92 |
| Rater reacts to the other person | Walling off | .41 |
| Rater focuses on the other person | Affirming | .92 |
| The other person reacts to the rater | Walling off | .83 |
| Rapist with me at best | | |
| The other person focuses on the rater | Loving but freeing | .89 |
| Rater reacts to the other person | Independent but loving | .91 |
| Rater focuses on the other person | Loving | .88 |
| The other person reacts to the rater | Loving | .87 |
| Rapist with me at worst | | |
| The other person focuses on the rater | Blaming | .90 |
| Rater reacts to the other person | Angrily hides self, views | .87 |
| Rater focuses on the other person | Lets go and doesn't care | .82 |
| The other person reacts to the rater | Very separate | .92 |
| My cousin with me when I was age 5 to 10 (at best) | | |
| The other person focuses on the rater | Attacking | .88 |
| Rater reacts to the other person | Recoiling | .85 |
| Rater focuses on the other person | Conflict: controlling vs. letting go | .74 |
| The other person reacts to the rater | Walling off | .91 |
| My cousin with me when I was age 5 to 10 (at worst) | | |
| The other person focuses on the rater | Attacking and rejecting | .87 |
| Rater reacts to the other person | Recoiling | .86 |
| Rater focuses on the other person | Lets go and doesn't care | .76 |
| The other person reacts to the rater | Very separate | .77 |

*Formulation Using SASB Intrex Questionnaires* • 161

**TABLE 6.3. Intrex Summary Report for Miriam (*Continued*)**

| Rated relationship | Label | Fit |
|---|---|---|
| Mother with me when I was age 5 to 10 | | |
| The other person focuses on the rater | Attacking | .63 |
| Rater reacts to the other person | Conflict: submit, trust vs. withdraw | .76 |
| Rater focuses on the other person | Loving but freeing | .87 |
| The other person reacts to the rater | Walling off | .78 |
| Father with me when I was age 5 to 10 | | |
| The other person focuses on the rater | Affirming, protective, and controlling | .92 |
| Rater reacts to the other person | Loving | .89 |
| Rater focuses on the other person | Loving | .92 |
| The other person reacts to the rater | Loving | .92 |
| Mother and father when I was age 5 to 10 | | |
| Rater sees mother focus on father | Controlling vs. letting go | .87 |
| Rater sees father react to mother | Conflict: submit, trust vs. withdraw | .89 |
| Rater sees father focus on mother | Affirming | .86 |
| Rater sees mother react to father | Walling off | .73 |

*Note*. For brevity in descriptions of rated relationships, *focuses* indicates focus on other, and *reacts* indicates focus on self.

at worst. Profiles available in the general report provide additional helpful detail. Figure 6.5 presents Miriam's ratings of her ex-fiancé. At best, the two had a high degree of complementarity (within-subject $r = .72$), as seen in the similar profiles at the top of Figure 6.5. The primary difference is that she did not complement his 1-6: **Blame** with 2-6: Sulk. While complementary, their interactions are outside IRT-defined normative relating. Fitting Miriam's description of him in her interview, her fiancé showed marked 1-5: **Control**, 1-6: **Blame,** and 1-8: **Ignore** as well as low 1-1: **Emancipate** compared with available norms. Miriam's pattern compared with norms involves high levels of 2-5: Submit and she is walled-off (2-8: Wall-Off).[3] When at best, the parallel cognitive and affect models would predict that Miriam felt scattered and looked to her partner for guidance and also felt overwhelmed and alienated. These predictions are consistent with her report in therapy.

At worst, a still more disturbed pattern of relating was reported (bottom half of Figure 6.5). High levels of hostility are rated but now the profiles

---

[3]Notable deviations are defined here as values falling more than 1.5 *SD* from normative means. The raw data that clinicians will typically interpret and discuss with patients are given in Figure 6.5. The text notes significant departures from norms to supplement understanding of the profile.

162 • *Observing, Assessing, and Formulating Patient Patterns*

**FIGURE 6.5. Ex-Fiancé's Focus on Miriam and Her Reaction at Best and Worst**

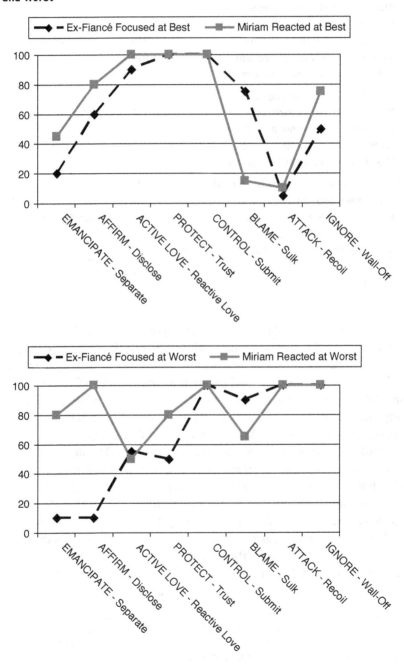

*Formulation Using SASB Intrex Questionnaires* • 163

have low complementarity (within-subject $r = .18$). Miriam saw her partner as very controlling and hostile. Meanwhile, compared with norms, Miriam rated a rare profile that involved unusually high degrees of open disclosure, coupled with unusually high levels of submission, fear, and distancing. This complex profile involved opposing elements of friendliness, hostility, enmeshment, and distance. The fit value of .41 in Table 6.3 suggests that this profile is not a good match to any of the standard prototypes. A confusing mixture of centeredness, alienation, overwhelm, and terror would be predicted in her affective responses.

The Intrex ratings make sense in light of the clinical narrative around Miriam's relationship with her ex-fiancé. Initially, it was the best relationship she had ever experienced. Later, she described her ex-fiancé's jealous rages, accusations, and constant monitoring of her email and phone messages for evidence of contact with other men (1-5: **Control**, 1-6: **Blame**, and 1-8: **Ignore**). She responded by giving him access to her phone and email accounts (2-5: <u>Submit</u> and 2-2: <u>Disclose</u>). His jealousy only seemed to escalate. She faulted herself for the relationship problems (3-6: *Self-Blame*), taking his blame. She finally broke off the relationship, reasoning that she could never please him and he would be happier without her. She recalled the demeaning statements the rapist said to her years earlier, which included that she could never please a man, especially sexually. After the rape, Miriam became suicidal (3-7: *Self-Attack*) in a manner that, as rated on the Intrex, paralleled attacks and rejection she perceived with her ex-fiancé.

**Miriam's Copy Processes**

Knowing Miriam's story in narrative terms, it is easy to see how her recent significant other relationship echoed earlier abusive relationships with the rapist and her cousin. Within-subject correlations can help test these hypotheses. Figure 6.6 shows strong matches for profiles with each of these men in a way that suggests the copy process of recapitulation: Miriam repeatedly finds herself in close relationships with men who behave the same as her cousin in childhood. Even though her ex-fiancé was not reported to have abused her physically, the codes of his verbal behavior show direct parallels with abusive figures on the Intrex. In addition, he appears to have shown some love and protection even at worst, likely contributing to Miriam's sense that he was the best relationship she could hope for.

Returning to the summary report labels in Table 6.3, Miriam's focus on her ex-fiancé when the relationship was at its worst was 1-2: **Affirm**. This fits with her description in therapy of trying to be open and show her love to him even as his jealousy was escalating. On the Intrex, Miriam rates herself

**FIGURE 6.6. Miriam's Relationships With Her Cousin, the Rapist, and Her Ex-Fiancé and Their Focus on Her at Worst**

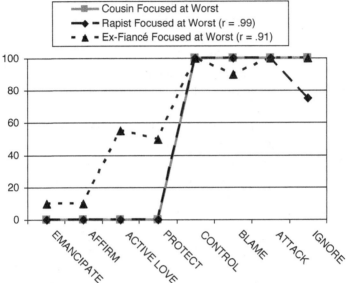

as being warm and caring toward her partner, despite inordinate levels of hostility. She is trying to offer a pattern of secure relatedness to a partner whose baseline involves aggression, blame, and coercion. Copy process theory suggests that Miriam "comes by it honestly" and has learned to affirm aggressive, out-of-control others in attempts to appease them. Miriam's narrative suggests that her mother's support for the aggressive cousin modeled this behavior, and that her assignment to take responsibility to manage him gave ample opportunity for practice.

Additional profile comparisons in Figure 6.7 present two other relationships in which it appears that Miriam's assignment is to offer friendliness to hostile figures. Her behavior with the ex-fiancé recapitulated the relationship she had in childhood with her mother, and it also suggests identification with the way her father approached her mother. Meanwhile, the ex-fiancé, like Miriam's mother in childhood, reacted with sulking and hostile distance (bottom of Figure 6.7).

A final observation about Miriam's copy process is shown in Figure 6.8. Striking parallels exist between Miriam's perceptions of the rapist when their relationship was at best and of her father. Both show a predominantly loving well-attached profile. The main difference is in the degree of control each exerted over Miriam. When Miriam and the rapist were together in the social

**FIGURE 6.7. Parallels Between Miriam and Her Father as She Recapitulates Patterns With Her Mother in a Recent Significant-Other Relationship**

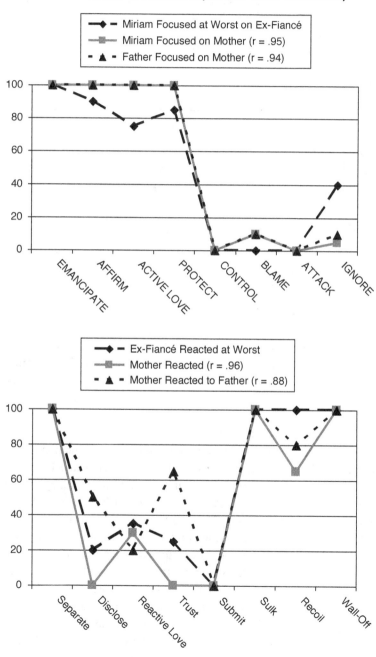

166 • *Observing, Assessing, and Formulating Patient Patterns*

**FIGURE 6.8. Miriam's Ratings of the Rapist and Her Father at Best**

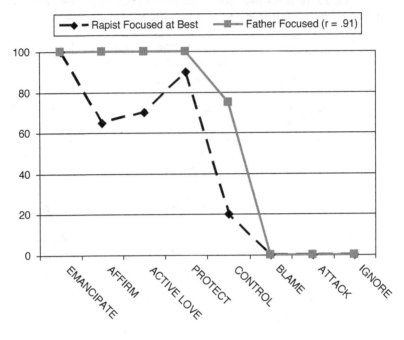

group, she may have been attracted initially to qualities she saw in him that were similar to qualities of her father. Unfortunately, and commonly for people who engage in intimate partner violence, the rapist switched to a profile more like her abusive cousin, enacting it to murderous extremes.

### Summarizing Miriam's Results

Key pieces of Miriam's overall pattern on the Intrex, supplemented by details from the clinical interview, suggest that she has almost always been abused by men she trusted. The pattern is that at first, men seem kind and even reminiscent of her father—the opposite of her abusive cousin. When men become abusive, Miriam appears to adopt the strategy she saw her father use with her mother of returning loving affirmation in the hope that they will be appeased. This pattern eventually leads to self-blame and self-rejection, as she applies the rapist's words and actions to herself. Suicidal actions, depression, and PTSD all make sense in light of these patterns.

IRT theory posits that a key factor in maintaining these maladaptive patterns is not just a person's early learning but also their sense of love and loyalty to the early figures with whom the patterns were learned. Treatment recommendations would involve revisiting thoughts and feelings related to

*Formulation Using SASB Intrex Questionnaires* • 167

the attachment figures to the degree that they interfere with Miriam's learning of more adaptive ways of seeing the self and others. One small example comes from a later therapy session, in which Miriam described a long-held value of noticing people "on the edges." She would work hard to be extra kind and caring so those people would feel comfortable and participate. She associated this way of being with her father and felt proud of her ability to do this. Although kindness of this sort is by no means a bad thing, Miriam was able to understand how caring for those who were either excluded by others or chose to remain aloof also helped her select some of the abusers. A therapy goal is not for Miriam to now choose the opposite value and become hard-hearted. Instead, she will need to learn to use judgment about when to decide to help, how to engage with others in ways that are well bounded and self-preserving, and how not to expect and tolerate abuse as if it were part of a healthy relationship. Other therapy goals would involve reclaiming and building on Miriam's rebellious self-esteem. The area of how to relinquish her parents' tradition of giving love for hostility will require sensitivity to avoid fueling the blame-the-victim stance held by Miriam's family in the head.

## PRESENTING INTREX FINDINGS TO PATIENTS

The Intrex can be a powerful tool for focusing discussion in therapy, and it gives a sense of which patterns and relationships may be worth further exploration based on their effects on current functioning. Taking a session or two to review Intrex findings can help with visualizing patterns, discussing implications, and setting treatment goals. This approach has been used in multiple variations of SASB-guided group therapy (Benjamin, 2000; Canate, 2012; Dobner-Pereira, 2021; MacKenzie, 1996).

Again, as part of the feedback process, it can be helpful to provide patients with a copy of the SASB model and explain its basic structure before reviewing select Intrex profiles. This includes a description of therapy goal behaviors. In any such review, it is important to avoid blaming IPIRs. The goal of the review should be to describe and understand patterns, and then explore implications that might help with steps toward treatment goals.

The Intrex manual (Benjamin, 2000) provides a model for the process:

> You see that you have learned to expect and deal with attack and rejection by trying to control things by trying to keep everything in good order. That was a reasonable way to try to deal with your situation. Now . . . you need not continue that tradition. An entirely different way of relating would be described by these behaviors over here (point to the region of friendly autonomy . . .),

168 • *Observing, Assessing, and Formulating Patient Patterns*

where you can have your own different point of view and still be friendly (give a concrete example involving her particular story). Here, people are connected because they want to be, not because they are obligated or forced to be. Once you can give up the need to protect yourself in the old ways (and let go of all you do to try to get the mother in your head to change), you might be able to try new patterns like these. Here is how it can work: Have you ever noticed that on days you smile, people will smile back? That is complementarity. What you send out affects what comes back. If we can somehow help you to feel you don't have to have things turn out a certain way and can let them happen instead—and that you are fundamentally friendly—friendly exchanges are more likely to come your way. (p. 40)

Using this approach, Miriam was helped to understand her current self-concept as being a function of input from her mother as well as the abusive male figures in her life. She was also supported in envisioning how her self-concept might have been different, and still could be, had her birthright self been given the chance to internalize secure-base messages instead. At the end of that session, Miriam reported motivation to engage in self-care and acceptance and, as she put it, "to be my own best mother." Her subsequent progress in treatment involved success at doing this and is reviewed in Chapter 8.

## RESEARCH FINDINGS

Intrex ratings and output have the considerable advantage of providing testable data with clinical and research utility. As noted in Chapter 1, the Intrex has been applied extensively in research to study interpersonal and intrapsychic differences in a variety of clinical populations. These include mood and anxiety disorders (Erickson & Pincus, 2005; Essex et al., 1985), eating disorders (Björck et al., 2003; Forsén Mantilla, Clinton, & Birgegård, 2019; Forsén Mantilla, Norring, & Birgegård, 2019; Wonderlich et al., 1996), substance abuse (Cushing, 2003; Humes & Humphrey, 1994; Ichiyama et al., 1996; MacDonald et al., 2007), personality disorders (Benjamin & Wonderlich, 1994; Klein et al., 2001; Ruiz et al., 1999), dissociative disorders (Alpher, 1996), first-episode psychosis (Harder, 2006), relationships with voices in schizophrenia (Thomas et al., 2009), and more. Researchers have typically emphasized dimensions measured as affiliation/autonomy (AF/AU) over profiles or clusters, due to parsimony and ease of use for analytic purposes. They commonly find differences between pathological and normal groups along the affiliation axis, with patient groups tending toward disrupted attachment positions on the left of the model, and mixed findings for the vertical axis that appear to depend on context (see Chapter 2). More specific focus on profiles and their relation to copy processes has also been explored and is closer to the level of analysis recommended in this chapter for clinical interpretation and understanding links to symptoms for individual patients.

## Profile Differences

As mentioned earlier, interpersonal profile differences are associated with depression, anxiety, and anger (Benjamin, 2018). When the self is rated in relation to a significant other, depression is associated with a deficit in friendly clusters, whereas anger problems are associated with higher levels of hostility. Anxiety has a profile between that of depression and anger and is significantly associated with 2-7: <u>Recoil</u> (Benjamin, Wamboldt, & Critchfield, 2006). Benjamin (2005) reported results by Goedken (2004) showing that depression is more strongly associated with deficits in parental affirmation (1-2: **Affirm**) and love (1-3: **Active Love**) in childhood, whereas anxiety is associated with the presence of more parental hostility. Benjamin (2005) concluded:

> Thus, although anxiety and depression are highly comorbid, there are important differences in their interpersonal templates. According to IRT, procedures for repairing deficits in positive interpersonal experience would not be the same as procedures for addressing damages from excessive negative interpersonal experiences. (p. 196)

A few studies have explored profiles. For example, Benjamin (1989) observed differences in roughly 30 patients for ratings of the relationship with their auditory hallucination. The rated relationships were coherent, and specific profiles differed qualitatively by diagnostic category. Patients diagnosed with borderline personality disorder or depression with psychotic features tended to hear voices that engaged in 1-5: **Control**, 1-6: **Blame**, and 1-7: **Attack**. Individuals with bipolar disorder tended to have affirming (1-2: **Affirm**) and protective (1-4: **Protect**) voices. Patients with schizophrenia showed more complex patterns of individual relating with their hallucinations. Figure 6.9 presents an IRT patient's relationship with her hallucination and with an abusive uncle. The patterns are nearly identical and very hostile. Consistent with prior findings by Benjamin (1989), this patient's profile is paired with the diagnosis of major depression with psychotic features. Clinically, this suggests the need to better understand the patient's family in the head generally and key experiences with this uncle in particular.

**FIGURE 6.9. Intrex Evidence for Internalization as an Auditory Hallucination of an Abusive Early Figure**

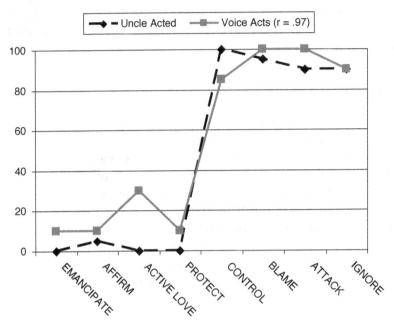

In conclusion, the SASB-based Intrex questionnaire can be used to gain a clear and nuanced understanding of a patient's interpersonal patterns, including those that suggest copy process and gift-of-love links to key attachment figures. Beyond its utility in research, the Intrex is designed to inform clinical work by enhancing awareness and facilitating collaborative dialogue about the relational themes with the self and others that are central to IRT case formulation. As the clinical case examples of Tomas and Miriam made clear, additional nuance in the ability to understand and validate findings comes from direct patient narratives about their relationships. Chapter 7 provides further input about the process of developing an interpersonal case formulation using clinical interview methods.

# 7 USING STRUCTURAL ANALYSIS OF SOCIAL BEHAVIOR TO FORMULATE PATTERNS FROM CLINICAL INTERVIEWS

How can I help my patient with an eating disorder or one who cuts or is hearing voices? What can I do to help a patient who is severely depressed or one who has a suicide plan? How do I treat a patient whose children steal her medication or one who reports intense anger toward others almost daily? In Interpersonal Reconstructive Therapy (IRT), the answer to questions like these is typically, "It depends on the case formulation."[1] As described in Chapter 5, the IRT approach to case formulation begins with the assumption that clinical problems usually make sense. How they make sense depends on the meaning and patterning of the problems in light of the patient's learning history with important other people. Structural Analysis of Social Behavior (SASB) is used to track and understand patient problems in interpersonal terms. Interventions are then chosen to address how patient symptoms relate to ongoing dialogue with important persons or their internalized representations (IPIRs).

---

[1]The clinical material used in this book is adequately disguised to protect patient confidentiality.

https://doi.org/10.1037/0000403-007
*Structural Analysis of Social Behavior (SASB): A Primer for Clinical Use*, by K. L. Critchfield and L. S. Benjamin
Copyright © 2024 by the American Psychological Association. All rights reserved.

172 • *Observing, Assessing, and Formulating Patient Patterns*

This chapter builds on discussions of case formulation in Chapters 5 and 6 but focuses on using SASB to organize material from clinical interviews. The here-and-now process of relating as well as the content of clinical conversation are considered. Treatment implications and in-session uses of the case formulation will be pursued more intensively in Chapters 8 and 9.

## INTERVIEWING STYLE: COLLABORATIVE PURSUIT OF THE RIGHT LEVEL OF DETAIL

As noted in Chapter 3, the clinician can enhance the interpersonal clarity of patient narratives to make them SASB codable. The recommended interviewing style involves open-ended following of the patient's experience, coupled with using moderate structure to steer the interview process when needed. The patient's unconscious, free-associative flow is actively tracked and used as a means for understanding the world from their point of view. The clinician should seek to be transparent and straightforward, ensuring that the patient is informed and comfortable with the interview, interviewer, and planned use of the information they disclose.

An IRT clinician will typically start with an open-ended question that invites disclosure without determining content to any great degree (e.g., "What do you need?"). The clinician then follows up with what emerges by carefully tracking what the patient says and empathically reflecting details to encourage further back-and-forth elaboration at the level of specific statements and behaviors in sequence. Language from the SASB model can be helpful when reflecting relational themes (e.g., "You felt ignored by her" [1-8: **Ignore**]).

The clinician also steers the process of the conversation when needed to help moderate affect. For example, the clinician may shift the focus to less difficult details of the narrative for a time. Such steering can also be directed toward repair of apparent failures of collaboration. For example, the clinician may interrupt the flow to check in with a patient about how they are feeling or perceiving the conversation, to comment if the patient seems tuned out or overwhelmed, and so on. In SASB terms, the clinician's process should stay interpersonally focused on the patient in the here and now, be basically friendly, and be neither too enmeshed (as in a single-minded desire to change, control, or "figure out" the patient) nor too separate (as in being aloof, impatient to finish and get to other matters, or uncaring).

Overall, the baseline SASB codes for an optimal interviewer process are 1-2: **Affirm** and 1-4: **Protect**. The first question of the formulation interview

*Using SASB to Formulate Patterns From Clinical Interviews* • 173

is often something like, "What do you need?" or "What do you need help with?" These questions are interpersonally complex in a benign way, simultaneously communicating both 1-4: **Protect** as a clear intent to be helpful and steer a conversation, coupled with 1-1: **Emancipate**, encouraging the patient to respond in whatever way and in whatever terms make sense to them. As the individual begins to talk about their view of what is needed, the clinician should keep an attitude of curiosity and a desire to detect primary themes and understand their details. We briefly illustrate the recommended interview style next and then describe the content pursued by the clinician.

### Illustration of the Recommended Interview Process

The first few seconds of the IRT consult interview conducted with Joe (Chapter 3) are presented next. Joe was referred for a consult interview during an inpatient hospital stay precipitated by a serious suicide attempt. His speech is slowed and affect blunted, yet he maintains good eye contact and seems to be engaged.

THERAPIST: Okay, thank you [referring to signed consent]. Why don't we start with what you need?

As discussed earlier, the second sentence ("Why don't we start with what you need?") conveys 1-4: **Protect** plus 1-1: **Emancipate**. The therapist structures the interview to be helpful by encouraging the patient to express.

JOE: What I need?

THERAPIST: Yeah.

JOE: I suffer from severe depression.

THERAPIST: Is—, so you have depression. So, what do you need?

Here, the interviewer first reflects the patient's statement, engaging in a process of 1-2: **Affirm**, and then reiterates the question, coded 1-4: **Protect**. Use of 1-2: **Affirm** in the form of reflections, interest in, and careful tracking of the patient comprises a major part of the IRT interview style. Through the principle of complementarity, this approach invites open disclosure (2-2: Disclose). More direction (1-4: **Protect**, and occasionally 1-5: **Control**) is used to change direction or steer the conversation as needed, much like a river guide works to keep the boat in a good part of the stream. If things are moving along well, little influence is needed; but a more active approach is sometimes needed to guide the way. The question "So, what do you need?" serves that purpose in a small but important way. Joe's prior experience of

174 • *Observing, Assessing, and Formulating Patient Patterns*

psychiatric care may have led him to think that only certain kinds of answers are wanted to a question like this one. The therapist uses a combination of warm control (1-4: **Protect**) plus encouragement to express beyond what might usually be expected (1-1: **Emancipate**).

JOE: I need to find a mechanism, cope with life.

THERAPIST: So, you suffer from severe depression, and you need a mechanism to cope with life.

This is another reflection that precisely uses the patient's own words, continuing with the recommended process of 1-2: **Affirm**.

JOE: Mm-hmm.

THERAPIST: Um, what are some things you need help coping with?

The interviewer continues to communicate interest, curiosity, and a desire to understand and follows the patient's subtle shift of content from depression to coping (coded 1-2: **Affirm**).

JOE: Ways to keep myself from being come [sic], becoming so depressed that I try to commit suicide.

THERAPIST: Okay, so you have a sense that you could manage yourself a little better. If you could, you wouldn't want to commit suicide so much. Is that correct?

The therapist might experience the patient's responses here as frustrating, as he is making only small conversational steps forward from the topic of depression to needing to cope better with life, then to wanting to cope so that he doesn't try suicide—none of which really answers the question ("What do you need?") very well. Joe's slow process may be a function of depression, medications, oppositionality, or other factors. In the first few seconds of his interview, this is not yet known. The interviewer's approach is one of careful reflection and tracking, summarizing, and checking for accuracy of understanding, staying mainly with 1-2: **Affirm**.

JOE: Right.

THERAPIST: Um, are you willing to talk about how you understand your wish to commit, commit suicide?

Here, the interviewer expresses interest and asks permission to talk about crucial content introduced by the patient. Permission-asking is a way to address the possibility that Joe's answers reflect reluctance to talk about

*Using SASB to Formulate Patterns From Clinical Interviews* • 175

difficult details while continuing to grant autonomy (1-1: **Emancipate** plus 1-4: **Protect**). Very little of the content of Joe's narrative thus far is SASB codable. He may want to cope better, suggesting that 3-4: *Self-Protect* is wanted as an antidote to suicidality. In addition, 3-7: *Self-Attack* likely characterizes his suicide attempt, but more detail is needed.

JOE: Yeah.

THERAPIST: What do you know about that? Can you tell me what that's like when you do it? Let's take the last time.

The optimal interviewing style seeks specific examples. Good options might involve the most recent, the first, the most intense, or the best remembered of any particular example.

JOE: Plan it out, gather the pills, the way I've been doing it, and uh, the last two times uh, get ready and take them all at one time real quick and chew them up so you get the best benefit out of them and go to sleep.

This is good detail from a safety-planning perspective and makes clear some specific behaviors constituting Joe's suicidal 3-7: *Self-Attack*, but it gives the clinician little insight into Joe's mindset. The interviewer goes on to use an open-ended question aimed at cognitions associated with suicide, consistent with tracking each domain of cognition, affect, and behavior. The interviewer has several possible directions available at this point, including asking about types and amounts of medications used, whether Joe is actively suicidal now, how he feels about the attempt, or how he might wish to have coped differently with it. The clinician will opt instead to first stay close to Joe's words to try and see the situation from Joe's point of view, possibly cuing to Joe's paradoxical use of the words "best benefit" and "go to sleep."

THERAPIST: What, what goes on in your mind when you do that?

JOE: Well, you feel completely hopeless, and you feel like there's no other way out.

THERAPIST: What is it that you feel hopeless about?

The earlier question about cognitions produced information about an affect: hopelessness. A follow-up question presses further about the perceived context linked to suicide.

JOE: Oh, things that are happening in the last year, you know, no control of things.

176 • *Observing, Assessing, and Formulating Patient Patterns*

THERAPIST: What would be an example?

JOE: Health problems

THERAPIST: Health problems.

JOE: A big one.

THERAPIST: What are the health problems?

Not all interviews move as seemingly slow as this, but the transcript illustrates the basic steps of the recommended "dance." The focus is on seeking clear and precise detail that is usually elicited in specific examples. The process does not usually demand detail, but instead moves between careful tracking and persistent curiosity about details of the patient's view. It can be helpful to disclose this aspect of the interviewing style to patients: "I like to be concrete. I'm trying to see the world as you do."

Regarding the content of Joe's narrative, it is often important to identify and be curious about apparent contradictions. For example, the therapist may offer the following:

THERAPIST: Earlier you said that your mother was really helpful, always there for you and looking after you. But we've been talking just now about long periods when she left you alone to fend for yourself and watch over your siblings. It's almost like you're describing two different people. Can you help me understand that?

Content codes of the mother's behavior to young Joe contrast 1-4: **Protect** with 1-8: **Ignore**. Here is another brief example:

JOE: I had no choice. I was just doing what I was told [Joe to Mother: 2-5: <u>Submit</u>] . . . I'm responsible for everything that happened [3-6: *Self-Blame*].

THERAPIST: Help me understand how you had no choice, and yet are responsible for everything?

In each example, the clinician conveys a deep sense of having followed and considered the content of what Joe offered, tracking the interpersonal patterns in his narrative. In terms of the here-and-now process, the clinician steers the conversation in part through what is reflected and tracked (primarily coded as 1-2: **Affirm**) with selective use of influence to steer the process, usually involving 1-4: **Protect** and, in some instances, blended with 1-1: **Emancipate**, as in the clinician's last statement ("Help me understand how you had no choice, and yet are responsible for everything?").

## PULLING TOGETHER THE INTERPERSONAL CONTENT TO DEVELOP A COPY PROCESS FORMULATION

A matrix like the one in Figure 7.1 can be imagined for each narrative or relationship story comprising inputs, responses, and impacts on the self, with each having potential affective, behavioral, and cognitive elements. Filling in the template can typically be done informally in the interviewer's mind, although use of a scaffold like Figure 7.1 to cue clinician awareness can be useful when starting. Across the course of a consultative interview or a therapy session, various relationship narratives may be elaborated and discussed or returned to in a nonlinear fashion until each cell contains specific quotes, examples, or SASB-codable details.

A general rule of thumb is to follow the patient's affective responses and free-associative flow but prioritize focus on inputs, responses, and impacts on the self related to presenting symptoms. Control of the process and direct questions about the early history and home life are recommended if they do not arise naturally from opportunities while discussing present problems. For example, an interviewer can ask about responsibilities and discipline in the home ("What chores were assigned to you? Your siblings? What would happen if you didn't do them? How were you disciplined?") or what others in the family thought ("Who else knew about that situation? What did they think about it?").

As described in Chapter 5, *input* typically refers to the actions of specific others but can include groups of people, situations, or contexts that are important. *Responses* are the patient's thoughts, feelings, and behaviors in the situation described. *Impact on self* refers to behaviors toward the self and implications of input and response for the patient's self-concept. Cognitive and affective elements are also important and should be followed carefully as well. Next, a sample case is used to show how detail described early in a consult interview can be summarized for input, response, and impact-on-self elements, using SASB codes of the content to track relational themes.

**FIGURE 7.1. Heuristic for Gathering Narrative Interpersonal Detail**

|  | Input | Response | Impact on self |
|---|---|---|---|
| Affect |  |  |  |
| Behavior |  |  |  |
| Cognition |  |  |  |

178 • *Observing, Assessing, and Formulating Patient Patterns*

## Clinical Case: Annette

Annette is a 32-year-old Caucasian woman. She is recently separated from her husband of 12 years with whom she has three sons, ages 11, 8, and 4 years. She was hospitalized following a suicide attempt by overdose of pain medication. In an interview, Annette said, "I am a worthless person. I want to end this pain. My heart hurts so bad. Life is not worth living." She reports two previous suicide attempts. One of these was at age 14 after a boyfriend left her. She told no one and "slept it off." Another was with pain medication roughly 3 years ago after a close friend discovered Annette had had sex with the friend's husband. According to the medical record, Annette has a long history of depression and experiences anxiety and panic attacks. At one point, she was provisionally diagnosed with bipolar disorder in response to reports of anger and impulsive actions, which included giving a friend a large amount of money for gambling and having an affair. She is prescribed antidepressants as well as opioid medications for chronic back pain after a car accident in her twenties.

Annette reports that what precipitated the recent suicide attempt was a "bad day." She was sexually assaulted by a male acquaintance in a locked break room at work. She resisted and he stopped but laughed at her as he left. She concluded, "I'm just a joke to him." Later, she forgot an important certification exam at work and berated herself ("See, I knew I couldn't do it"), and then took a dangerous amount of her pain pills. Another acquaintance saw that Annette was not well and offered to take her to the hospital, but then also tried to take advantage of her sexually. When she resisted, he became angry and said, "You're old and ugly. Who would want you anyway?" The acquaintance took Annette to her car and left her. She eventually made it home and her husband brought her to the hospital. The interview described next took place while she was an inpatient. The reader is encouraged to make judgments about the SASB codes of her content in this passage and compare them to the summary that follows, divided into input, response, and impact-on-self components.

THERAPIST: Let's begin with what you need?

ANNETTE: What do I need?

THERAPIST: Yeah, what do you need?

ANNETTE: Boy, that's a broad question. Um, healthy relationships; you know, know my boundaries; not getting ticked off really easy.

THERAPIST: Oh, are those three things related?

*Using SASB to Formulate Patterns From Clinical Interviews* • 179

ANNETTE: Yeah, they are to me.

THERAPIST: Uh-huh. Help me understand that. Tell me about that.

ANNETTE: Well, I'm finding that I have a hard time expressing my feelings until, and I like to make sure everybody is happy around me, so they'll like me.

THERAPIST: Uh-huh.

ANNETTE: So I do whatever it takes, even jeopardize my own self.

THERAPIST: In order to please them?

ANNETTE: In order to please people.

THERAPIST: What would be an example of that?

ANNETTE: Um, by cheeking my pills so that I give them to other patients that need them worse than I do.

THERAPIST: What?

ANNETTE: You asked. [*laughs*]

THERAPIST: So that's how you see it.

ANNETTE: Yeah. Somebody else needs them. Because their doctor doesn't give them enough and so, and they're in pain and detoxing, and so I stuck a pill in my cheek and took it back to my room and gave it to somebody who needed it. Because they only wanted one thing and I wasn't going to give them that thing. But I would give them my pills because they, to make them feel better.

THERAPIST: What was it you wouldn't give them?

ANNETTE: Um, myself.

THERAPIST: Are we talking about something sexual or what?

ANNETTE: Yeah.

THERAPIST: Somebody on the ward wanted sexual contact with you? And you said, "No, but I'll get you a pill." Is that basically it?

ANNETTE: [*nodding yes*]

THERAPIST: Do you want to talk more about that?

ANNETTE: If you want to.

180 • *Observing, Assessing, and Formulating Patient Patterns*

THERAPIST: I'm kind of interested in that.

ANNETTE: Just some poor guy needed, he was detoxing really bad and he, I just know where he was. And he was hurting and he wasn't in his right mind. And, where I was at when I first came here was where I felt needed. Instead of having to worry about taking care of myself, I could take care of everybody else.

THERAPIST: Okay.

ANNETTE: And, you know I take, open the little salt and pepper things for the little old ladies that couldn't, couldn't do it. And this young guy he came in and he was just . . . he kept coercing me to come into his room at night. And I say "no." And so instead, I would give him my extra sleeping pill. [omitted discussion of who else on the unit knows about this situation]

THERAPIST: Okay. So, the message then about you is that you were feeling badly about yourself, and you feel better when you're helping people for whatever they need, and that's what's important about you here. Right?

ANNETTE: [*nods yes*]

THERAPIST: And this is an example of where you put others before yourself, or an example of how you define yourself at least. You feel better about yourself if you can put others before.

ANNETTE: Yeah. I define myself. My mother says I'm self-centered, so I don't think that I put myself before others completely or she wouldn't come up with that. So, I must do it with everybody else outside my relationship with my family. Because I know my family loves me, but I want so desperately to have relationships on the outside that, whether they be healthy or not, I just am so desperate for attention and caring and love and somebody to like me, that I do stupid things.

THERAPIST: Wow. Like what?

ANNETTE: Like give people medication that should not have it.

THERAPIST: Okay. On the outside you do the same thing?

ANNETTE: Probably.

THERAPIST: Can you think of a recent example?

ANNETTE:     Yeah. I loaned my neighbor $700, and she ran off to gamble with it.

Table 7.1 summarizes details about Annette's interactions with the male patient who wanted sex. The primary interpersonal theme is of wanting to help a coercive male in order to try to gain approval, both submitting to and avoiding his demands, then blaming herself.

In SASB terms, the male on the unit was both coercive (1-5: **Control**) and, as she Annette saw it, also dependent on her for help (2-4: <u>Trust</u>). Annette complemented this position with 1-4: **Protect** and 2-5: <u>Submit</u> but also was 2-1: <u>Separate</u> in that she "protected" him, just not in the way he wanted. Her introject involved 3-8: *Self-Neglect* by compromising herself and putting his needs before her own, and then she 3-6: *Self-Blame* about the whole situation. Codes could be further clarified if more details were known about what Annette and the other patient said and did exactly. For example, Annette's word "coercing" was coded without knowing precisely what was done by the other person. It seems likely that her cognitive stance followed parallel logic of the SACB model, to be a mix of concentrating (cluster 1-4: **Protect**), being guided (cluster 2-5: <u>Submit</u>), and also being internally directed (cluster 2-1: <u>Separate</u>). However, these details are not known, and it is not feasible to elicit complete information about every interaction mentioned in a single interview. What is essential for our present purposes is to listen for primary relational themes, repeating patterns, and links to early history.

**TABLE 7.1. Annette's Interaction With Another Inpatient**

|  | Input | Response | Impact on self |
| --- | --- | --- | --- |
| Affect | "He was hurting." | Nurturant response: "I just know where he was." | Not known during interaction; angry at herself afterward |
| Behavior | Male patient tried to "coerce" her to come into his room, wanting sex.<br><br>1-5: **Control** plus<br><br>2-4: <u>Trust</u> | Gave her own sleeping pills to male patient.<br><br>1-4: **Protect** plus<br><br>2-5: <u>Submit</u><br><br>"[Sex was] something I wouldn't give."<br><br>2-1: <u>Separate</u>, 2-8: <u>Wall-Off</u> | "I take care of others instead of worrying about myself."<br><br>3-8: *Self-Neglect* |
| Cognition | "He wasn't in his right mind because he was detoxing." | Not described | "I do stupid things for approval."<br><br>3-6: *Self-Blame* |

182 • *Observing, Assessing, and Formulating Patient Patterns*

## Summary of Annette's Current Problem-Linked Interpersonal Themes

As Annette's interview progressed, the experiences leading up to her hospital admission were explored. The details are summarized with examples and brief quotes in Table 7.2. The themes are remarkably similar to her story on the inpatient unit. Others, usually male individuals, are initially seen as friendly but then pressure her for sex. Examples with her husband are similar in the way he is jealous and controlling about sexuality.

Time and again, Annette encounters people whose approval she wants and who try to exploit her in some way. Her focus on "helping" others by providing what they want, or trying to, usually involves passive submission to their desires, combining 1-4: **Protect** and 2-5: Submit. In all of her examples, this includes some form of 3-8: *Self-Neglect*. Annette has limits, but the pattern is that when she resists others (2-1: Separate), she is denigrated, mocked, or rejected, and then blames, rejects, or attacks herself. Recently, she has begun to have angry explosions at her husband and children. In one example, Annette refused demands for sex from her husband and told him, "Go get another wife." He then decided on a separation. As the interview develops, she reports losing friends, employment, and finances from

**TABLE 7.2. Overarching Themes for Annette's Current Problem Patterns**

| Input | Response | Impact on self |
|---|---|---|
| Annette initially sees others as friendly | Annette tries to be friendly and help others | Annette makes attempts to develop herself at work |
| 1-4: **Protect** | 1-4: **Protect** | |
| 1-3: **Active Love** | 1-3: **Active Love** | 3-4: *Self-Protect* |
| But then pressure, intimidate, and attempt to exploit her, especially men who want sex | She gives them what they want in order to be loved | She criticizes herself for failures to make others happy: "I will never, never, ever forgive myself for that, ever" |
| | 2-5: Submit | |
| 1-5: **Control** plus 2-4: Trust | She occasionally resists and/or "blows up" | |
| 1-5: **Control** plus 1-7: **Attack** | 2-1: Separate or 2-8: Wall-Off | 3-6: *Self-Blame* |
| | 1-7: **Attack** | She attempts to destroy herself through cutting, or overdose: "I'm a worthless person who has no business living." |
| They abusively insult, humiliate, and ultimately abandon her if she resists | When met with condemnation or disapproval, she despairs, gives up, or acts impulsively, giving whatever others they want at the expense of her "own self" | |
| 1-6: **Blame** | | |
| 1-7: **Attack** | | 3-7: *Self-Attack* |
| 1-8: **Ignore** | 2-5: Submit (or 2-6: Sulk), plus 3-8: *Self-Neglect* | |

Using SASB to Formulate Patterns From Clinical Interviews • 183

repeated attempts to serve and please others, always described from her point of view as attempts to receive love or acceptance.

Figure 7.2 provides an additional view of the details described in Table 7.2. In it, a set of prototypic sequences can be recognized. These sequences span input, response, and impact-on-self domains, with specific shifts occurring in relational patterns over time (depicted from top to bottom within each domain). For example, as loving input from others turns into coercion, Annette may respond with a parallel shift from appeasement to resistance (while blaming herself), for which she is ultimately rejected. She then responds with forms of fearful self-sacrifice and self-rejection (including self-harm and suicidality). By simply sorting Annette's narrative into the three major domains of input, response, and impact on self, more complex sequences such as these can sometimes be brought into view and used to further inform understanding of cyclical patterns in the present as well as their precedent in the learning history.

### Surveying Important Past Relationships for Links to the Present

The IRT consultative interview elicits links between present functioning and past learning. To do this, past relationships must be reviewed to assess what learning has taken place. The clinician should inquire about typical relationships, such as those involving romantic partners and childhood caregivers. Other important figures should be discussed as well, especially when brought up spontaneously and identified as important in the interview.

For Annette, her mother is a particularly important figure. Exhibit 7.1 contains quotes about her mother excerpted from the same interview. Prominent themes are 1-5: **Control** (mother is always right, do not talk back), with Annette submitting (2-5: Submit) and taking care of her mother (1-4: **Protect)**. For example, Annettee gives her mother rides to places to avoid unmoderated 1-7: **Attack** and 1-6: **Blame**. When Annette deviates from what her mother wants (2-1: Separate), she is called a "horrible daughter" (1-6: **Blame**). She sometimes gets acceptance for following her mother's rules (e.g., a shopping trip for dieting), and so receives intermittent reinforcement for the pattern of pleasing through self-sacrifice.

Figure 7.3 uses the SASB model to organize the major patterns Annette described with her mother. There is substantial similarity between patterns with her mother and those listed in Table 7.2 for current patterns. She recapitulates the early experience with her mother with others. There is also a strong similarity between her mother's input and Annette's current self-concept, suggesting introjection (i.e., she blames and attacks herself for

184 • *Observing, Assessing, and Formulating Patient Patterns*

**FIGURE 7.2. Prototype Sequences of Input, Response, and Impact on Self for Annette**

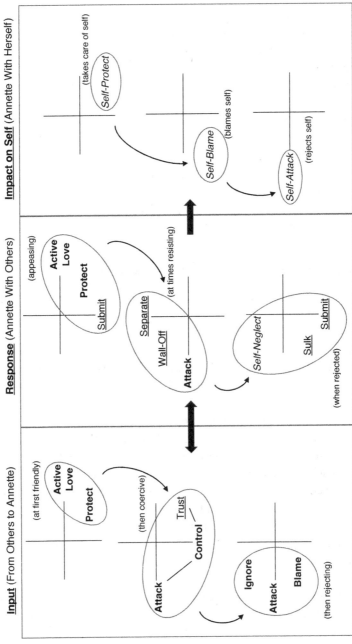

*Using SASB to Formulate Patterns From Clinical Interviews* • 185

**EXHIBIT 7.1. Annette's Mother**

| Quote |
| --- |
| She is my worst enemy and my best friend. |
| She is educated, beautiful, smart, intelligent. |
| Acceptance from her is important. |
| I first began dieting at age 15. Mother was pleased and took me to buy nice clothes. |
| She is always right. Do not talk back, or she will deck you, hit you with her fist, drag you, kick the s-- out of you. |
| My father was on my side. After he supported me, they would fight. |
| She says I am worthless because I have no college degree. All the family has degrees. |
| She told me I was a horrible mother when my youngest son was an infant. She said I paid more attention to my girlfriends than my baby. I did the best I could. I bought him what he wanted. I loved him. Sent him to preschool. I don't think I did wrong. |
| She says I am self-centered. When I won't drive her around, she calls me a horrible daughter. She is disgusted with me. I don't contribute to the family. |

failure to please others). Identification might also be suggested in recent angry explosiveness at her husband and children.

The full case formulation for Annette was summarized in a written report as outlined in Chapter 5. The following sample paragraph captures the predominant themes related to Annette's mother. The use of SASB to organize the themes in writing should be apparent:

> Annette reports many examples of being subject to forms of severe criticism, punishment, and rejection by important people in her life, most notably her mother, from a very early age. Her mother was very controlling and would use severe punishments if her rules were not followed. The patient reports having always desired her mother's approval, trying hard to win it, and being very hurt when it was not forthcoming. She currently shows signs of having internalized her mother's hostile control and rejection in a few different ways, including (a) treating herself like her mother treated her, in the form of vicious self-criticism and a belief that she is worthless and unlovable, even to the point of suicide, (b) behaving with others as if mother was in charge and her rules still applied by placing a high value on pleasing others "so that they like me" (even to the point of allowing herself to be abused and exploited).

## Linking Patterns to Symptoms

As noted in prior chapters, a person's interpersonal patterns and symptoms are seen as relating in sensible ways. For example, inordinate self-criticism, loss, and overwhelm are all understandable ways to become depressed. Anxiety is understandable as the result of a perceived need to persist in

186 • *Observing, Assessing, and Formulating Patient Patterns*

**FIGURE 7.3. Interpersonal Patterns Described Between Annette and Her Mother**

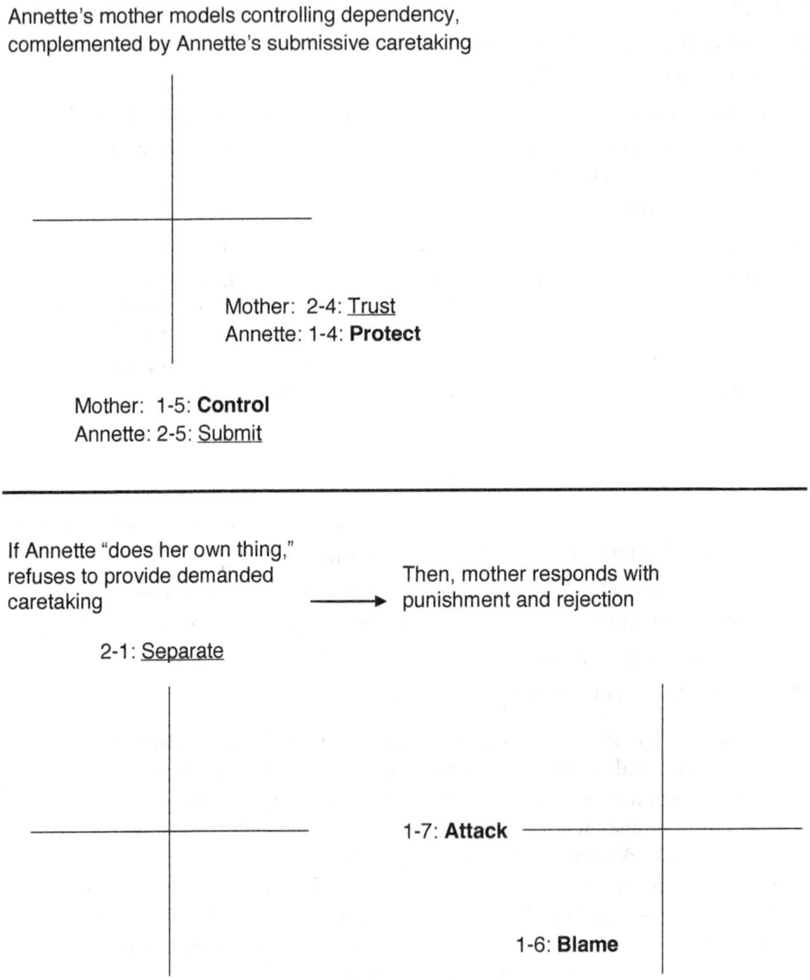

Annette's mother models controlling dependency, complemented by Annette's submissive caretaking

Mother: 2-4: <u>Trust</u>
Annette: 1-4: **Protect**

Mother: 1-5: **Control**
Annette: 2-5: <u>Submit</u>

If Annette "does her own thing," refuses to provide demanded caretaking

Then, mother responds with punishment and rejection

2-1: <u>Separate</u>

1-7: **Attack**

1-6: **Blame**

handling overwhelming tasks, especially when success seems unlikely. Perceived external threats and a need to fend off attacks or dreaded outcomes also links strongly to panic and anxiety. As Zinbarg et al. (1992) summarized:

> Fear says, "A terrible event is happening and I need to take action right now to stop it." Anxiety says, "A terrible event may happen; I may not be able to deal with it, but I've got to be ready to try." Depression says, "A terrible event may happen; I won't be able to cope with it, so I won't bother trying." (p. 238)

Manic symptoms can result from a sense of responsibility and presumed capability to handle absolutely everything, with impulsive choices and anger showing the fraying edges of failing attempts at mastery and control. Benjamin and colleagues described and provided evidence for these common ways to arrive at each symptom type (Benjamin, 2003, 2006, 2018; Benjamin, Wamboldt, & Critchfield, 2006), and evidence of links between symptoms and patterns in Intrex data are reviewed in Chapter 6.

A SASB-based summary of Annette's copy processes with her parents is shown in Figure 7.4. For Annette, depression, anxiety, manic periods, and suicidality all appear to be linked in different ways to attempts at trying to please abusive, coercive others, only to fail and be blamed for it. Links between her patterns and symptoms are summarized as follows:

> Her suicidality reflects rejection and condemnation . . . renewed and reinforced by others (husband, sons, attackers), for apparent failure to please, especially sexually. . . . A belief that she is worthy of punishment and worthless, coupled with a belief that she will not be believed or rescued, is a likely source of her long-standing depression. Anxiety may be a function of anticipating how she will be evaluated by those she is trying to please. Heroic efforts to please may at times have resulted in manic expenditures of energy.

## Articulating the Gift of Love

The interview process elicits information about present and past relating so that a person's copy process links can be traced relative to symptoms, and so that their motivating gifts of love may be understood. In Annette's full case formulation, relational patterns with her father, husband, children, and other important figures are also summarized. However, for Annette, the primary gift of love (GOL) relates to her mother and is explained like this:

> Repeating scenarios in which Annette sacrifices and even harms herself in order to take care of others, expecting acceptance for it from figures who only control, criticize, and reject her, reflects her desire to get it right with her mother. It is as if she is saying to her mother (and current others who repeat the pattern with her), "When you see the lengths I go to in order to care for you, you will love me." Annette confirmed this hypothesis, saying, "Gaining acceptance from my mom was extremely important to me, even when I was little. And I do whatever I can now."

Annette's father is another important person in her life. Early on, he protected Annette from her mother's rages, but later doubted her descriptions of her mother's abuse and withdrew from protecting her. A GOL is also hypothesized for him:

> Strong fondness plus copying with father may suggest a gift of love to him in addition to mother. It is as if she is saying, "If I do not protect myself from

**FIGURE 7.4. Case Formulation for Annette in Terms of SASB Codes and Copy Processes (Only Mother and Father Shown)**

| Person copied | Copy processes | Behavior/s copied |
|---|---|---|
| **Mother:** | Introjection of | 1-6: **Blame** as 3-6: *Self-Blame* |
| | | 1-7: **Attack** as 3-7: *Self-Attack* |
| | | 1-8: **Ignore** as 3-8: *Self-Neglect* |
| | Identification with | 1-7: **Attack** |
| | Recapitulation of | Self: |
| | | 1-4: **Protect**, 2-5: <u>Submit</u> |
| | | Others: |
| | | 1-5: **Control**, 2-4: <u>Trust</u> |
| | | When Self is 2-1: <u>Separate</u> or 2-8: <u>Wall-Off</u> |
| | | then others: |
| | | 1-6: **Blame** |
| | | 1-7: **Attack** |
| | | 1-8: **Ignore** |
| **Father:** | Introjection of | Others: |
| | | initially 1-4: **Protect** (as 3-4: *Self-Protect*) |
| | | but then 1-8: **Ignore** (as 3-8: *Self-Neglect*) |
| | Recapitulation of | Others: |
| | | initially 1-4: **Protect** |
| | | but then 1-8: **Ignore** |

*Note.* SASB cluster codes added here to enhance clarity. SASB = Structural Analysis of Social Behavior. Adapted from "Reliability, Sensitivity, and Specificity of Case Formulations for Comorbid Profiles in Interpersonal Reconstructive Therapy: Addressing Mechanisms of Psychopathology," by K. L. Critchfield, L. S. Benjamin, and K. Levenick, 2015, *Journal of Personality Disorders, 29*(4), p. 560 (https://doi.org/10.1521/pedi.2015.29.4.547). Copyright 2015 by Guilford Press. Adapted with permission.

exposure to danger in intimate relationships, see myself as not needing, or not being worth such protection, and repeatedly lose close relationships through their loyalty to others over me, then I show agreement, loyalty, and understanding of your choice not to believe that I was being abused. When you see how I agree with your view of me, you will see my loyalty to your views and love me for understanding your choice."

When possible, GOL hypotheses are checked out directly with the patient during the interview or soon after in the process of treatment. In many cases, the sense of being "seen" in this way is so organizing for a patient that it can appear as though it should have been self-evident. Reactions like, "Yes, that's it exactly," are common. In other cases, the GOL may feel more complicated to approach and consider, perhaps because the idea is new, it would entail a great deal of grief to face at the given moment, or the therapist has not gotten it quite right and it either does not apply or not in the way proposed. In these circumstances, the GOL motivation needs to retain status as a hypothesis. As noted previously, the GOL hypothesis must never be imposed or be used to confront. Exploration of copy processes, where they were learned, and what purposes they may serve in the present is the way to explore the possibility. Ultimately, if the patient does not agree about this motivation, then it is not considered correct (Benjamin, 2003, 2006).

Toward the end of Annette's interview, the interviewer reflected the primary GOL theme they had been discussing: "So the reason you stick with it [i.e., repeated suicidality, attempts to appease controlling, exploitative others] is you still want mother to love and approve you. Is that right?" Annette agreed with the interviewer's summary and decided to continue working with the idea in therapy. A key treatment implication was then to help Annette differentiate from the internalized version of her mother sufficient to be able to make her own decisions. Annette, like so many others, will likely need a great deal of support to reach that goal, since it means giving up on hopes of having mother's approval according to the old family rules for her.

## SASB, CASE FORMULATION, AND PERSONALITY DISORDER DIAGNOSIS

Part of the reason Annette was referred for a consultative interview was to get diagnostic clarity, especially around the suspected presence of personality disorder. The IRT approach to case formulation allows a SASB-based bridge by matching an individual's patterns to an interpersonal prototype

190 • *Observing, Assessing, and Formulating Patient Patterns*

for each of the personality disorder profiles. To facilitate this bridging, Benjamin (1996) defined each of the personality disorders (PDs) in the fourth edition of the *Diagnostic and Statistical Manual of Mental Disorders* (*DSM-IV*; American Psychiatric Association, 1994) according to their characteristic interpersonal features. She explained that the positions around the SASB model can be thought of like notes in music, with each PD prototype having its own recognizable rhythm and melody. Individual patients each have their own "song" that can be compared with these prototypes. More concretely, when PD is present, the associated patterns are usually apparent from SASB codes of the copy process formulation, which in turn suggests which PD diagnostic categories might be present. An array of Annette's copy process codes, with all IPIRs included, is shown in Table 7.3 and can be compared directly (i.e., using a correlation coefficient) to similar arrays from Benjamin's (1996) PD definitions. This interpersonal prototype-matching approach has been useful in research and clinical work characterizing individual profiles in terms of overlap with the PD prototypes (Critchfield, Dobner-Pereira, & Stucker, 2021;

**TABLE 7.3. Annette's Case Formulation Arrayed as the Set of SASB-Defined Behaviors Involved in Her Symptom-Linked Copy Process Formulation (All IPIRs Included)**

| SASB code | Others to me | | Me to others | | Me to me |
|---|---|---|---|---|---|
| | Past | Present | Past | Present | Introject |
| Emancipate | | | | | |
| Affirm | | | | | |
| Active Love | | | | | |
| Protect | | | X | X | |
| Control | X | X | | | |
| Blame | X | X | | | X |
| Attack | X | X | | X | X |
| Ignore | X | X | | | X |
| Separate | | | X | X | |
| Disclose | | | | | |
| Reactive Love | | | | | |
| Trust | X | X | | | |
| Submit | | | X | X | |
| Sulk | | | | | |
| Recoil | | | | | |
| Wall-Off | | | X | X | |

*Note.* X indicates the corresponding behavior was observed and is implicated in a copy process. IPIR = important person or their internalized representation; SASB = Structural Analysis of Social Behavior.

*Using SASB to Formulate Patterns From Clinical Interviews* • 191

Critchfield, Panizo, & Benjamin, 2019). The method has also been used to empirically test and validate predictions of Benjamin's interpersonal model of PD based on predicted patterns of comorbidity among PD definitions (Critchfield et al., 2015; Panizo Jansana, 2020).

Annette's SASB-based, copy process profile shows the strongest overlap with Benjamin's empirical prototype for passive-aggressive (PAG) PD ($r = .51$). All other profiles were much lower ($r$ values $< .30$), with paranoid PD being a relatively distant secondary match ($r = .35$).[2] Benjamin (1996) described the interpersonal translation of the PAG prototype as follows:

> There is a tendency to see any form of power as inconsiderate and neglectful, together with a belief that authorities or caregivers are incompetent, unfair, and cruel. The PAG agrees to comply with perceived demands or suggestions but fails to perform. He or she often complains of unfair treatment, and envies and resents others who fare better. His or her suffering indicts the allegedly negligent caregivers or authorities. The PAG fears control in any form and wishes for nurturant restitution. (p. 267)

Confirming the patterns observed in her case formulation, Annette qualified for the formal *DSM-IV*[3] definition of PAG by responding in the affirmative to the following criteria when asked about them during the consultative interview: (1) passively resists fulfilling routine social and occupational tasks, (2) complains of being misunderstood and unappreciated by others, (3) is sullen and argumentative, (5) expresses envy and resentment toward those apparently more fortunate, and (7) alternates between hostile defiance and contrition.

Annette's profile is not a perfect match to every element of the interpersonal PAG prototype, just as she does not fulfill every *DSM-IV* criterion.

---

[2] As described in Benjamin (1996), the PAG and paranoid PD prototypes each share an early history involving salient 1-5: **Control**, 1-6: **Blame**, and 1-7: **Attack** from attachment figures, producing in adulthood tendencies to be wary and withdraw defensively from others (2-8: <u>Wall-Off</u>) and to view them critically (1-6: **Blame**). However, the SASB codes of the two prototypes differ in other behavioral clusters, allowing them to be distinguished by their unique, nonoverlapping features. Benjamin (1996) used SASB-based definitions of each PD to explain how an interpersonal lens helps explain diagnostic comorbidity in the *DSM-IV* PDs. Panizo Jansana (2020) validated Benjamin's theory by comparing theoretically predicted and empirically observed degrees of overlap in patients with PD diagnoses.

[3] PAG was moved to the appendix in the *DSM-IV* and was removed from the *DSM-5* (American Psychiatric Association, 2013). The interpersonal pattern nonetheless persists in clinical work. The blend of passive resistance and ambivalence relative to authority figures makes this pattern difficult to assess and to work with clinically. Interested readers are encouraged to read about the pattern in a chapter dedicated to it by Benjamin (1993).

192 • *Observing, Assessing, and Formulating Patient Patterns*

Nevertheless, key elements of her internalized copy processes overlap with the PAG pattern. In many of her narratives, Annette alternates between submission and defiance, sometimes combining the two, such as when she provided the coercive patient with a cheeked pill to avoid having sex with him (also suggested in details of the episode, not reported here, involving sleeping with her friend's husband). In Annette's life, this instance illustrates not "chaotic behavior" or avoidance of potential abandonment so much as a desperate pattern of indirectness and "compliant defiance." Her pattern time and again is to receive abuse in exchange for self-sacrifice, to which she reacts with suffering and rage (usually kept inside, but sometime erupting toward the self or others) about the unfair coercion and unpredictable reversals from others.

Benjamin's (1996) interpersonal PD profiles were developed in part to aid in differential diagnosis. Annette's clinical presentation could suggest diagnosis of borderline personality disorder (BPD), along with other comorbid possibilities. For example, Annette has made multiple suicide attempts and has a seemingly chaotic pattern of disturbed relationships; she wishes for love and nurturance and tried suicide after being rejected and denigrated by two men not long after her husband left her. In that respect, her narrative suggests identity disturbance, anger problems, and recklessly impulsive actions that may be seen as consistent with BPD. However, the overlap of her SASB-coded copy process formulation with the BPD prototype is quite low ($r = .17$). Benjamin (1996) described the interpersonal prototype for BPD as follows:

> There is a morbid fear of abandonment and a wish for protective nurturance, preferably received by constant physical proximity to the rescuer (lover or caregiver). The baseline position is friendly dependency on a nurturer, which becomes hostile control if the caregiver or lover fails to deliver enough (and there is never enough). There is a belief that the provider secretly if not overtly likes dependency and neediness, and a vicious introject attacks the self if there are signs of happiness or success. (p. 119)

A necessary feature of BPD is fear of abandonment, usually handled by coercion of the other person so that they will be compelled to provide nurturance. Another necessary feature is evidence of self-sabotage following happiness or success. An exclusionary descriptor is tolerance of aloneness on a long-term basis (from Benjamin, 1996, p. 119). To simplify the distinction, BPD has a fear of abandonment as a primary motivational theme, whereas PAG has a fear of being unfairly controlled and condemned. Despite her craving for nurturance and approval, Annette did not report fearing abandonment. Instead, she was most fearful of indictment and condemnation that seemed to ensue no matter her choice. Rather than a chaotic shift from idealization to overt devaluation on the horizontal SASB axis, Annette's codes instead tended to emphasize the vertical interpersonal dimension of close enmeshment versus separation.

## THERAPY GOALS

Recommended therapy goals for Annette, in the most general sense, are to reduce red ways of being, mostly traceable to the GOL with her mother, and to increase access to green ways of being as defined by the therapy goals. During the interview, Annette repeatedly says that being affirmed by mother is very important to her. In an IRT-based analysis, this wish to please mother is related to the maintenance of many of her problem patterns, including suicidality. The idea is that when Annette tries to follow her mother's rules and values, she does things as her mother does, treats herself as her mother treats her, and relates to others as she relates to her mother. For example, it seems that Annette's suicidality (3-7: *Self-Attack*) represents the ultimate testimonial to the belief that mother (along with other condemners she noted, including her husband and sons) are "right" and that the patient is unworthy, despicable, and so on. If that is her reasoning, then Annette will need help forming her own self-evaluation and more freedom in choosing whether to comply and please others on their (often inappropriate) terms. In the effort to develop a separate, strong, well-socialized self that is both independent yet connected, Annette could benefit by learning more about how to relate to others with friendly autonomy. That could allow her to make her own decisions and still not necessarily be alienated from her mother and others. Annette will likely need a great deal of support in doing this, however, since this also means giving up on hopes of having her mother's approval according to the old rules. To help sustain motivation for these important tasks, Annette offered an important healing image for herself that involved finishing her degree and returning to her previous career teaching young children: "I want to be a teacher even if it takes me until I'm 108 to get there . . . we just have to keep me alive long enough." She understood that the image of herself as a nurturant and competent teacher could be applied to her own self-treatment—that is, to treat herself with compassion and caring when angry or in pain, as she would one of the children in her class, rather than with condemnation and harsh punishments as she had personally experienced in childhood.

Similarly, Annette reported that she no longer wishes to rage and be angry at others. That too could be facilitated by helping Annette decide as to whether she wants to be like her description of her mother. Behaviorally, she might be helped by learning alternative ways (a) to encourage others

194 • *Observing, Assessing, and Formulating Patient Patterns*

to meet her needs and (b) to consider whether she is angry in service of controlling them and whether and if such control is or is not appropriate. Alternative ways would involve assertion rather than aggression, request rather than demand, connection rather than win or lose, and so on.

## SASB AND IRT CASE FORMULATION RESEARCH

A fine-grained level of analysis using SASB helps to organize patient patterns (with supportive data) so that treatment is accurate. It also helps sustain therapists and patients in their work toward treatment goals by being able to invoke concrete, observable examples of red and green patterns. Being grounded in behavioral data about relationships separately allows researchers to test and validate IRT's proposed clinical processes. For example, Critchfield et al. (2015) asked trainees to independently view video of consult interviews, like those conducted with Annette (and usually conducted by Benjamin), but leaving out the interviewer's verbal summary of copy processes and links to symptoms. Raters then generated their own SASB and copy process–based case formulations using a structured format to allow direct comparison of its various facets. The results are reproduced in Table 7.4 and show very good interrater agreement for (a) identities of

**TABLE 7.4. Mean Interrater Agreement Computed With Cohen's κ Coefficient (SD) for Central Case Formulation Elements**

| Formulation element | Graduate-level IRT therapy trainees (*n* = 13) | Undergraduate research assistants (*n* = 7) | Average for primary site (*n* = 20) | Cross-site comparisons (*n* = 8) |
|---|---|---|---|---|
| 1. Key figures | .90 (.11) | .82 (.18) | .88 (.14) | .86 (.13) |
| 2. Copy processes | .81 (.13) | .78 (.27) | .80 (.18) | .77 (.18) |
| 3. Key figures link to specific symptoms | .78 (.35) | .77 (.34) | .78 (.33) | .56 (.60)/ .91 (.19)* |
| 4. Key figures link to specific symptom via specific copy process | .75 (.16) | .64 (.14) | .71 (.16) | .77 (.18) |

*Note.* IRT = Interpersonal Reconstructive Therapy. From "Reliability, Sensitivity, and Specificity of Case Formulations for Comorbid Profiles in Interpersonal Reconstructive Therapy: Addressing Mechanisms of Psychopathology," by K. L. Critchfield, L. S. Benjamin, and K. Levenick, 2015, *Journal of Personality Disorders, 29*(4), p. 563 (https://doi.org/10.1521/pedi.2015.29.4.547). Copyright 2015 by Guilford Press. Reprinted with permission.
*The second set of values reflects comparisons made after clarification of the formulation instructions (*n* = 6).

key figures; (b) copy processes; and (c) links between symptoms and key figures, with average Cohen's κ values ranging from .71 to .88. A separate team of experienced clinicians using IRT at another site also provided formulations of a subset of the interviews. Cross-site agreement ranged from κ = .77 to .91. Even trained undergraduates with little clinical experience did well at the interpersonal aspects of formulation. Their disagreements usually involved links to specific symptoms, which they were less well trained in recognizing.

The same study showed strong agreement for assignment of SASB content codes (Critchfield et al., 2015). Average correlations between SASB-based profiles generated across the two training sites were $r = .99$ for behaviors that both teams agreed were part of the case formulation. Profiles that included behaviors one team thought was relevant, but the other did not, were lower for intransitive behavior ($r = .66$) but not for transitive behavior ($r = .99$).

Additional analyses showed that copy process case formulations can be used to uniquely identify patient profiles. To do this, raters were asked to match five interviews to seven formulations summarized like the one shown for Annette in Figure 7.4. Only SASB labels and copy processes for parental figures were included. Of 40 clinical trainees who attempted the task, half made a perfect set of matches, while another 25% made only one mismatch. The probability of getting three or more correct on this task through random guessing alone is less than $p = .05$. Ninety percent of raters exceeded that threshold. These findings support the idea that SASB-based, IRT case formulations provide an excellent basis for unique tailoring of the treatment approach to a patient's attachment history and needs. Chapter 8 focuses on the in-session therapeutic process and how clinical decision making is optimally informed and adapted to each patient's relational history and case formulation.

PART IV

TREATMENT: CONNECTING WITH PATIENTS AND OPTIMIZING INTERVENTIONS USING STRUCTURAL ANALYSIS OF SOCIAL BEHAVIOR-BASED FOCUS ON PSYCHOTHERAPY PROCESS, CASE FORMULATION, AND THERAPY GOALS

# 8 DIRECTING IN-SESSION RELATIONAL PROCESSES TOWARD THERAPEUTIC GOALS

Interpersonal processes can be directed toward therapeutic goals during sessions.[1] This chapter examines the Structural Analysis of Social Behavior (SASB)–based profile of optimal therapeutic relating, explaining how the relationship process can only be optimized if used in support of reaching green goals. Therapy goals using SASB, including how the process of therapy can be used to enhance their pursuit, are also discussed.

## PATTERNING OF THE THERAPY RELATIONSHIP

Optimal patterning of the therapy relationship is consistent with secure attachment in the following key respects: It has friendliness as its baseline. It also offers moderate degrees of enmeshment, which facilitates connection and communion, and differentiation, which helps foster and allows development of a separate, agentic self (Bakan, 1966). Therapist interventions at the moment-by-moment level are primarily in clusters 1-2: **Affirm** and 1-4: **Protect**.

---

[1] The clinical material used in this book is adequately disguised to protect patient confidentiality.

https://doi.org/10.1037/0000403-008
*Structural Analysis of Social Behavior (SASB): A Primer for Clinical Use*, by
K. L. Critchfield and L. S. Benjamin
Copyright © 2024 by the American Psychological Association. All rights reserved.

Patients are usually in complementary positions of 2-2: Disclose and 2-4: Trust. The largest distinction between other types of attachment relationships and the therapy relationship is that its focus is asymmetric: The therapist's primary attentional focus is on the patient, while the patient's focus primarily concerns themselves and their own experience. Another important difference is that direct and intense expressions of love (1-3: **Active Love** and 2-3: Reactive Love) occur only in limited and highly contextualized ways.

This therapy relationship pattern is presented in Figure 8.1, in which average percentages of patient and therapist SASB clusters are reported across multiple studies using formal coding of observed therapy process. Figure 8.1 includes codes from 205 sessions of psychodynamic treatment (Coady, 1991a, 1991b; Henry et al., 1986, 1990; Tasca et al., 2011; Ulberg et al., 2009), cognitive behavior therapy (CBT; Ahmed et al., 2012; Critchfield et al., 2007; Tasca et al., 2011), and process-experiential treatment (Maramba, 2005; Wong & Pos, 2014). Most therapist statements involve 1-2: **Affirm** and

**FIGURE 8.1. Empirical Baseline of Therapy Relationships**

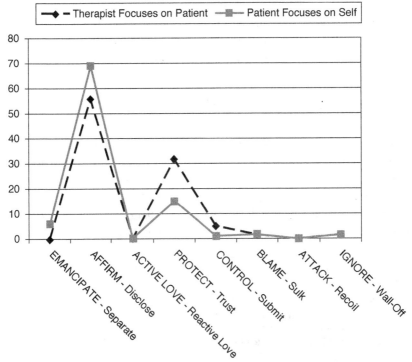

*Directing In-Session Relational Processes Toward Therapeutic Goals* • 201

1-4: **Protect**, which patients usually complement with 2-2: <u>Disclose</u> and 2-4: <u>Trust</u>. These SASB clusters make up approximately 88% of all patient and therapist statements and have an aggregate profile correlation of $r = .94$, which indicates overall strong complementarity.

Much less common in psychotherapy processes are therapist use of 1-5: **Control** (7%), patient use of 2-1: <u>Separate</u> (6%), and therapist use of 2-2: <u>Disclose</u> (5%; not shown in Figure 8.1). The other SASB clusters have an average occurrence rate of 2% or less. Codes involving any form of hostility are even rarer, occurring at a rate of roughly 4% each for therapists and patients and usually in complex combination with another behavior. For therapists, hostility is primarily seen as 1-6: **Blame** and 1-8: **Ignore**; for patients, it takes the form of 2-6: <u>Sulk</u> and 2-8: <u>Wall-Off</u>.

To illustrate optimal dimensions of therapy relating, the next sections discuss the therapeutic process relative to the SASB clusters most commonly observed.

### Cluster 2: Affirm and Disclose

The most frequently observed therapist behavior is friendly autonomy granting, or 1-2: **Affirm**. This cluster position is most consistent with Rogerian expressions of empathy, acceptance, and positive regard. It also characterizes how a therapist typically engages in accurate reflection, active listening, and nonpossessive support. The therapist often seeks to understand a patient's experience from the patient's point of view, without adding significant new ideas or interpretations. According to the parallel cognitive and affective models (SACB and SAAB), this behavior should be accompanied by the therapist's internal experience of being oriented toward understanding their patients and feeling accepting of them. In addition to straightforward expressions of warm autonomy granting, formal research coding often includes less intense or more implicit expressions of cluster 2, such as brief confirmation that the therapist is listening ("Mm-hm") and genuinely wants to know more about the patient's experience ("Tell me more about that").

The complementary position, 2-2: <u>Disclose</u>, is the most frequently observed patient behavior. Disclosure typically involves the patient openly sharing their own thoughts, feelings, and views. It also involves being and expressing in ways that are not attempts to appease or manage fear of the therapist. According to the parallel affective model, the associated feeling is of being centered, while the cognitive style is expressive. These behaviors typically involve introducing new and relevant material, rather than simply following minimal demand characteristics of the situation.

202 • *Treatment: Connecting With Patients and Optimizing Interventions*

SASB-based research supports the idea that the tendency to relate in cluster 2 is linked with positive outcomes. Therapist affirmation has been associated with improved outcomes (Ahmed et al., 2012; Henry et al., 1986). Patient disclosure also increases in response to a therapist's affirming statements, and this effect has been observed in both individual (Muran et al., 2018; von der Lippe et al., 2008) and group (Tasca et al., 2011) therapy settings. In turn, patient disclosure has been associated with psychodynamic therapy outcomes (Coady, 1991a; Henry et al., 1986, 1990; Jørgensen et al., 2000), improved alliances in humanistic and existential treatment (Wong & Pos, 2014), and increased expectations of success in CBT (Ahmed et al., 2012). Evidence suggests that therapist affirmation is also internalized over time as patient 3-2: *Self-Affirm* (Bedics et al., 2012a, 2012b; Harrist et al., 1994; Quintana & Meara, 1990).

Cluster 2 is not at the extreme of the SASB model's vertical dimension and still involves a degree of interdependence. For example, the therapist can often steer a conversation to important issues through a relatively gentle process of expressing interest and attending to some topics over others. The term *reflective interpretation* is sometimes used to describe the technique of selectively focusing on and amplifying key elements to enhance awareness and motivation for change.

In the following transcript segment, there are many examples of cluster 2 affirmation and disclosure. The therapist carefully listens and tracks, gently but persistently bringing the conversation to the tension between red and green parts of the patient's identity and the relevance of those parts to her history of dependence on her mother (now deceased). The transcript is from the second session held during an inpatient hospitalization, as reported in Critchfield and Mackaronis (2016, pp. 201–203).

THERAPIST: I'd really like to just follow up on our meeting yesterday, sort of what thoughts and feelings you've had about that discussion, and maybe figure out where to go from here, or whether to go from here.

PATIENT: Okay, I know it brought out a lot of emotions and a lot of feelings, some good, some bad, especially when we talked about how I needed to learn to cope on my own because I'm so dependent on people. That kind of freaked me out.

THERAPIST: Really? In what way?

PATIENT: Because I just, I don't think I can do it. I'm terrible at talking with people, so I don't know.

*Directing In-Session Relational Processes Toward Therapeutic Goals* • 203

THERAPIST: So, you feel freaked out by the idea.

PATIENT: Yeah, that I could help do it on my own and learn how to not depend on people and I just don't know how I - I've always had someone to help me.

THERAPIST: What would that look like? I mean, what would it be like to try and cope with things and build a life? Do you have any . . .?

PATIENT: Well eventually I felt more suicidal. I hate to say that. But the thought of just doing it made me even more unsure. Because right now I'm dealing with the pain and trying to manage on my own, and trying to manage without pain pills . . .

Later in the interview, the patient is remembering her mother.

PATIENT: We all just laughed and that made her even madder. [*laugh*] We lived with her drama queen scene so much that it was just like every time she did something we ended up laughing, so . . . [*pause*]

THERAPIST: Do you miss her?

PATIENT: A lot.

THERAPIST: I imagine. I imagine it would be hard not to.

PATIENT: Mm-hmm.

THERAPIST: You said that even if she couldn't figure out a way to advocate or take the pain away, she'd be up here helping in whatever way she could think of.

PATIENT: Mm-hmm. She was really knowledgeable, and she didn't believe in medicine and drugs. But she advocated for me because she saw I couldn't function and when it became that I was in too much pain she said, okay, this needs to be done. But other than that, like with her cancer just got into all these different things and so she'd probably get, if she couldn't find a doctor to prescribe or help with my pain, she would try to find a way to bring me out of it, instead of feeling like giving up . . .

THERAPIST: So, it sounds like it just makes everything that much more intense that she isn't here, not just as your advocate, but as your mother.

PATIENT: Mm-hmm.

THERAPIST: And the idea of trying to take over some of that role for yourself.

PATIENT: I've lost all hope. I just don't care. There is a tiny piece in there that cares because I would have left here already and ended it. But the majority of me has said, "I'm sick of this. I hate the way doctors treat me. I hate going in and out. I have to live like this the rest of my life." It makes it hard to have a relationship or friends or anything so I feel like, there is that little bit that would like to try, but the majority of it is still thinking to end it.

THERAPIST: Well, I hear you. And there's no one who could stop you if you make that choice in the long run, and you know that as well as anyone does. I do appreciate your honesty in just saying it how it is. And I hope you feel like I'm hearing you.

PATIENT: I do.

THERAPIST: And I also hear the tension in you between that hopeless part of you and the little part that has made it this far.

PATIENT: Mm-hmm.

A positive shift occurred over the next few sessions of daily inpatient work, sufficient to draw surprised comments from other staff who worked with this patient. Her focus between sessions began to parallel that of her in-session conversations, shifting over time from an initial position of hopelessness, suicidality, and craving for a return of her mother's protection to a more centered commitment to the process of building a new, self-chosen, life.

### Sometimes Affirmation Is Not Helpful

Affirmation can also be used in ways that are iatrogenic in the sense of supporting red goals rather than green ones. To illustrate this, let us revisit research discussed in Chapter 4. Bedics and colleagues (2012a, 2012b) reported on two contrasting treatments for borderline personality disorder (BPD): dialectical behavior therapy (DBT) and community treatment by experts. In the DBT condition, therapist affirmation was followed by better self-treatment and reduced self-harm and suicidality, whereas affirmation levels in the community treatment had the opposite effect. The issue was one of what precisely was being affirmed:

> The present findings lend support to the hypothesis that DBT therapists may utilize validation strategies as a method of confirming or modeling a positive self-view for their patients (Lynch et al., 2006). The opposite effect for CTBE

therapists may be indicative of a less precise use of validation that may, unintentionally, reinforce a hostile view of self (e.g., Swann, 1997). (Bedics et al., 2012a, p. 75)

The issue raised here is not the same as concerns over the accuracy of expressed empathy per se. Rather, empathy can have potentially variable effects depending on how patients perceive it (Elliott et al., 2018). Vague, diffuse, or poorly timed expressions of empathy risk being perceived as support for red rather than green. For example, a therapist might make the brief affirming comment, "Mm-hmm," intending to convey empathy ("This sounds important. Please tell me more"). However, the brief comment is unclear and may be perceived as affirming the patient's content instead ("I agree with the view you are expressing"). Karpiak and Benjamin (2004) provided data showing that maladaptive views (e.g., "I'm hopeless," "No one will listen or help," and "It's too hard") can be reinforced and supported when immediately followed by 1-2: **Affirm**. In CBT for generalized anxiety, affirmation of maladaptive statements was associated with worse symptomatic outcomes at termination and 1 year later. In psychodynamic treatment, affirmation of problem patterns was associated with worse relating with a significant other but unexpected improvements in self-concept. Karpiak and Benjamin (2004) noted the following:

> it is feasible that affirmation of a patient's complaints or other maladaptive statements about a significant other might correspond with both a feeling of acceptance of the self and ongoing difficulty with the significant other. (pp. 671–672)

In sum, theory and evidence converge to suggest that therapist affirmation is an important baseline position and generally beneficial. This view is supported by meta-analytic findings regarding the correlation between expressions of empathy and positive therapeutic outcomes (Elliott et al., 2018). However, as the meta-analytic work on empathy also confirms, the benefits of 1-2: **Affirm** are not universal and can have heterogeneous effects. As Karpiak and Benjamin (2004) noted, differential effects seem to be a function of the reinforcement value of affirmation. Therapeutic errors may consist in accidental reinforcement of red, maladaptive patterns. Therefore, it is crucial to keep a patient's case formulation in mind when using 1-2: **Affirm** in support of green goals.

### Cluster 4: Protect and Trust

Cluster 4 comprises protection and trust, the second most common behaviors among patients and therapists across therapy approaches. For therapists, this encompasses forms of friendly influence over the patient. Relevant positions on the SASB full model include 144 Sensible analysis and 145 Constructive stimulate. The associated cognitive stance is one of concentrating on the patient, whereas the associated affect is one of nurturance. The prototype might involve the therapist providing advice, didactic input, or homework assignments and leading in-session practice with exposure-based activities or mindfulness exercises. Therapist 1-4: **Protect** is observed with most instances of transference interpretation (Marble et al., 2011) and is relevant across techniques of multiple orientations. For patients, the complementary position of 2-4: Trust consists of taking in input, following and relying on what is offered, or requesting help or advice. The associated cognitive style (SACB) for patients is to expect to be well directed, and the associated affect (SAAB) is to be hopeful.

Correlation between therapist 1-4: **Protect** and indicators of outcome are less consistent than for affirming statements, with statistically significant findings in only three of nine available studies (Coady, 1991a; Henry et al., 1986; Jørgensen et al., 2000). Research suggests that the timing and context of its use matters greatly. For example, Ahmed et al. (2012) found that patients have lowered expectations of therapy when their therapist responds in an initial session with warm persuasion (coded 1-4: **Protect**) rather than empathic listening. Gender may moderate the effect of cluster 4 on clinical processes as well. For example, MacDonald et al. (2007) observed that male individuals with substance use disorder were less likely to engage in subsequent treatment when the initial interview had more 1-4: **Protect**. Along similar lines, the only study in which 2-4: Trust was associated with poorer outcomes involved a predominantly male psychotherapy sample (Henry et al., 1986).

Data on internalization of therapist 1-4: **Protect** also exist, but again seem to be highly context specific. Bedics et al. (2012b) found evidence for internalization of warm control by therapists in successful DBT treatment for BPD. This may be because provision of warm structure helps counteract the internal dysregulation and the sensitivity to abandonment that are defining features of BPD (Benjamin, 1996). Parallel findings have not been reported in studies of heterogeneous outpatient samples, but more research is needed on the topic generally.

When used well and in an appropriate context, the behavior coded in cluster 4 can have powerful and immediate effects. In the following transcript segment, the therapist uses friendly control to help a patient withstand the impact of difficult session material (traumatic memories, activation of hostile internalized voices). Prior to the interaction described in the transcript

*Directing In-Session Relational Processes Toward Therapeutic Goals* • 207

segment, the interview involved discussion of the basis for collaboration and trust to understand current problems. The patient then began speaking about painful memories of early sexual abuse and rejection by her father that had clear links to her current symptoms and self-concept. In the following passage, the therapist continues to track this material empathically but adds 1-4: **Protect** (underlined statements) to enhance support for the patient's green self.

PATIENT: Yes, of course. It was my father and I wanted his approval.

THERAPIST: Right.

PATIENT: So, I guess that somewhere along the line, I'm like, I just feel like I was numb and I would do it anyway. If this is what made me get my love from my father, then that's what I would do.

THERAPIST: Okay. Right. Okay, so he gave you some kind of love if you would go along.

PATIENT: Yeah.

THERAPIST: Of course. <u>But you didn't have much choice, did you?</u>

PATIENT: No, I didn't.

THERAPIST: <u>You did not.</u> So, but it was a good/bad experience, or bad/good, because for once you got something affirming.

PATIENT: Right, exactly. I think as, yeah, it could be, as sick as this might sound, it was like at least I had some kind of time with daddy.

THERAPIST: <u>You bet. I've heard that so many times, "At least I had this." But what a price, what a price.</u>

PATIENT: [*crying*] And that's why my mom told me it was my fault, because she said I should have told her.

THERAPIST: <u>Well you were going to get beaten, right?</u>

PATIENT: [*nods*]

THERAPIST: <u>And you would have lost this little bit that you had. So, I wouldn't have told her either. So, but she can't, she can't be a mom about it, can she?</u>

PATIENT: I don't know, she just, I just in my head it's like I knew she was going through a lot too.

THERAPIST: Yeah. She had her own, she had her own struggles too. <u>That's for sure. We'll talk about that in a bit. Um, this is not a court of law and I'm not the Department of Health and Social Services. I'm not going to hear this and call the police in. We're just trying to describe how it happened.</u>

PATIENT: Okay.

### Cluster 3: Love

Love, in the form of attachment gone awry, is at the core of the Interpersonal Reconstructive Therapy (IRT) theory of psychopathology. The internalized versions of caregivers and lessons learned with them essentially control the safety and threat system that links so powerfully to symptoms. However, as depicted in Figure 8.1, the extremes of friendliness (1-3: **Active Love** and 2-3: <u>Reactive Love</u>) are rare events in psychotherapy process. Some evidence suggests that although the base rate is low, expressions of interpersonal love may still enhance the therapy bond in ways that are linked to outcomes. For example, Wong and Pos (2014) found that in the first sessions of experiential therapy, cluster 3 behaviors are associated with better alliances. In the study of DBT for BPD described earlier, the patient's perception of a therapist's degree of 1-3: **Active Love** was associated with increases in self-love and reduced self-harm (Bedics et al., 2012a, 2012b).

When patients are asked to rate their view of the therapeutic relationship on the Intrex questionnaire, cluster 3 items receive moderate to high ratings and are experienced as being present, which is in contrast with observational research. It is possible that when the less-frequent expressions of relatively intense warmth (expressions of caring, enjoyment of the work, joint laughter and delight, celebrations of accomplishments) occur in and support a relationship context with high levels of 1-2: **Affirm** and 1-4: **Protect**, the tendency is for their overall effect to enhance attachment and be perceived as more meaningful than a simple frequency count in a transcript would suggest. A patient's perception of 1-3: **Active Love** from the therapist may help the relationship become introjected in support of 3-3: *Active Self-Love*. It may also help explain how the well-bounded, secure-base relationship offered in therapy can sometimes be experienced by patients in romantic or sexual terms. A similar kind of psychological averaging was noted by Kaslow and colleagues (1989) on the opposite side of the SASB model. In their study, a suicidal adolescent experienced parent input that involved a relatively high frequency of observer-coded 1-6: **Blame** and 1-8: **Ignore**;

however, the adolescent seemed to have internalized their combination in the form of suicidality, 3-7: *Self-Attack*.

### Deviations From Therapeutic Baseline Are Often Linked With Poor Outcome

SASB-based studies of therapeutic process have repeatedly shown that deviations from the empirical baseline presented in Figure 8.1 are associated with poorer outcomes. This is particularly the case when forms of hostility are involved. For example, Henry and colleagues (1986, 1990) found that even small amounts of therapist 1-6: **Blame** and 1-8: **Ignore** or complementary patient behaviors of 2-6: Sulk and 2-8: Wall-Off predict poor symptomatic outcomes and more hostile self-treatment. In these studies, therapist hostility was rare and usually subtle, appearing as part of a complex communication paired with friendly clusters. The basic finding was replicated in additional studies (Muran et al., 2018; Schut et al., 2005; von der Lippe et al., 2008), and complex communication has been linked with poorer outcomes (Coady, 1991b).

Other studies have found fewer links between SASB-defined hostility and poor outcomes, likely because they had lower overall rates of hostility (e.g., Ahmed et al., 2012; Critchfield et al., 2007; MacDonald et al., 2007; Maramba, 2005; Muran et al., 2018). These studies instead identified contexts in which therapist use of interpersonal directiveness (1-4: **Protect** and 1-5: **Control**) and patient resistance or disagreement (2-1: Separate) were linked with poorer prognosis or outcomes (Ahmed et al., 2012; Hara et al., 2022; MacDonald et al., 2007). Treatment methods may differ in terms of the types of relationship ruptures they invite, whether a struggle involving power and a resistance to control or to subtle expressions of hostility. In any case, the pattern of evidence confirms that deviations from the usual baseline of therapeutic relating can affect outcomes, especially if left unaddressed.

Deviations from the therapeutic baseline may be indicative of an alliance rupture (Eubanks et al., 2019; Muran et al., 2018). These ruptures are often, but not always, marked by (usually subtle) forms of interpersonal hostility from the patient or therapist. They can also involve an unusual sense of going along passively or submissively without much agency, or the opposite in terms of assertive pushing off from a therapist, perhaps in relation to the goals, tasks, or processes of therapy. Both sets of problems also fall outside of the therapy goal ways of relating.

In terms of SASB clusters, when patient behavior falls in any cluster away from moderate friendliness, this may suggest a type of alliance rupture. Clusters 2-6: Sulk and 2-7: Recoil may be the more recognizable markers of a

210 • *Treatment: Connecting With Patients and Optimizing Interventions*

problem, in that they typically involve expression of fear or resentment about the therapist or what they have done or might do. A more difficult-to-detect marker of an alliance rupture involves cluster 2-8: Wall-Off, which might be sensed in a subtle pattern of nondisclosure or in more obvious forms such as tuning out, withdrawing, or shutting down in sessions or missing sessions. It is important to note that dissociation may also present as 2-8: Wall-Off. However, dissociation is typically best understood as appearing in conjunction with 3-8: *Self-Neglect*, and it may represent less of a walling off from the therapist than from the therapy process when overwhelmed. Clusters 2-1: Separate and 2-5: Submit do not involve hostility, so their salience to therapy outcomes may be more dependent on context than the other interpersonal positions.

## Reversed Focus

Reversals of focus also deviate from the recommended therapy baseline. These behaviors occur in roughly 5% to 6% of all statements in SASB-based therapy studies, with most taking the form of therapist self-disclosure. Research on therapist self-disclosure suggests that it may function similarly to expressions of love and enjoyment in SASB cluster 3 as described earlier, converging on the idea that even a few instances can be profoundly beneficial in the right context. Hill (1989) noted this impact and also provided clarity: In a study of experienced therapists, helpful disclosures typically "kept the focus on the client and helped to clarify the client's experience. . . . These disclosures generally helped clients to become more aware of their own feelings or behaviors" (p. 317). In SASB-based terms, beneficial use of therapist 2-2: Disclose involves a simultaneous focus on the patient that reinforces or amplifies some other message in the region of 1-2: **Affirm** or 1-4: **Protect**. Therapist disclosure can even be used to help support work at the level of the gift of love (GOL):

> I know a little about what that's like, to struggle with getting some distance from a loved one too wrapped up in their own thing to really see us, wishing that maybe they still finally will. Sadly, it's far more common and human than it probably feels right now. The fact is I think you are doing great work and can get through this.

Patients may also reverse focus in friendly ways that are benign, such as expressions of interest about the therapist that are socially normative and fit the immediate context (e.g., "Are those new glasses?" or "How was your vacation?"). As with so much in IRT, the meaning of any such behaviors needs to be considered within the context of the individual's history and

*Directing In-Session Relational Processes Toward Therapeutic Goals • 211*

case formulation, including when affirming or protective stances are taken toward the therapist. Consider the following therapist response:

> I hear you wanting to sort of take care of me right now and make sure I'm okay after [recent event]. I appreciate you offering that help and advice. At the same time, I can't help but think about[2] how your assignment in the family was always to take care of others in hopes of getting some of your own needs met. I wonder if you see any connections to that idea in what we were talking about before we kind of shifted to me?

In contrast, reversals that involve hostility (e.g., patient 1-6: **Blame** or therapist 2-6: <u>Sulk</u>) have been linked to poor outcomes and usually must be addressed right away. The predictive principles can be helpful in thinking about how to get a therapy process back on track. For example, Figure 8.2 begins with a patient's blaming and sulking comment about perceived therapist neglect. The pull of complementarity will be for the therapist to blame the patient in return, become defensively apologetic, or both. Figure 8.2 illustrates a better option in which the therapist responds with nondefensive disclosure about the issue and seeks understanding. In other words, the opposite and the antidote positions are used to invite the patient into friendlier territory (process channel) while also addressing the topic (content channel) and providing the opposite of neglect.

### Using the Case Formulation to Support Green More Than Red

As described in Chapter 5, an adherent IRT therapist's goal is to support green more than red whenever possible, without failing to attend to what red is saying or doing within the patient's experience. By implication, this means that there is a narrow set of circumstances in which interpersonal hostility can be used beneficially. Examples include when hostility is directed toward red while green is clearly protected, affirmed, or set free in the process. Critchfield and Mackaronis (2016) provided an extended case example involving management of a suicidal crisis through a process of differential response to the red and green parts of the self. The following transcript selection provides another illustration involving sarcasm (underlined in the transcript) that serves a similar function.

PATIENT:   That's true. Just sitting here, I just like kind of almost feel guilty about telling, saying things about my mom and my dad.

---

[2]In addition to its content, this example also contains the use of therapist disclosure (2-2: <u>Disclose</u>) to briefly accept and acknowledge the shift with some warmth before returning the focus to the patient.

212 • *Treatment: Connecting With Patients and Optimizing Interventions*

**FIGURE 8.2.** Regaining Collaboration After Alliance Rupture Involving Reversal of Usual Structural Analysis of Social Behavior Focus

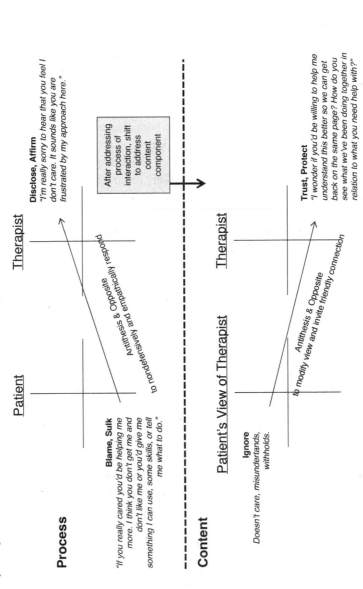

*Directing In-Session Relational Processes Toward Therapeutic Goals* • 213

THERAPIST: Yeah. Who, but now who would scold you for saying this?

PATIENT: [*smile*] The red?

THERAPIST: Yes. You hear the red.

PATIENT: Yeah

THERAPIST: You've got a mom in your head there and she's. It's like she's sitting over there [*points at nearby chair*] and she's talking to you.

PATIENT: Oh yeah, trust me she is. [*laughing*]

THERAPIST: Okay, well let's hear you talk back to her.

PATIENT: I don't know what to say.

THERAPIST: You're so unfamiliar with that, you don't know what to say.

PATIENT: No.

THERAPIST: Give it a try.

PATIENT: Um, I just feel like I could tell her, "I don't care, you know I'm going to do this because I want to be able to let all this stuff go," and really, I just want to be mad and tell her I don't care what she thinks, I'm doing it anyway.

THERAPIST: Good!

PATIENT: You know, she can stay back there but I'm not going to do it.

THERAPIST: All right, you've got a good start!

PATIENT: That's how I feel.

THERAPIST: That's, that's good. That's healthy.

PATIENT: But then I feel guilty at the same time because I don't want to hurt my mom. Because I know she has stuff.

THERAPIST: <u>Oh, you're her therapist now?</u>

PATIENT: [*looks down, smiling*]

THERAPIST: <u>Where did you get that job?</u>

PATIENT: I don't know. I hired myself. [*laughs*]

THERAPIST: [*laughs*] <u>You hired yourself. Well, fire yourself, okay?</u>

PATIENT: Okay.

THERAPIST: You are really quick, you know that?

PATIENT: [laughs]

THERAPIST: You really are. You could really go with this. So, you're going to have to fire her but I want, I want just a little rehearsal here of telling, telling her she'd fired, uh, firing yourself for taking care of her.

PATIENT: Okay. I'd just tell her, "Mom, I'm not doing this anymore, you know. I'm tired of going through the same thing over and over with you." That's what I would tell her.

THERAPIST: And what would she say?

PATIENT: She'd probably start cursing.

THERAPIST: Yeah.

PATIENT: Yeah, for sure.

THERAPIST: And then what can you say?

### Summary of Optimal Relating

Across orientations, therapeutic process commonly involves the use of SASB clusters 2 and 4. When focused on patients in individual or group settings, the therapist's stance pulls for a complementary profile from patients; together, these are associated with better outcomes compared with deviations from that basic pattern. Evidence shows that timing and context also matter greatly at the level of moment-by-moment sequences. When used in the wrong contexts or directed toward the wrong content, even affirmation and protection can provide support for problem patterns. Predictive principles based on the SASB model's geometry are helpful for identifying and working with in-session patterns. Their use is enhanced when there is a clear sense of red, green, and therapy goals.

## ALIGNING PROCESSES OF RELATING WITH GREEN GOALS

In IRT, optimal relatedness is always oriented toward increasing a patient's ability to learn, access, and choose adaptive thoughts, affects, behaviors, and self-concepts while decreasing maladaptive ones. Part of this learning comes from explicit discussion of strategies, perspectives, and skills that may be useful in handling current relationships and stressors. An equally important part comes from directly experiencing and having the opportunity to internalize the secure-base pattern offered by the therapist and therapy. Because the old patterns often reflect learning with internalized figures, adaptive change typically involves getting distance from rules and ways of problematic attachments.

The circles at the bottom of Figure 8.3 depict the two sets of therapy goals in IRT, as discussed in Chapter 5. For relationships with the self and others in the present (labeled "in the world"), the therapy goal is a baseline way of relating that is consistent with secure attachment, represented on the right side of the SASB model. For relationships with internalized figures (labeled "in the head"), the goal is to be differentiated, at the top of the vertical axis.

When a patient is making sustained progress toward adaptive goals, there is little or no reason to discuss the in-the-head goals. However, when

**FIGURE 8.3. Two Types of Treatment Goals Each Related Directly to Individual Case Formulation**

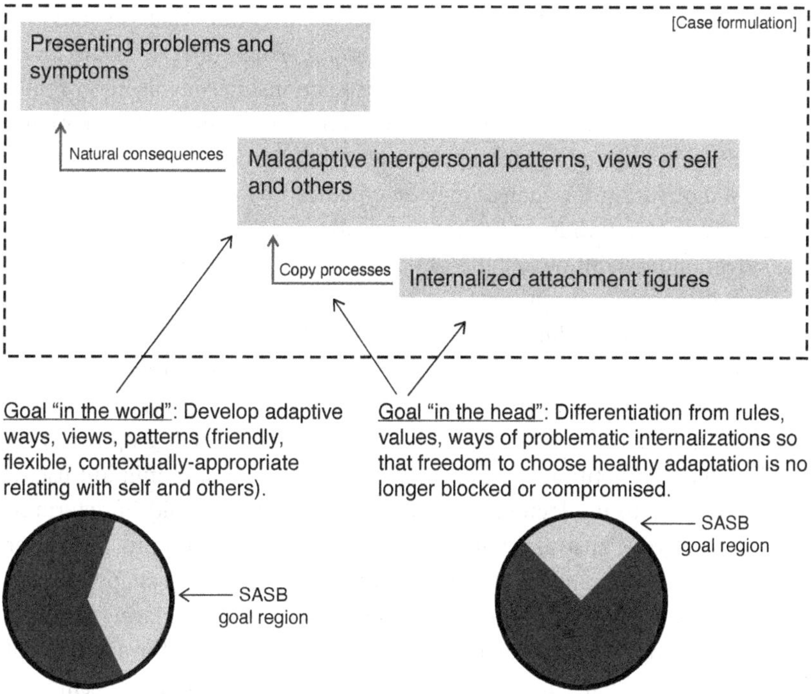

Goal "in the world": Develop adaptive ways, views, patterns (friendly, flexible, contextually-appropriate relating with self and others).

Goal "in the head": Differentiation from rules, values, ways of problematic internalizations so that freedom to choose healthy adaptation is no longer blocked or compromised.

*Note.* SASB = Structural Analysis of Social Behavior.

a patient is engaging in old patterns and motivation for change is unusually difficult to find, these may be signs that yearnings for some form of persisting connection to the associated figures is driving the behavior as a GOL to them. When this occurs, the therapist needs to be more active and take context-appropriate steps to enhance awareness of these links and the patient's ability to take steps that involve getting psychological distance from them. The goal, in essence, is for the patient to wrest permission from their internalizations to pursue healthy patterns regardless of what the family in their head thinks. The distinction between in-the-world and in-the-head goals is not the same as deciding to focus on past versus present events. Instead, it is about the often very here-and-now conflict between the patient's regressive loyalist (red) and growth collaborator (green) parts of the self.

In relation to goals for family in the head, people sometimes need to approximate the goal by first engaging in hostile distance before being able to practice friendlier and more moderate forms of differentiation. For example, the patient in the earlier transcript segment says, "I just want to be mad and tell her I don't care what she thinks, I'm doing it anyway." Another patient in Chapter 5 imagined putting her parents in the trunk (or threatening to) to have some distance from the family in the head while driving home after sessions. The friendlier forms might be reflected in a patient's understanding that their parents had their own injuries and reasons—that on some level, whatever had gone awry in the attachment relationship, "it was never really about me [the patient]." In any case, the crucial element is that patients have sufficient internal permission to make adaptive changes in the present. Patients' motivation for change may be enhanced by discussing the goal of healthy differentiation in ways that emphasize development of a self that is one's own, along with ownership of one's own choices and responses, even if others disagree or disapprove.

The therapeutic relationship should be directed toward enhancing (a) patient awareness of red patterns, their origins, and their functions in the present via the GOL; and (b) patient choice of adaptive, green alternatives. Just like the change process with addictions or habits, giving up red ways involves many repetitions and practice with deliberate and mindful use of new awareness to implement adaptive choices. SASB can aid in determining whether goal-consistent patterns are being modeled and practiced over time. Principles of complementarity can also be used to help shape existing relationships so that they better approximate secure-base relating patterns (e.g., expressing warm understanding of a partner can pull for a reciprocal response, rather than engaging in an old pattern of hostile enmeshment, demandingness, or alienation).

## Addressing Important Persons or Their Internalized Representations

Sometimes it is important to maintain a distinction between the internalized and present-day versions of loved ones. The goal of differentiation is not about enforcing distance from others in the present, nor is it to assign blame about the past. Instead, differentiation is about gaining separation from the seemingly present, remembered representations of attachment figures. This is done through a process of recognizing how lessons learned with these figures are echoed in the patient's current patterns and responses. That recognition in turn enhances the possibility of resisting red and choosing differently. In other words, therapeutic relating in IRT should be consistently and compassionately focused on enhancing the ability to know oneself and make adaptive choices, independent of the views, attitudes, rules, or ways of others. From this differentiated position, patients can choose preferred ways of being, preferred degrees of distance and closeness with others, and healthy ways of being connected in the present. Practice and repetition are usually required, since the internalized versions of loved ones have essentially been encoded as characteristic patterns of neurological and biological response, especially to seek safety when threat is perceived.

People braving the initial steps of change involving a GOL can often experience considerable ambivalence, regression, grief, and temporary exacerbations of symptoms. These can be understood through tracking and exploration of patient phenomenology, in terms of what the internalizations say about each step toward differentiation (Benjamin, 2018). From a biological perspective, as successful treatment progresses, the threat system is being slowly re-cued through imaginal and behavioral practice with forms of being or choosing separately from (and sometimes in defiance of) the internalized attachment figures. This occurs in large part through provision of a secure base offered by the therapist, which is specifically oriented toward enhancing awareness of the patterns as well as their sources and functions in the present. That awareness is in turn used to support practice with more adaptive ways of being.

## Example of the Role of Differentiation Relative to Therapy Goals

Miriam, described in Chapter 6, rated her self-treatment and the internalized version of her mother in the head at various points throughout IRT. As shown in Figure 8.4, her results were characterized initially by suicidal self-attack and self-blame. She referred to treatment goals such as taking care of herself or understanding and having compassion for herself as "rebellious" because they opposed what her mother thought she deserved. At the end of treatment, Miriam rated herself as aligning well with the therapy goal region.

**FIGURE 8.4. Change in Miriam's Self-Treatment From the Beginning to End of Therapy**

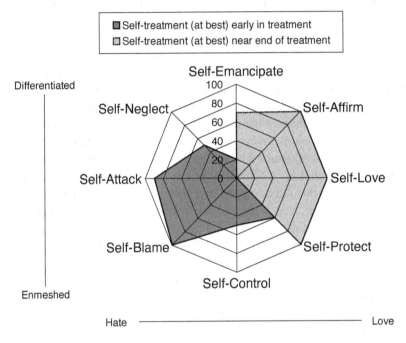

Figure 8.5 shows a parallel set of Miriam's ratings in relation to her mother. At the beginning of treatment, Miriam's ratings mirrored her in-session comments about wanting her mother's love and approval, which she often sought through submission to her mother's rules and ways (the essence of her GOL). Miriam understood and agreed with this basic formulation. One treatment implication, explicitly discussed with Miriam, was that she needed help to find internal permission and risk being more separate from her mother's rules for her. Miriam agreed with and participated in developing this goal, but she initially feared her (internalized and current-day) mother's reaction. Recurrent suicidal ideation and other trauma responses, including periods of intense anger and ambivalence about the treatment goals, characterized the early phase of Miriam's treatment. Over time, Miriam increasingly began to engage with the possibility of change by relinquishing the GOL to her mother in particular. A turning point occurred after multiple sessions of collaborative focus on links between wishes to finally be accepted by her mother and Miriam's symptoms of intense anger (usually directed at herself), suicidality, and self-blame. Consider this example from Miriam:

**FIGURE 8.5. Miriam's Relationship With Her Mother (Focus-on-Self Behaviors)**

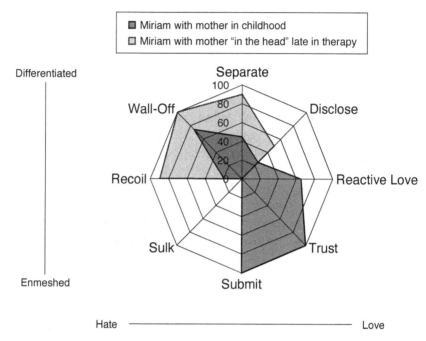

I made a decision I should probably tell you about. I decided it's time for me to stop being angry with my mother. I want her to love me no matter what, and so I should give that in return. I think she did the best she could; she just didn't do a good job. And that's not her fault, it's just, that's the best she could do. So, I need to be more understanding, I think. I made that decision and I'm going to work on it. It's going to take a while.

Figure 8.5 presents Miriam ratings of the relationship with her mother in the head. She had successfully shifted her position to one of distance and differentiation (albeit relatively hostile forms). Once Miriam mobilized her will to let go of her pursuit of the GOL, therapeutic interventions related to her self-concept seemed to have more impact. Miriam's self-treatment shifted reliably away from hostile self-control to the much more friendly and self-accepting position shown at the end of treatment in Figure 8.4. Over the next few months of therapy, Miriam's suicidal ideation abated, as did her symptoms of posttraumatic stress disorder and anger. Her formal ratings of anxiety and depression, which had been sustained at very high levels (between 2 and 3 $SD$ above the norm) for over a year, dropped below normative means and stayed there reliably, even in the face of new stressors. Findings in IRT are accumulating to suggest that letting go of the GOL is key to reliable change among patients who have not responded well to prior treatment attempts (Critchfield, Dobner-Pereira, et al., 2019).

### Optimizing Therapy Process Using the IRT Case Formulation and Treatment Goals

As discussed in Chapter 5, the optimal therapy session supports green more than red. A therapist's use of 1-2: **Affirm** can be directed systematically to this end. By directing attention and curiosity about "how it works" in relation to current patterns and relevant learning history, the therapist can heighten awareness of red, green, and any inherent conflicts between them. At other moments, empathy and understanding can be directed to support and reinforce attempts to practice and sustain green ways of being, thinking, and feeling. In line with this, preliminary findings from IRT research suggest that when therapists are adherent to IRT, they are more likely to bring up the topic of differentiation and/or interdependence with attachment figures. In turn, their patients are more likely to refer to green aspects of self-concept and to be assessed as speaking in a green state during their sessions.

This process can include some forms of "cozying up" to red by expressing understanding of maladaptive perspectives and responses (e.g., that red patterns have the intent of seeking safety and belonging or can be understood when seeing things through the lens of a patient's history) but without going so far as to endorse them. In some cases, red empathy can also be used strategically to enhance connection and trust to press for change later. However, simple expressions of empathy for red, if offered without context that ties back to the case formulation and goals, usually serve to reinforce maladaptive patterns (Karpiak & Benjamin, 2004). The therapist's ability to discriminate between red and green matters a great deal in IRT work. An example might be the decision to offer empathic support for a patient's rage over perceived slights. For some patients, this type of empathy may fuel a pattern of entitled narcissism (red pattern); for others, it may provide a basis for an emotional experience that corrects previously being forbidden to ever have, express, or "own" feelings of any kind (enhancing steps toward a greener pattern).

Similarly, use of influence in the form of 1-4: **Protect** has optimal impact when it occurs in a collaborative context and is directed toward enhancing green therapy goals. Interpretations, homework, and other forms of influence that reinforce red values and views are to be avoided or, if necessary, should be framed clearly so that green views are still supported and help the patient distinguish them. For example, it may be reasonable to encourage Miriam to take self-defense classes in service of enhancing self-efficacy and her ability to recognize and protect herself from abusive men, while also likely finding a supportive community that would counteract her mother's internalized views. If this were pursued without further comment and context, there is great danger that the plan would be "taken over" by red as reinforcing the internalized version of her mother's input: "Your assignment is to manage the actions of dangerous men. You are to blame for anything that may go wrong." If self-defense classes are co-opted by red values, Miriam's may respond by becoming still more anxious and depressed, eroding self-concept as she attempts to appease mother by blaming herself and working ever harder to fearfully monitor others and control what they do. To have a positive effect, any such assignment must be framed so that Miriam actively understands and agrees with the intervention as a method of enhancing a green self that is well differentiated from her mother's views. If Miriam disagrees with the suggestion, alternative methods could still be pursued if they served goals of (a) accepting herself as she is and (b) refusing the old assignment of managing aggressive and critical male individuals, because that would be more consistent with her case formulation. If Miriam then wishes to increase skills to provide her own safety, then she may do so once the choice is truly hers rather than an echo of her mother's critique.

As suggested earlier, separation of the patient into red and green parts suggests potential uses of interpersonal hostility and complexity, with the caveat that they should only be directed toward red and in clear ways— never to green. Critchfield and Mackaronis (2016) provided examples of a therapist's selective use of 1-8: **Ignore** to help dampen the impact of red while still providing support for green. A sarcastic, ironic, or humorous tone can sometimes be helpful to question red patterns and to help motivate green alternatives. Consider this example:

> I hear you that you're so frustrated by all this that you'd like to punch your boss's lights out. It could cost your job and your retirement, but I'm sure your father [who did essentially the same thing] would be very happy about that one!

If delivered the right way, such a statement could be used to then pivot and invite patient reflection about potential choices and potential identification with the father's ways. Sarcasm and interpersonal complexity can be presented in ways that convey refreshing irreverence and help the cause of wresting freedom for green. However, this is only true when the collaborative and green part of the patient has enough strength to take it in as support. Such interventions are risky. If they are offered in a decontextualized way or with the wrong tone and timing, the same comment could be perceived as an expression of contempt or frustration at the whole self of the patient rather than selective targeting of red in clear support of green. If the statement is heard as an attack on the patient's total self, then that would be wounding and a major alliance rupture would be expected. As noted previously a bit of misdirected hostility can go a long way toward poor outcomes (Henry et al., 1986, 1990). Therefore, great care must be taken to ensure that sarcasm and humor do not arise from a therapist's own frustration or other counter-transference feelings. The patient's immediate response should be followed up carefully to ensure understanding and offer repair if there is any doubt.

## Summary

Tracking of SASB dimensions and clusters can be used to enhance clinical decision making about the timing, context, and framing of moment-by-moment interventions. It offers precision and accuracy to help choose language for reflecting and discerning a patient's experience. When used optimally from an IRT perspective, these codes also help with choices to direct empathy and skill building systematically to enhance adaptive, green patterns and reduce maladaptive, red ones. Chapters 9 and 10 provide deeper description of the IRT process, including case examples of the change process and procedures for monitoring goals and outcomes cued to the individual's case formulation.

# 9 ACTIVELY APPLYING THE INTERPERSONAL RECONSTRUCTIVE THERAPY CASE FORMULATION

In their classic work, Alexander and French (1946) described the relationship between case formulation and treatment this way:

> Especially in the first hours of an analysis, there are pressing considerations that should demand of the analyst a very active intellectual initiative toward the goal of arriving at an adequate dynamic formulation just as soon as possible. . . . The analyst during this period may be compared to a traveler standing on top a hill overlooking the country through which he is about to journey. At this time it may be possible for him to see his whole anticipated journey in perspective. When once he has descended into the valley, this perspective must be retained in his memory or else it will be gone. From this time on, he will be able to examine small parts of this landscape in much greater detail than was possible when he was viewing them from a distance, but the broad relations will no longer be so clear. . . . A still more important reason for attempting an early and comprehensive formulation, however, is the need, as soon as possible, to sketch out a therapeutic plan. (pp. 109–110)

To extend their metaphor and link it with major themes of Chapter 8, Structural Analysis of Social Behavior (SASB) is a compass while on the therapeutic

---

https://doi.org/10.1037/0000403-009
*Structural Analysis of Social Behavior (SASB): A Primer for Clinical Use*, by
K. L. Critchfield and L. S. Benjamin
Copyright © 2024 by the American Psychological Association. All rights reserved.

224 • *Treatment: Connecting With Patients and Optimizing Interventions*

journey.[1] SASB provides clarity about two key directional elements: (a) the nature of the current situation, especially the ability to recognize copy process patterns; and (b) the direction a patient needs to move from in the present moment in order to reach therapy goals. This chapter focuses on navigating the change process across sessions of Interpersonal Reconstructive Therapy (IRT).

## USING THE CASE FORMULATION TO GUIDE MOMENT-BY-MOMENT INTERVENTIONS: MILANA

Milana is a 30-year-old, single White woman. She is highly intelligent, has always done well in school, and rose through the ranks of her profession quickly. She is well traveled, speaks several languages, and has a charming and iconoclastic flair. Milana began treatment for significant depression and anxiety after an unexpected breakup with her romantic partner at the time. The central red pattern in Milana's case formulation involves chronic and recurrent anger at others. She is usually the "person in charge," giving advice to friends, family, and romantic partners (1-4: **Protect**). She usually views them in a benevolent light. They in turn are seen by Milana as taking in her advice and appreciating the ways she generously offers resources to them (2-4: Trust). However, when she is angry, she departs from the relatively benevolent baseline just described and becomes demanding, often coercing the people closest to her to give her protection or caregiving. This is especially the case with romantic partners. When at worst, her pattern can therefore be characterized as one of demanding dependency involving 1-5: **Control** and 2-4: Trust. Milana's style has been met with a variety of responses in the past. Romantic partners she accepts usually offer the kind of loving caregiving she wants (1-4: **Protect** and 2-5: Submit). But over time, this pattern changes to accusations of her being "bossy" and "needy." As Milana's partners become burned out with her perceived demands, they angrily reject and leave her. A significant relationship ended this way just prior to treatment.

Milana's early history set the prototype for this pattern and can be seen in part in her Intrex profiles (Figures 9.1 and 9.2). Milana describes her mother as "emotionally absent" and addicted to prescription painkillers; she also says that her mother generally focused on her with hostility and

---

[1] The clinical material used in this book is adequately disguised to protect patient confidentiality.

Actively Applying the Interpersonal Reconstructive Therapy Case Formulation • 225

**FIGURE 9.1. Milana's Ratings of the Remembered Childhood Relationship With Her Mother**

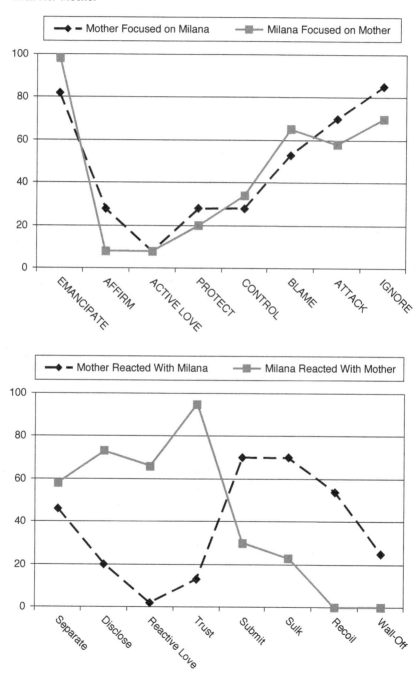

226 • Treatment: Connecting With Patients and Optimizing Interventions

**FIGURE 9.2. Milana's Ratings of the Remembered Childhood Relationship With Her Father**

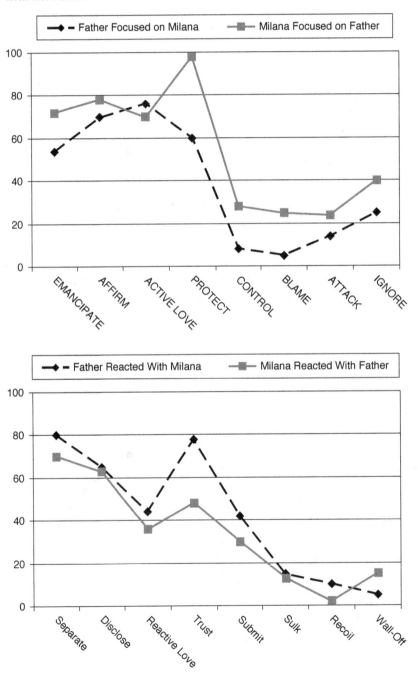

distance while intransitively submitting and sulking, which demonstrates her mother's hostile dependency on her. As such, Milana's ratings of the remembered childhood relationship show a substantial departure from a secure attachment profile. She rates herself as being very much like her mother in childhood, returning hostility and distance (profile $r = .91$). Milana's ratings differ in that her reaction to her mother is one of 2-4: <u>Trust</u> and relative warmth that approximates secure attachment, despite the lack of complementary input recalled from her mother (profile $r = -.58$).

Meanwhile, Milana recalls in the interview that she felt very close to her father in childhood, trusting him while he warmly guided and protected her. She valued being able to provide him with advice and support, taking care of him in ways that were friendly but were also outside developmental norms. Figure 9.2 shows the similarity perceived between Milana and her father (both profile $r$ values > .90). Overall, she reports having a great deal of influence and power in the early family and enjoying her father's warmth and protection. That picture changed in adolescence. Milana reports that her father rejected her after learning that she had had sex and used drugs. He changed at that point, and Milana says that he has been critical and controlling ever since then.

Milana now tends to see herself as living in a control-or-be-controlled world. Many of the closest relationships discussed in therapy involve her feeling overwhelmed by the need to care for or advise others and being frustrated and angry when others do not comply with her help (whether requested or not). Dramatic actions, harsh punishments, and sudden ends to relationships have occurred, sometimes initiated by others and sometimes by Milana. She describes yearning for a male rescuer. She is also keenly sensitive when others go their own way, perceiving it as intolerable abandonment. When this happens, she reports being vulnerable to a sense of worthlessness and "loss of myself." Despite the sensitivity to abandonment and sudden shifts in her esteem of others (based on their compliance), when Milana's SASB-coded copy process patterns are compared with Benjamin's (1993, 1996) personality disorder (PD) prototypes, they overlap most with narcissistic PD ($r = .53$), followed at a distance by the other Cluster B patterns (histrionic, $r = .34$; borderline, $r = .29$; antisocial, $r = .25$) in the fourth and fifth editions of the *Diagnostic and Statistical Manual of Mental Disorders* (American Psychiatric Association, 1994, 2013). Milana's emphasis on control of others, expectations of caregiving and adoration from them "no matter what," and use of anger to coerce compliance are consistent with a narcissistic pattern (Benjamin, 1993, 1996).

228 • *Treatment: Connecting With Patients and Optimizing Interventions*

Early in the session presented next, Milana provides a description of her current situation. Her affect is distressed. She appears angry, confused, and anxious. She has a new boyfriend who recently moved in with her.

PATIENT: [*rapidly, upset*] Maybe I should be alone. I just don't think. I'm not a thinker, I'm a doer. I don't learn because I tune things out. He [my boyfriend] always needs to explain things to me. I need to have control, change needs to be slow. We argue too much. My friend says we need communication skills. Can I bring him in with me for a session?

THERAPIST: This sounds important. Can you tell me more about what's been going on?

PATIENT: He's very critical. He's an emotional person. He really loves me, but he likes things the way he likes them. He's bipolar. He says, "Why is it always about you?" He's tired of dealing with me crying all the time. I want to be with someone who treats me well, not so critical.

There is little SASB-codable content up to this point in the conversation. There is urgency about a relationship but only brief, traitlike labels have been provided thus far, without a sense of the context. There is emphasis on what sounds like themes of control and blame. Milana alternately criticizes herself and her boyfriend and also complains about how he criticizes and controls her. Her affects as she relates the above are agitated, overwhelmed, and scornful (SAAB), whereas her cognitive style is narrowly focused on details and looks to find fault and condemn (SACB). There is potential for overlap between these clusters and her case formulation. However, more detail is needed to understand precise locations relative to the case formulation. The therapist attempts to get oriented in the next sequence.

THERAPIST: Okay. Well, I think I need to get to where I can see things the way you do. Could we take an example of a recent argument and walk it through from the beginning? Like "he said, she said." Let's take your last argument. When was it?

PATIENT: It was last night. He wanted his things upstairs. I didn't know that. He didn't tell me. I wasn't ready for that.

THERAPIST: What did he say about that?

PATIENT: He said he was leaving, that he couldn't take me anymore.

THERAPIST: Why did he say that? What was going on?

*Actively Applying the Interpersonal Reconstructive Therapy Case Formulation* • 229

PATIENT: I was crying. He was just going out for a little while because he was upset.

At this point, the narrative is still fragmentary. Clearly there has been some kind of conflict and both partners are very upset. New information suggest that the topics involve enmeshment, territory (crying about the boyfriend putting his things somewhere in the house), and distance that is possibly used in a complex way to punish (the boyfriend is leaving and can't "take me anymore"). Also, the story thus far is mostly focused on the boyfriend's actions.

PATIENT: He said, "Why is it always about you?"

THERAPIST: About you?

PATIENT: I was worried because he was leaving. I said, "I need to know when you're coming back. How long are you going to be gone? Is this minutes, or hours, or days?! I need to know!"

THERAPIST: So, he was leaving to get some space because of whatever was going on between you two.

PATIENT: Yes.

THERAPIST: And you were worried because you didn't know when he'd be coming back.

PATIENT: Exactly.

THERAPIST: So, if I understand this right, he wanted to get some distance, but you were panicking about this and wanted some reassurance from him about when he would come back. It sounds like you wanted to make him take care of your feelings, even while he was trying to get some distance to cool down after this big argument about where he could put his stuff. Is that about right?

In this sequence, the therapist reflects back what Milana has said, with some changes in emphasis that reflect areas of overlap with themes in the case formulation. For example, the phrase "wanted some reassurance from him" emphasizes Milana's dependency (2-4: <u>Trust</u>), while "make him take care of your feelings" highlights 1-5: **Control** in the context of her perceived dependency. The summary reflection ends with a question to see if this understanding fits Milana's experience. Here is her response:

PATIENT: [*with a sense of recognition*] I hadn't thought of it that way. It's true. I'm afraid he's not coming back, even though I know he is. . . . He just needs some space sometimes.

This response helps confirm that a central theme of Milana's case formulation theme is present. It involves her pattern of complex dependency plus control. In essence, "I will make him take care of my feelings, rather than deal with them myself. I will not let him leave me and be separate. I will not let him have his own way." Having tagged this familiar landmark in her case formulation, the therapist's goal now becomes one of helping Milana see the copy process connections to the family in the head more clearly. From there, if her will to change is sufficiently enabled by the therapy process, she can then address the implications for her relationship with her boyfriend, including taking steps to make repairs and prevent recurrences.

Other elements of the conflict suggested in this passage likely will need to be unpacked across the session, and they could be helpful in clarifying how this incident relates to red patterns on the one hand and green goals on the other. This process of unpacking includes the preceding context to this part of the story, which will likely involve struggles over boundaries and the need to share decision making and relinquish some control as her boyfriend moves in (i.e., who can put what where, and who can leave or stay if someone is upset). Also, the boyfriend's distance is most salient to Milana, but the context implies that they both want to be closer (i.e., the choice to move in together). As noted already, deeper exploration could help Milana see the copy process repetition in this conflict and how she will need to get distance from internalized ways and values learned with her parents. At this point, Milana has already had collaborative therapy discussions about how she wants to be in charge in order to feel secure and how this desire ends up pushing other people away. She is aware that as others begin to retreat from her control, she typically escalates, becoming more hostile and critical but also more desperately needy. She has also seen that she becomes like both her mother and father, behaving just as she recalls them responding to conflict when this kind of thing happens. Despite these prior conversations, it is not at all surprising that her red pattern still jumps up powerfully and without her full recognition.

Changing a set of overlearned and attachment-linked patterns that are associated with a sense of threat to an alternate set of healthy responses takes many repetitions and deliberate rehearsal. A therapist's role in IRT is often to patiently facilitate this process of recognizing and resetting. Benjamin (2018) referred to the *Five R's* required for change, the first part of which is modeled by Milana's therapist so far: "(1) recognize specific instances of problem patterns, (2) review their historical roots, (3) resolve to change them, (4) resist urges to repeat them, and (5) rebuild the agreed-upon secure base alternatives" (p. 129).

*Actively Applying the Interpersonal Reconstructive Therapy Case Formulation* • 231

As the session unfolds beyond the transcript segment presented earlier, the therapist continues to reflect back and expand Milana's narrative in SASB-codable terms. This is difficult in part because Milana is angry and anxious as she tells the story. However, over time, she becomes less upset and more centered (the affect expected to accompany cluster 2) as she begins to recognize the familiar themes of her case formulation.

The job of listening, clarifying, and reflecting themes can also help a therapist feel settled and calm in the face of strong affect, sense of urgency, and fragmented narratives. Further into the session, Milana and her therapist share a recognition that she copes with difficult feelings by relying on others or controlling her environment to the extreme; failing that, she copes by escaping completely and not thinking at all about what is happening. Her boyfriend, meanwhile, is seen as having an equally problematic pattern for Milana, consisting of fuming compliance, followed by angry outbursts and extreme distance—a pattern very close to that described earlier for her mother. The therapist primarily uses Milana's own language, plus SASB concepts, to help her put things together. At one point Milana remarks, "How did you figure that out? That's like magic!" A brief review of the SASB model follows, to help Milana work the same magic going forward. With shared recognition and collaboration in place, future sessions increasingly build on the foundation of awareness to help Milana address and change the pattern itself, including considering her choice of partner (given his own apparent red patterns overlapping with her family's patterns).

The therapist's approach is consistent with the IRT core algorithm: (a) pursuing input, response, and impact-on-self elements of the narrative; (b) attending to the in-session relational process; and (c) making links to the case formulation to enhance awareness and choice about patterns. The therapist's statements primarily 1-2: **Affirm**, with occasional use of 1-4: **Protect** when brief interpretations are offered or when a nudge away from mere "venting" about the boyfriend is needed.

The goals for Milana involve moving away from hostile enmeshment and toward friendly differentiation. This includes Milana having greater comfort with her boyfriend's reasonable needs for space(physical and psychological) and also finding ways of communicating her own boundaries, needs, and desires using 2-2: <u>Disclose</u>. In a later session, the therapist's note reads:

> Couple session held at patient's request. They have been actively trying to accommodate each other's styles since last session. No "big blow out" arguments despite some tensions. Patient noted she is "like my father," insisting others think and behave like her. She notes he was her only attachment, but she is questioning his ways. She can see how bothered she and others get. Patient and boyfriend both agreed about her father's ways. Boyfriend notes

he is not taking it so personally when she wants reassurance; relayed how his own history makes "commitment" confining and so he pulls away. Patient recognized that by clinging to old ways, she gets what she most fears; unusually open about vulnerability to feel "stupid and inadequate" when shut out; tearful while discussing it.

Much remains to be done in terms of helping Milana finally come to terms with the family in the head and to allow a new way of being to take root in her relationships. However, in this session, the connections are being tagged explicitly and are supported by both therapy work and the couples' process. Milana is using awareness of her patterns and their origins to contemplate change, questioning ways of being that were learned with her parents in the direction of greater differentiation. It is expected that as she does this, she will be able to adopt more moderate self-concepts in addition to more adaptive relational patterns with others. And they will serve as antidotes to the red pattern of fragile narcissism in place at the beginning of treatment.

## EVERY MAJOR CLINICAL DECISION HAS REFERENCE TO THE CASE FORMULATION: MIRIAM, JENN, AND SARA

Techniques, like therapy goals, can be thought of as being directed variously toward a patient's inner and outer worlds. Optimal interventions take into account the family in the head as well as real-world relating with the self and others. The general idea is to support green more than red with all interventions and to be mindful about input from both green and red parts of the patient. In addition to enhancing awareness about patterns and their origins, IRT interventions should seek to generate and build on intrinsic motivation to pursue change once awareness has been achieved. In IRT, the therapist's role involves active use of the case formulation to find interventions that support green more than red. In preliminary data, the ratio of support for these two parts of the patient appears particularly linked to patient progress with the gift of love and eventual outcome (Critchfield et al., 2011; Karpiak et al., 2011; Stucker et al., 2020).

In this section, we provide examples of how the case formulation was used to select very different interventions for three patients with contrasting circumstances. The primary purpose of these examples is to clarify how clinical decision making should take into account the individual formulation, related treatment goals, and strength or vulnerability of the existing therapeutic relationship. Our extended examples revolve around the question of whether a hospitalization is needed to ensure patient safety. However, a parallel set of contrasts could be made for a wide range of other clinical choices, such as recognizing and repairing alliance ruptures, allowing or disallowing requests for between-session contacts, responding to missed sessions, and more. Our hope in choosing this topic of suicidality and hospitalization is in part to model highly contextualized thinking in relation to a topic that is often alarming for therapists and tends to come with a sense of urgency that might override all else. The topic nonetheless needs to be approached in a tailored and context-specific way to have optimum effects, just as with all the other potential topics that could be discussed here. The goal is, of course, to preserve life and with it the ability to continue therapeutic work. It is also to ensure that green is supported more than red, even in a circumstance where it is feared that red will ultimately triumph. As shown in these examples, the IRT approach uses hospitalization to preserve safety and the ability to continue working together but does not invoke it as an optimal solution for every situation; instead, IRT draws on or strengthens, when possible, a patient's green internal resources to remain safe. Again, this means an approach to safety planning that incorporates the case formulation, the therapy relationship, and the patient's motivation to pursue green (Critchfield et al., 2022).

Benjamin (2003, 2006) detailed the uses and indicators of the need to hospitalize for safety, along with some additional ways to safely manage crisis and preserve both patient autonomy and safety in the short term. IRT safety plans in individual outpatient contexts usually consist of an agreement for the patient to call the therapist if in crisis and to wait for a response that is promised within 24 hours, or else to present at the hospital for evaluation or to call 911 if too unable to safely wait for the therapist's return call. If the latter occurs, debriefing will be required about the situation before resuming IRT. The phone call is relatively brief (10 minutes or so), is oriented to assessing the situation and helping a patient find strength, and, if possible, to contain red safely until the next session. Otherwise, an agreement is made to meet face to face as soon as can be arranged to discuss matters in more depth, including whether hospitalization would be helpful. The hospital is seen as an important tool in preserving safety, but like most interventions, it can be used to enhance good adaptation and functioning (support for green) or to reinforce old patterns (support for red), as shown in the following examples.

### Example 1 (Miriam): Averting Hospitalization

This example picks up 1 day after the difficult session with Miriam presented in Chapter 5 as an example of high IRT adherence. This was near the beginning of Miriam's IRT work, and it had been not quite 2 months since the discharge from her prior hospitalization. She called in sick at work, contacted her psychiatrist to arrange for readmission, and had a neighbor bring her to the hospital. She sent a text to her IRT therapist, saying that she didn't feel safe and so was readmitting herself. The IRT clinic was located in the same building Miriam was admitting herself to, so the therapist was able to intercept Miriam. She accepted her therapist's invitation to first discuss what was happening and then make a decision together about whether to proceed to hospital admitting. For about 72 hours, she had been suffering traumatic re-experiencing, sleeplessness, anger, panic, and a desire to harm herself. As a reminder, this response was triggered by sexual comments and lewd gestures made by men who pulled up in a truck as she was walking outside. These events were discussed productively in session the day before, but the symptoms persisted unabated. As detailed in Chapter 6, Miriam's case formulation involves rules to be strong and be the peacemaker, especially regarding violent and degrading men. In this crisis session, Miriam elaborated further that she feels expected to "confess her sins" (meaning to take the blame for whatever men do) and show she is broken and "crazy" in order to appease her family. It became clear early in this crisis meeting that Miriam saw going to the hospital as a form of appeasing her family in the head by blaming herself for what these men did. In terms of her SASB-based IRT case formulation, Miriam's response to the internalized version of mother emphasizes 2-5: <u>Submit</u> and 3-6: *Self-Blame*. Based on this assessment, hospitalization would repeat this response and be a victory for red, 180° from the therapy goal regions of the model. By being rehospitalized, Miriam would verify her mother's pronouncements that she is "broken and crazy." It was a positive sign that Miriam was seeking safety in the hospital. However, it would be best if red were not supported in the process of keeping her safe, as this would likely maintain the overall pattern of chronic vulnerability to suicide and undermine green goals.

The therapist took the approach of helping Miriam understand her reaction in terms of recognizing the red aspects of her response. She was helped to explore alternatives she had for safety and also for her approach to the family in the head. These options included hospitalization. They also included Miriam finding internal strength to refuse the assignment by the internalized version of mother to blame herself for what these men did.

Ultimately, after what was clearly a difficult process for her, Miriam decided against hospitalization and instead to pursue strengths on an outpatient basis. She stabilized with implementation of daily sessions (using the outpatient hospitalization approach described by Benjamin, 2003, 2006). Miriam was able to return safely to the usual therapy schedule after about 3 days of the more intensive approach to support green.

*Actively Applying the Interpersonal Reconstructive Therapy Case Formulation* • 235

The SASB codes of Miriam's decision not to be hospitalized are understood to be green because they included a defiance of her mother's internalized view of her (2-1: <u>Separate</u>), trust in herself (3-2: *Self-Affirm*) that she could, with help, handle this differently, and 2-4: <u>Trust</u> in her therapist. These SASB positions are opposites of the red ones used to pursue hospitalization, and so were optimal for enhancing green and moving toward overall therapy goals. Of course, hospitalization would have still been pursued if Miriam and her therapist felt that she could not safely use the support offered or if she lost motivation to pursue healthy adaptation during the subsequent daily sessions. Fortunately, Miriam got through this episode with an intact belief in herself, the therapy, and the therapist. Her subsequent treatment process and outcome is described in Chapter 10.

### Example 2 (Jenn): Encouraging Hospitalization

The meaning of a proposed hospitalization can differ widely in context of a different internalized family history. Jenn's adjustment to an abusive early family environment was to take care of others and manage them despite their abuse of her. In this respect, her experience overlaps with Miriam's. Historically, Jenn's experience is that any sign of "weakness" merits an escalation of her father's mockery, rejection, and abuse for being "not like my boys." Jenn believes the hospital is a place where her history will be recapitulated: "no one would believe" even if she were to allow them to help her; she would simply be told to "be strong" and "pretend" in parallel with the rules of her internalized family. Unfortunately, this was her experience in prior hospitalizations. As a result, Jenn now prefers suicide as "a fix" for life's problems. But she has a requirement that suicide should look like an accident so that it serves the purpose of "helping others" (as she sees it) by removing herself as "a burden" on them. Apart from this perception, objectively, she functions at a high level of competence in a caregiving profession.

SASB codes for Jenn's formulation include elements of 2-8: <u>Wall-Off</u>, coupled with neglectful self-control (3-5: *Self-Control* plus 3-8: *Self-Neglect*). She believes her actions are in service of 1-4: **Protect** to others. However, her "protective" behaviors, seen objectively, usually parallel her self-treatment and involve 1-5: **Control** plus 1-8: **Ignore**. Jenn decides what others need from her, keeps her suicidal plans secret, and ultimately expects that they will not care or will soon move on (again recapitulating aspects of her early childhood learning).

Given this history and her perceptions, Jenn avoids hospitalization when she becomes suicidal. During past involuntary hospitalizations, she reports thinking, "I'll show them. I can just get out and kill myself anyway. I know what they want to hear." Therefore, when she is dangerously suicidal, a better approach is to encourage a voluntary process of going to the hospital based on practicing good self-care.

For Jenn, it can help reduce reactance and support personal autonomy to acknowledge that (a) she is ultimately in charge and (b) in the long run no one can stop her from killing herself if she really wishes it. She will simultaneously need to hear about her therapist's concern for her welfare and a desire to provide help. Together, these two messages counter her expectation of complex control and neglect by instead providing their opposites: 1-1: **Emancipate** and 1-4: **Protect**. Her "reflex" is to neglect and sacrifice herself, so "cozying up to red" might involve noting that there is no "hurry" to commit suicide, and that hospitalization might allow a return to deeper work in therapy rather than "mere" symptom management. In SASB terms, this would encourage Jenn to 3-1: *Self-Emancipate* plus 3-4: *Self-Protect* (the opposite of her usual self-treatment), coupled with 2-4: Trust in hospital staff (rather than walling off from them). On occasions when she consented to hospitalization to preserve her life and the therapy, a helpful emphasis was on how to approach the hospitalization in terms of self-care and how to view the inpatient unit in a more helpful way than through the lens of her own family dynamics and history.

Without SASB and each patient's individual case formulation to use as a guiding framework, it is difficult to discern between these two contrasting situations. In both examples, the assumption is that long-term safety ultimately derives from a patient's willingness to preserve an option involving future growth and development. To summarize, the differential process of clinical decision making (whether regarding hospitalization or any other intervention) should be based on (a) sensitivity to patterns in the case formulation; and (b) a focus on how to *motivate* the individual, *based on that individual's point of view*, to move away from red copy process patterns and toward SASB-specified green goals.

Benjamin (2003, 2006) extended these ideas further to describe *dynamic crisis management* as working directly with motivations that relate to the family in the head. For example, the therapist can ask the patient to walk them through the suicidal fantasy and articulate what key figures in the case formulation would think of the suicide, how the patient would respond to them, and what they would say in response. Motivation to commit suicide can be blocked by awareness that the wish for ultimate love and acceptance from the family in the head cannot be met, not even in the afterlife, or that the costs of pursuing it are not worth the desired payoff. Other red acts, such

*Actively Applying the Interpersonal Reconstructive Therapy Case Formulation* • 237

as substance abuse, self-harm, harm to others, and self-sabotage, can be addressed in a similar fashion. In each case, the "right" intervention will be consistent with the case formulation, using it to access and enhance motivation to leave red wishes and yearnings behind, grieve the losses, and pursue adaptive change instead (Benjamin, 2003, 2006; Critchfield et al., 2022).

### Example 3 (Sara): Enhancing Motivation for Treatment Upon Hospital Discharge

A final example illustrating the use of SASB and the case formulation to work with motivation involves another hospitalization. This time, the context is a planned discharge to outpatient care. Sara had been rehospitalized several times in a short period for suicidal ideation. She feared she had "burned out" her previous therapist with chronic suicidality. Sadly, this may have been true and also was a recapitulation of key themes in her case formulation. Sara perceived many losses in her life (including suicide by a sibling) as being Sara's fault for being "a burden" to that sibling. The patterns of her case formulation suggested a passive-aggressive profile. So, in addition to traumatic losses and wishes for care and concern from others that were rarely forthcoming in her experience, she also felt substantial resentment and fear about being controlled by others (usually a setup to be betrayed or let down). The treatment team and the previous therapist were happy to transfer care to an IRT clinician, but Sara was uncertain about the "different approach." If she felt that she was "being dumped," was abandoned, and had no choice in the matter, then the treatment would begin with a very serious recapitulation of her case formulation likely to fuel additional suicidality.

Fortunately, the IRT clinician was able to explore and discuss Sara's case formulation with her, including the therapy goals. While doing so, they were able to identify a part of Sara that seemed to really understand and want to pursue change. Green was recognizable through Sara's comments that the approach made sense to her and that she decided she wanted to give it a chance. A reasonable basis for treatment was provided by recognition that the following SASB positions were present in relation to the new therapist: 2-2: <u>Disclose</u> plus 2-4: <u>Trust</u> and desires to 3-4: *Self-Protect*. Her associated affects and cognitions from the parallel models appeared centered and expressive (SAAB) as well as hopeful and well directed (SACB).

Sara's prototypic red response entailed being resentfully submissive and suspicious, recognizable in SASB terms as 2-6: <u>Sulk</u>, 2-8: <u>Wall-Off</u>, and 3-8: *Self-Neglect*. Her sentiments might be along these lines: "I was rejected by my past therapist and so have no choice now but to reluctantly go along."

On the parallel affective and cognitive models, red affects would be recognizable as agitation and alienation, while red thought styles would be scattered and secretive. If this was her stance with the new therapist, additional efforts would be necessary to make a successful referral.

Use of SASB to judge interventions, as well as a patient's response to them, allows a therapist to be empathic and precise when making decisions involving an internal conflict between red and green parts of the self. To do this, in-session process needs to be directed strategically to support green growth and use it to replace and diminish red whenever it is possible to do so safety and collaboratively. Chapter 10 pulls together use of the case formulation, navigation of therapeutic process, and measurement of in-the-world and in-the-head goals for two IRT treatments.

# 10 TRACKING CHANGE AND ASSESSING OUTCOMES

This chapter focuses on using Structural Analysis of Social Behavior (SASB)–based methods to track the change process and determine whether therapy goals have been met.[1] In doing so, it brings together consideration of problems, treatment processes, and outcomes in SASB-based terms (Henry, 1996; Strupp et al., 1988). A set of contrasting case examples are used to illustrate the relevant procedures and issues. This chapter concludes with consideration of how to know when therapy is complete. It also provides an overview of future directions and ongoing research linking Interpersonal Reconstructive Therapy (IRT) adherence to outcomes in a sample of patients defined as CORDS (or comorbid, often rehospitalized, dysfunctional, and suicidal; Critchfield et al., 2015).

---

[1] The clinical material used in this book is adequately disguised to protect patient confidentiality.

https://doi.org/10.1037/0000403-010
*Structural Analysis of Social Behavior (SASB): A Primer for Clinical Use*, by K. L. Critchfield and L. S. Benjamin
Copyright © 2024 by the American Psychological Association. All rights reserved.

## TRACKING CHANGE USING REPEAT INTREX ASSESSMENTS

Through repeat administration, the Intrex questionnaire can be used to measure changes in a patient's self-concept over time. Self-concept has in turn been linked to symptom change (Benjamin, Rothweiler, & Critchfield, 2006; Henry et al., 1990). The two patients discussed next (Jenn and Miriam) both provide an example of this use of the Intrex. Their therapies were conducted as part of a long-term outpatient research protocol investigating IRT. Sessions were videorecorded and periodically archived for study, producing a rich and detailed picture of their change processes.

### Jenn

Jenn, who was also discussed briefly in Chapter 9, is a 50-year-old, White woman who manages a nursing home. At the time of referral, she was going through a difficult divorce. Jenn was anxious and suicidal and had been hospitalized three times in the preceding year. Her medical chart includes diagnosed bipolar II disorder, posttraumatic stress disorder (PTSD), and panic disorder and a variety of medical diagnoses involving chronic pain. Jenn received medication that was periodically monitored and adjusted by prescribers. She explained that problems began after she was injured in a fall and asked her husband for help around the house while she recovered. His response was to leave her for another woman and convince his sons (from another marriage) to have no further contact with her. After this, Jenn began to have panic attacks, flashbacks, and nightmares of early childhood trauma, odd experiences, delusions of reference, and severe depression. She reported deep humiliation, feeling "bad" and "selfish" for "causing" her husband to leave. Despite all this, Jenn functioned well at work and managed to keep her employer and coworkers from knowing anything was wrong. In the formal Structured Clinical Interview for *DSM-IV* Axis II Personality Disorders interview (First et al., 1996), she qualified for paranoid, schizotypal, and borderline personality disorder diagnoses.

### Developmental History

Jenn's early history involved recurrent, violent, and humiliating abuse by two older brothers, including sexual abuse. Her brothers nearly buried her alive on one occasion to back up a threat on her life if she were to tell their parents (Figure 10.1). Jenn believes that her mother was aware of their abuse but did not intervene, offering only "boys will be boys." Her father also seemed to provide tacit support of the boys' abuse. He sometimes

*Tracking Change and Assessing Outcomes* • 241

**FIGURE 10.1. Case Formulation for Jenn Using Structural Analysis of Social Behavior Codes and Copy Processes**

| Person copied | Copy processes | Behavior/s copied | | |
|---|---|---|---|---|
| **Mother:** | Introjection of | 1-5: **Control** as 3-5: *Self-Control* | | |
| | | 1-8: **Ignore** as 3-8: *Self-Neglect* | | |
| | Recapitulation of | Others: | Self: | |
| | | 1-8: **Ignore** | 1-4: **Protect** | |
| | | 2-4: <u>Trust</u> | 2-5: <u>Submit</u> | |
| **Father:** | Introjection of | 1-5: **Control** as 3-5: *Self-Control* | | |
| | | 1-6: **Blame** as 3-6: *Self-Blame* | | |
| | | 1-8: **Ignore** as 3-8: *Self-Neglect* | | |
| | Recapitulation of | Others: | Self: | |
| | | 1-6: **Blame** | 2-5: <u>Submit</u> | |
| | | 1-8: **Ignore** | 2-6: <u>Sulk</u> | |
| **Brothers:** | Recapitulation of | Others: | Self: | |
| | | 1-6: **Blame** | 2-5: <u>Submit</u> | |
| | | 1-7: **Attack** | 2-6: <u>Sulk</u> | |
| | | 1-8: **Ignore** | 2-7: <u>Recoil</u> | |
| | | | 3-5: *Self-Control* | |
| | | | 3-8: *Self-Neglect* | |

provided praise and admiration to Jenn, only to follow it with bitter sarcasm and humiliating mockery, telling others she was "weak" and "not like my boys." Jenn recalls crying in her room for hours as a young child, hoping that her mother would come in and comfort her. She would instead be ignored or told to take care of her younger brother. Hugs for her were rare. She reports learning that having needs or feelings is "selfish" and "bad." The only times Jenn felt accepted by her family, which she wanted very much, were when she was "strong" and managed to give the impression that she was unaffected by their abuse, neglect, and degradation.

242 • *Treatment: Connecting With Patients and Optimizing Interventions*

In copy process terms in the present, Jenn recapitulates the early experience of her brothers and father when she repeatedly suffers or expects abuse and invalidation at the hands of others (especially male individuals). Jenn appears to introject and recapitulate the remembered relationship with her mother by forcing herself to ignore her own needs and instead focus on attending to others. For example, Jenn believes that her husband left precisely because she did not follow her family-of-origin's rules for her and instead asked for help. As a result, Jenn blames herself for his departure. She introjects her father's view of her, feeling humiliated for not being "strong." She becomes anxious when mobilizing to accomplish tasks (e.g., preparing divorce papers), but then panics and has increased physical pain at the thought that no justice will ever come from her efforts. Other times, she is overwhelmed and hopeless, aware only of immense loss. Jenn justifies her chronic and severe suicidality with the beliefs that (a) her current suffering and fear will stop and (b) her deceased parents will respond to her life of uncomplaining and selfless (self-neglecting) service by finally providing relief and comfort to her in the afterlife. As therapy progresses, she discloses that she believes her parents are sending coded messages through day-to-day events (e.g., songs that would come on the radio while driving) that meant she should kill herself and join them. Therapy sessions were difficult and had a sense of being "touch and go" in relation to her safety, even with agreement about the case formulation and its implications for reaching green therapy goals.

Figure 10.2 shows Jenn's "when red" pattern from repeat administrations of the Intrex questionnaire. The pattern shows little progress over time. The measures were administered approximately every sixth session. With few exceptions, Jenn rates herself as highly self-attacking, making little progress in relation to herself across 157 sessions. This is consistent with her reports in therapy of persistent symptoms of self-harm and suicidal ideation through the same period.

Figure 10.3 provides additional information about Jenn's course of treatment across approximately 2 years. The session numbers are listed along the horizontal axis of both the top and bottom graphs. The top graph shows progress in terms of gift of love (GOL) awareness and choice; the bottom graph shows Jenn's depression as self-rated with the Beck Depression Inventory and expressed as T scores ($M = 50$, $SD = 10$). Ratings of the GOL to the family in the head are given from statements made in each recorded session. The Gift of Love Awareness and Choice scale (top graph) follows the Stages of Change model (Prochaska & DiClemente, 1983), commonly applied in addictions research but here applied to the GOL. The stages in the graph are indicated by ratings of 0 = unawareness, 1 = precontemplation,

Tracking Change and Assessing Outcomes • 243

**FIGURE 10.2. Time Series of Jenn's Intrex Ratings for Self-Treatment (Introject) When Red**

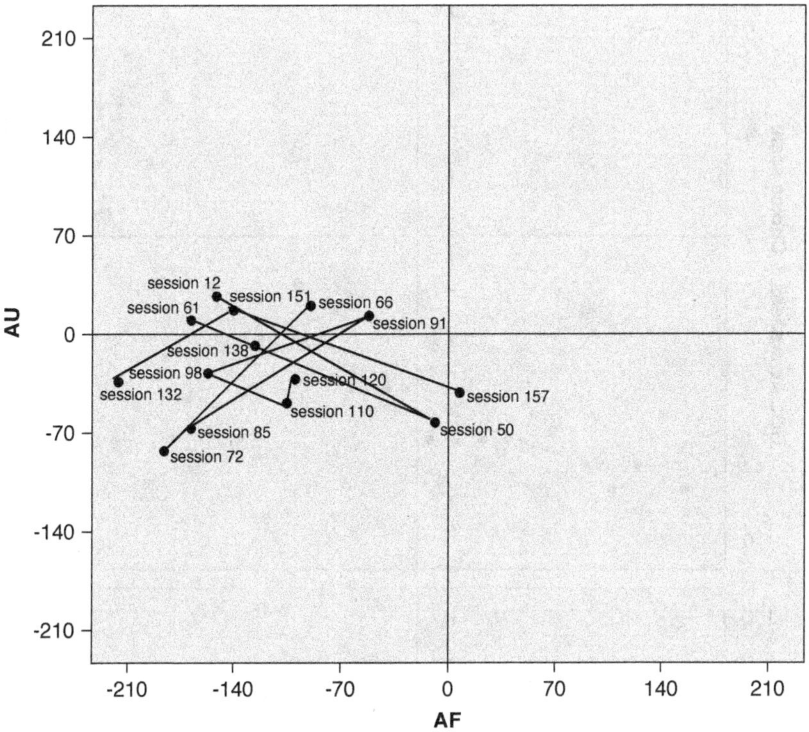

*Note.* AF = affiliation; AU = autonomy.

2 = contemplation, 3 = action, and 4+ = maintenance. These terms characterize a patient's expressed level of awareness regarding copy processes and GOLs as well as decisions and actions that demonstrate the choice to give up quests for love and approval and to instead pursue more adaptive responses to present circumstances. The horizontal line in the top graph indicates the beginning of the action stage when a conscious decision is made to give up the GOL and differentiate from rules and values of internalized loved ones. The horizontal line placed in the bottom graph indicates the normative level of depression in a nonclinical sample (i.e., T score = 50).

Jenn received treatment from two therapists during the period shown in Figure 10.3. The first 60 sessions (top of Figure 10.3, left of the vertical line) were conducted by a trainee therapist. IRT adherence was low (3.1 on a scale from –10 to +10). This therapist provided a generally supportive relationship

**FIGURE 10.3. Relationship Between Progress With GOL and Self-Ratings of Depression for Jenn**

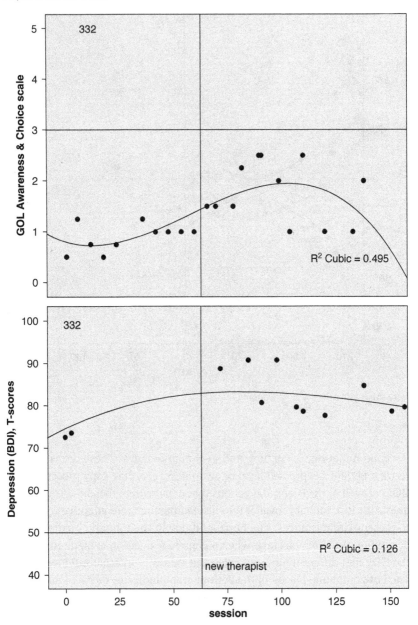

*Note.* Gift of Love Awareness and Choice scale ratings are as follows: 0 = unaware, 1 = precontemplation, 2 = contemplation, 3 = action, and 4 = maintenance stage. BDI = Beck Depression Inventory; GOL = gift of love.

and intervened in ways consistent with many standard approaches. However, clarity about interpersonal patterns was not often pursued, and interventions did not clearly reflect Jenn's case formulation. Efforts to motivate green and block red tended not to be effective and copy process patterns were not addressed. This phase of treatment ended with a series of crises and eventual unilateral termination by Jenn (Benjamin & Critchfield, 2010). She later described that termination as "pre-emptive," fearing she would be rejected by the first therapist after disclosing details of traumatic abuse. As can be seen in Figure 10.3, ratings of Jenn in this first portion of her treatment fell in the precontemplation range, reflecting little in-session awareness of her copy process patterns or their links to her history through the GOL.

Transition to a second therapist occurred after Jenn contacted the clinic again about a month later. Work with the second therapist was rated as much more IRT adherent (8.1 on a scale from –10 to +10). The pattern of crises and need for rehospitalization was reduced in this period and the therapy relationship appeared more able to sustain long-term work. However, Jenn's self-reported depressive symptoms show that they stayed at around 3 *SD* above the normative mean across the same period. As noted in Chapter 9, despite chronic and recurrent suicidal ideation, Jenn typically refused hospitalization or saw little benefit to her patterns, level of severity, and longer-term clinical risk when hospitalization was used. Jenn's session ratings placed her more often in the contemplation stage of change. Despite increased awareness, however, Jenn never quite makes it into the action stage during this part of her treatment. She appears instead to contemplate change and then back away, repeating this process a few times. During this period, her depression symptoms remain extremely high, and her self-concept remains very self-attacking.

Jenn's red GOL was discussed explicitly in this therapy and involved a desire to commit suicide and join her mother who died some years ago. The desire for a loving connection with her mother in the afterlife had Jenn focused on her suffering, its intensity, and perceived hopelessness of "a solution" to life's challenges. She responded to her mother's voice ("the siren song") when suffering, and she was being called to "peace" alongside her. Jenn would then ruminate over "perfect plans" for suicide and use suffering brought on by stressors and challenges to justify the plans. She resisted these calls, but often only because she felt the red obligation to "be strong and responsible" rather than becoming truly engaged with green therapy goals.

Jenn's in-the-head ratings of her mother during treatment (Figure 10.4) show Jenn's experience of her as demanding (1-5: **Control**) and neglectful (1-8: **Ignore**). In follow-up, Jenn explained that her mother tells her that killing herself would be for the best.

246 • *Treatment: Connecting With Patients and Optimizing Interventions*

**FIGURE 10.4. Jenn's Intrex Rating of Mother in the Head**

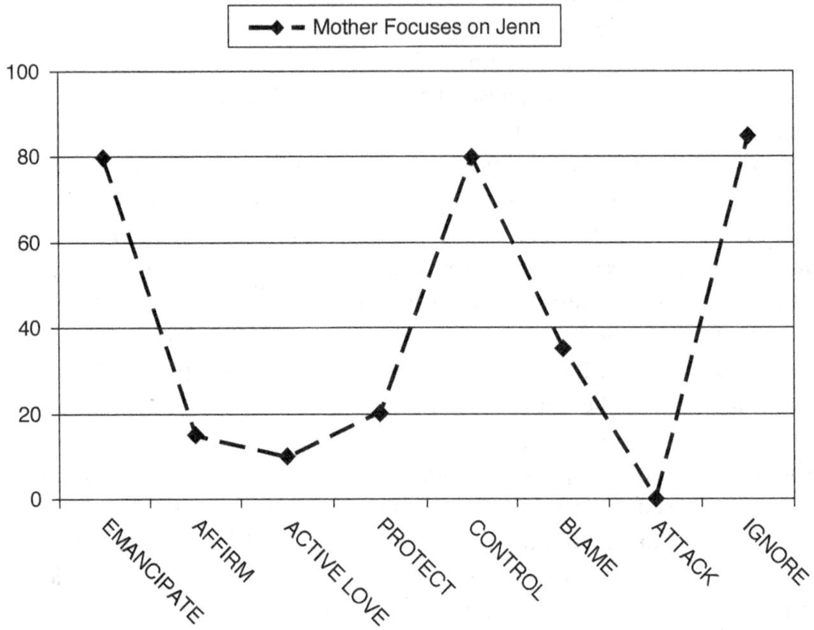

Jenn additionally characterized the relationships in a few words on the rating sheet, unpacking its complexity and the struggle of capturing it with a few Intrex items: "She feels warm and inviting and caring, but that's what I want, not what is 'truth.' I can't let go of the 'false' beckonings, although I am starting to realize it is not truth or safe." In SASB terms, Jenn experiences her mother as loving but "false" (1-3: **Active Love** plus 1-8: **Ignore**). She feels unable to resist her mother (2-5: <u>Submit</u>) and so is enmeshed with her. Unfortunately, what her mother demands is Jenn's death (behavioral 3-7: *Self-Attack* but framed as self-protection and facilitating a loving reunion). A small amount of green awareness seems to exist, in that Jenn should resist her mother's calls (2-1: <u>Separate</u>); Jenn recognizes them as false, but green is small compared with her red yearning for her mother.

Regarding her father, Jenn wrote:

> He is the master tricker—I am less tricked by him than Mom, but there are times I feel the love and support that was there on some selfish (his part) level. I'm willing to not be tricked as much as I am with Mom.

Jenn's father is characterized as exerting unfair, hostile control (1-6: **Blame** plus 1-8: **Ignore**). Although Jenn sometimes perceives him as loving, she says she mostly retains the ability to be separate and "willing to not be tricked" (2-1: <u>Separate</u>).

**Potential Blockers to Change**

Benjamin (2003, 2006) provided extended discussion (including flowcharts) of how to work with therapeutic impasses and address potential factors that block change. This work includes discernment about the need to discuss fears of change, negative views of the therapy or therapist, and eroticization of patterns. Giving up the GOL can itself be difficult and challenging. Jenn noted this in her own process:

> I know that if I let this go, I will feel better, be able to cope and have more peace. But it feels like if I do that, then they [abusers] win. It will just be like "whatever." I cannot allow that. I have to stay hypervigilant so that justice will be done.

Benjamin (2018) outlined the difficult process of supporting and motivating individuals so that they can move to (and through) the action phase of change. The costs of Jenn's felt need for justice could include her life. She worked, at first very ambivalently, to come to terms with the issue of justice-never-known and attendant grief, relative to her history of repeated traumas and losses at the hands of loved ones. This would require additional years of treatment for her journey.

Benjamin (2003, 2006, 2018) noted that eroticized patterns can also block progress in a way that is separable from seeking proximity to attachment figures. This is referred to as *Klute syndrome* and reflects that red patterns can be enacted and reinforced in sexual fantasy, persisting for reasons involving sexual neurochemistry and classical conditioning mechanisms that are separable from those tied directly to the GOL. The problem can be particularly difficult when attachment figures have also been sexual abusers and both motivational systems are activated. This possibility is suggested when change does not occur over time despite having collaboration and a clear, shared agreement about the case formulation and its implications.

The topic can be difficult to bring up, particularly with patients like Jenn who feel reluctance or shame about any discussion of sexual topics in therapy. Intrex ratings can sometimes be helpful in broaching the topic in a helpful way. For example, Jenn rated the Intrex relative to a boyfriend who she met later in therapy after her divorce was finalized and additional time had passed. She initially described him in sessions as focusing on her with kindness and understanding. She appeared to benefit from this input, treating herself as more deserving and worthy of self-care. This new attachment appeared to strengthen her green. Not long after, however, she provided Intrex ratings showing a strong parallel between her focus on him and ratings made previously of her focus on her father in childhood. Figure 10.5 shows the comparison in which Jenn simultaneously takes care of and stays distant from each of them. When her therapist noted this parallel, Jenn began to disclose long-held feelings of shame and confusion about a sexual side to the relationship with her father, not reported previously, resulting in a pattern learned with him of needing to simultaneously manage and keep distance from all men when sexuality was involved.

The availability of healthy sexuality in Jenn's new relationship appeared to be accompanied by re-emergence of problems in relation to herself, despite significant progress with her GOL to her father in other domains. She reported the following:

> I can't let myself progress or let [boyfriend] see the real me, because I know that I am dirty and wrong, and it would all be pretend. I feel I need to be punished. I have to end it with him before he sees too much.

Unfortunately, Jenn did end this relationship, siding with red (especially her internalized father) as she did so.

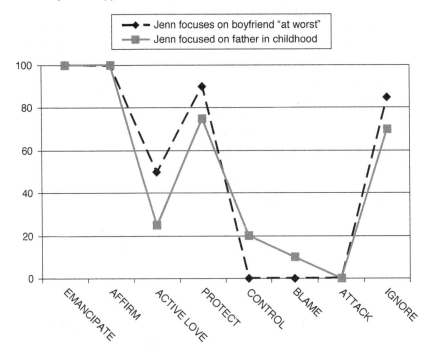

**FIGURE 10.5. Parallel, Problematic Interpersonal Relationships Involving Sexuality Can Suggest Eroticized Patterns (Klute Syndrome; $r = .95$)**

Enabling a patient's will to change is a crucial element of IRT. If a patient is unwilling to let go of wishes for love and acceptance from internalized attachment figures and continues to pursue the GOL via maladaptive means, then otherwise helpful interventions will likely fail to make a difference. Until Jenn is ready and able to come to terms with her yearning for love and protection by her parents, she can be predicted to continue feeling depressed and anxious, with keen awareness of the suffering, injustice, abuse, and help-lessness that links her to her (internalized) loved ones. Consistent with IRT theory, Jenn's chronic and potentially lethal suicidality changed very little during this first phase of treatment, while her yearning for loving union with her mother persisted.

Jenn went on to complete additional years in IRT treatment, which involved an uneven process of progress and setbacks, including the unfortunate addition of new, traumatizing events, as well as a loss and the onset of new physical health problems. With each new circumstance, red was happy to interpret them darkly, while her therapist continued to work to support green. Jenn eventually found her way out of the cage she was in. She offered this qualitative summary of her experience at the end of therapy that emphasized the quality of the therapy relationship:

> The most beneficial part of my therapy has been having a truly caring and empathetic listener as my therapist. I was validated and understood. That allowed me to spend more time processing rather than struggling to be believed and trying to internalize the trust needed for me to be able to ade-quately share.

In later communication with her therapist, Jenn reflected back further on her therapy process. Her words suggest a more secure baseline of relating with herself and with others in her life, while getting needed distance from early events (suggesting differentiation from the family in the head with whom many of them occurred).

> All in all, I feel better having purpose and feelings of validation for the person that I knew that I could be. . . . I am a strong, capable, creative, and giving person! As I just typed those last nine words I started to cry. Tissue break. . . . I now see the "stories" as just stories from the past. I learned from them. I am stronger because of them, and I can now share what I learned and how I learned how to move on. . . . I am good. . . . I wish that it [the therapy] had been shorter, but what I learned has made me a better [current role], and I appreciate that. So does [list of new people in her life].

### Miriam

Miriam's case was also tracked as part of a long-term outpatient research protocol. Her case formulation is provided in Chapter 6. Raters judged both

250 • Treatment: Connecting With Patients and Optimizing Interventions

Miriam and her therapist to show moderate to strong IRT adherence. She engaged in therapy and continued until she moved away for work in another state. Miriam and her therapist both agreed at the time that she was ready to "leave the nest." Her symptoms, which were initially very severe and chronic, had subsided to levels that matched nonclinical norms. These gains had been sustained over time, including in the face of significant stressors that she likely would not have been resilient to earlier in treatment.

Miriam filled out symptom measures and made periodic Intrex ratings of her self-concept "when red." This allows a view of her changing self-concept over time, presented in Figure 10.6. Her progress was not linear. There were steps forward, periods of consolidation, and periods of regression. This pattern

**FIGURE 10.6. Time Series of Miriam's Intrex Ratings for Self-Treatment (Introject) When Red**

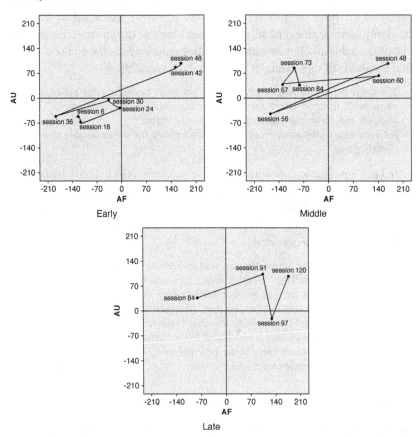

Note. AF = affiliation; AU = autonomy.

Tracking Change and Assessing Outcomes • 251

is consistent with the idea that in therapy, sometimes things may get worse before they get better.

In session 6 (shown in the lower-left quadrant of the left-most panel in Figure 10.6), Miriam's self-treatment is characterized by hostility and self-control. By session 24, she made progress with her self-concept. In session 36, she "relapsed" back to severe self-criticism, but then progresses dramatically forward to ratings characterized by self-affirmation and self-acceptance in session 42. She sustains this gain for a time until another relapse and recovery occur in sessions 56 and 60. After this, she moves to a fairly stable position of hostile self-neglect (sessions 67–84) before again making progress, this time steadily toward the SASB-based therapy goal region on the right of the model. It is informative to consider the content (see Exhibit 10.1) discussed in each of the sessions when Miriam made her ratings. The Intrex self-ratings are consistent with the topics discussed in therapy. Progress as well as setbacks can be seen to have meaningful correspondence with the relationship with her family in the head.

Figure 10.7 provides another timeline of Miriam's progress in therapy. The structure of this figure parallels the one provided for Jenn. Miriam's early sessions are rated in the "precontemplation" region of the graph, consistent with work in these sessions to establish a collaborative relationship, clarify goals, and work to understand her patterns, while also attempting to block red behavior that might lead to crisis and/or undermine collaboration. In these sessions, depression and other symptoms are prominent in Miriam's session notes and easily provoked by life events. Sessions 40 to 60 are rated at or near the action stage and are associated with dramatic steps forward, and with equally dramatic re-emergence of symptoms and negative self-treatment. Her pattern illustrates how attempts to differentiate can often seem stormy and fragile, especially at first, opposed as they are by fears of the unknown, retaliation by internalized loved ones, and grief over losses of identity and of connection with family in the head. In sessions 18 and 24 (Exhibit 10.1), Miriam attempts to be herself and choose her own life despite her mother's (internalized and actual) predictions of failure. In session 36, she has significant success that is recognized but immediately feels punished and left alone, in accordance with her mother's rules for her. At this point, her Intrex rating shows that she is more hostile to herself than at any other point in the sequence. Red is ascendant and her mother's rules for the self are held tightly.

By sessions 42 and 48, Miriam's tune is changing. In these sessions, she describes wanting to let go of her mother's messages, as well as anger toward her mother, in favor of choosing her own ways, values, and identities.

252 • *Treatment: Connecting With Patients and Optimizing Interventions*

### EXHIBIT 10.1. IRT Progress Note Excerpts for Miriam (Compare to Self-Ratings on Intrex in Figure 10.6)

**Session 6:** Went on date, felt "pretty." Next day was cat-called and propositioned from vehicle. Since then, panic attacks, unable to sleep. "I can't get control of it." "I'm tired of being singled out by guys." Resisting urge to "do something stupid" (cutting, suicide). Agreed recent progress (date experience, self-concept) made internalized mother and abuser angry. These men were the response. No wish to discuss. CBT techniques used to aid symptom management. [Patient requests rehospitalization the next day.]

**Session 18:** "Sparring with myself." "Making big decisions about who I am." "To go back to school. That's huge and I'm scared." Abusive cousin (supported by mother) linked to ex-boyfriend who said how life was to be: dismissive of patient's dreams, "when I asserted boundaries the relationship was destroyed." Progress now from "the rebel in me" "someday I'll have to do it just for me."

**Session 24:** Fears returning to school, that sleep and anxiety will lead to drop out, failure, suicidality. Mother predicts this. Patient reading family emails only once a week to deal with impact at a time she chooses. Likes idea of being friendly to self, rather than self-control and self-doubt about symptoms. Wants to view own fears of failure like resisting critical emails from family.

**Session 30:** Conference attendees defended patient when associate spread sex rumors. Feels bad she "didn't stand up for myself." "Sleeping is hard, eating is incredibly hard." "Went down to a lower dose of Depakote. My feelings are important, I need to feel them; after all these years of numbness, it's time." Fears about self-care and trusting self but notes progress.

**Session 36:** Depression and suicidal ideation after recognition for success at work. Noticed being treated differently, more distant. She is told, "This is how it goes when you get to a certain level." Resolves to be lonely, focus only on giving to others. Believes kind men do not exist or will not be attracted. Fears therapist will be critical and abusive because of sexual dream.

**Session 42:** Thriving at school and new job, self-care increasing, sleeping well, refreshed for "first time in years." Enjoying dating "kind" man. Wants to "let go" of long-standing anger toward mother. "It's not okay what happened," but says mother tried her best. Feels it hypocritical to want love and acceptance if not willing to give it. Does not expect mother to reciprocate.

**Session 48:** "Proud of myself" for asserting after groped while out with friends. Learned that negative interaction with co-worker related to the other person's poor performance. Concludes "okay" to be herself, questions belief that all problems show she is flawed. New, "kind" boyfriend. "Not listening" to red; internalizations ignored as patient pursues "experiment" of "being myself."

**Session 54:** No symptoms. Negotiating how to "be myself" in romantic relationship, resisting pull to submit or compromise to be accepted. Not wanting to "go back" to being "the unhealthy one" as labeled by her family and perceived in prior relationship.

**Session 56:** Self-critical for "not being over this depression." Bill for hospitalization coincides with anniversary of rape. Dropped school. Cousin and rapist in head, angry about progress. Ways to distance, ignore them; counter with self-care, self-affirm.

*Tracking Change and Assessing Outcomes* • 253

**EXHIBIT 10.1. IRT Progress Note Excerpts for Miriam (Compare to Self-Ratings on Intrex in Figure 10.6) (*Continued*)**

**Session 60:** Frustrated, boyfriend wants to stop dating yet have sex. Wants clarity but afraid to be firm lest he end contact. She does not feel exploited. Fears therapist will tell her how to feel, but says IRT is "only hope," places trust in the therapy process.

**Session 67:** Depressed, not working, minimal functioning. Mother demands she return home to "answer all your excuses with solutions." If lives a normal life, family will be "shocked." They believe she is "broken" and "psychotic." Reports commitment to own life and values, thinks she is a good person, has vision for life of "normalcy." Struggling against mother's "destiny" for her.

**Session 73:** Boyfriend ended relationship. Mother sent him email calling patient "crazy," "you should stay to help her." Perceives internalized abuser wants obedience, cut herself where he did, has "replay" of the abuse: chest crushed, hands shaking, tears but no affect. Cutting would appease, show she would never tell. Resisting, but fears escalation of problems for this "disobedience."

**Session 84:** Severe anxiety, sleepless, loss of appetite, dissociative experiences, daily suicidal ideation, desire to self-harm. Attributes symptoms to trauma reminders at work. Surprisingly, reports coping well with decision to feel and face memories, let them go. Discussed good self-care while attempting this. Reports increase in positive feelings and self-understanding as time goes on.

**Session 91:** No symptoms, functioning well. Tempted by out-of-state job. Mother would say she can't handle it. But choice of red or green seen as more important than to stay or go. Red may sabotage and "prove" she can't handle life, staying could agree with mother. Green sees staying as gaining stability, or going as trusting self to take healthy risks, accepting self even if problems arise.

**Session 97:** No symptoms despite big stressor. Had sex with colleague then learned he is engaged. Initially felt "a whore" "a homewrecker." Resolved by looking at information she had from him. Used anger at him to assert clear boundary. Seeks "reality" when old patterns emerge. "Everything I am doing is forbidden" from family's perspective, free to risk making healthy choices.

**Session 120:** Doing well. Pursuing balance of work and time for self, relaxed, fewer migraines. Reflects about religious differences in new relationship. Mother wrote, "you are living your life all wrong," "I tell you because I love you," "move home to see your father before he dies." Patient briefly angry but did not defend, decided it is fine to not seek their approval. Notes she used to grieve them, now sees past was never what she wanted, no need/way to change her family. Instead focuses on ways to improve her life.

**Session 127:** Last session. Patient excited about moving for new job. Family is disapproving, friends are happy for her. Reviewed therapy process. Long time since symptoms. Reports continued practice turning off harsh, critical internal voices, not appeasing and submitting. Reports valuing, cherishing, respecting herself, beyond simply "being normal." Committed to continuing this way.

*Note.* CBT = cognitive behavior therapy; IRT = Interpersonal Reconstructive Therapy.

254 • *Treatment: Connecting With Patients and Optimizing Interventions*

**FIGURE 10.7. Relationship Between Progress With GOL and Self-Ratings of Depression for Miriam**

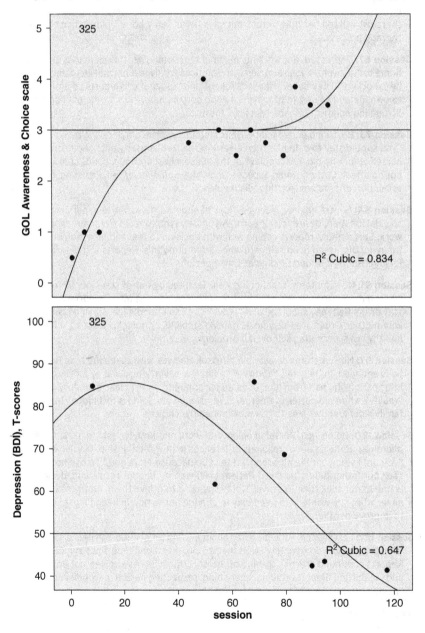

*Note.* BDI = Beck Depression Inventory; GOL = gift of love.

The interpersonal analysis of anger provided by Benjamin (1989, 1996, 2003, 2006, 2018) suggests that this affect typically accompanies and reflects desires to exert interpersonal control, get interpersonal distance, or both. In Miriam's case, the anger involved a wish for her mother to finally accept and understand her, treat her fairly, and support her as she goes her own way. "Letting go" of anger at her mother would equate to Miriam letting go of this quest for her mother to treat her differently, to realize the wish driving GOL behaviors. This could allow Miriam to truly go her own way with or without family permission. By session 54, Miriam reports no significant symptoms and talks in session about wanting to resist "going back" to the old way of being. Research ratings place her at this point in the "advanced action stage," expressing not only awareness of her patterns, along with their meanings and origins, but also a decision to no longer pursue the GOL that fuels them.

Miriam bounces back rapidly in session 60 after a regression to old patterns in session 56, but then loses a love relationship that for a time had offered a healthier kind of secure base for her. She then went through a long period where symptoms returned. Ratings of her commitment to change the GOL remained high, however, and she increasingly understood symptoms as clear recapitulations of the experiences she had with her mother, abusive cousin, and rapist. Eventually, after about session 84, she wrests internal permission to truly develop new views of herself and others and stands comfortably separate from family rules while learning new skills for relating. Her symptoms fall away and do not significantly return on any of the clinical or research measures. What is more, she describes centered feelings and even delight in getting to know herself and others in new ways, developing new interests and relationships. In session 120, she poignantly describes guilt-inducing input from her family, responding with statements that it is fine to not seek their approval and adding that she used to grieve them but could now accept that there was no way to change her family to finally be loved by them.

As shown in Chapter 8 (Figure 8.5), Miriam's change process involved a conscious decision to separate from her family in the present, as well as the internalized version in her head, to develop her own ways. Extreme separation is usually only required relative to the family in the head, built as it is out of memories of past experiences that may or may not allow for significant reauthoring in terms of their meanings in the present. Similarly, some relationships in the present may be too toxic, dangerous, or imbalanced to pursue. More often, patients have a real choice about whether they wish to salvage and strengthen relationships using therapy goal behaviors and principles of complementarity. Loved ones may also be growing and changing across developmental time, allowing new ways of relating. Once the GOL is relinquished, new relating can often take place on different footing, without

256 • *Treatment: Connecting With Patients and Optimizing Interventions*

so much dependency; relational patterns can be chosen better by patients and can be engaged in without illusions about who is being related with and why. The new patterns of relating with old attachment figures might be pursued in light of the SASB goal region for relating in the world. Miriam may or may not decide at some point in the future to try and rebuild bridges with her family members on new and more equal terms. If she chooses that path, it would be ideal for it to happen with therapeutic support, after she has gained more practice and comfort in her ability to do so without being overtaken by the old anger and the old yearning.

### Hannah

Hannah began therapy as an outpatient, seeking help for prolonged and severe anxiety. After a few weeks of therapy work, she disclosed to her therapist that this problem was frequently accompanied by suicidal ideation, that she had developed several specific plans for killing herself (overdose, driving off the road, using one of her father's guns, and combinations of these plans), and that seeing opportunities to enact those plans made both the anxiety and the desire for suicide escalate rapidly. She did substantial work in IRT therapy to recognize her red copy processes and over time relinquish her GOL with both parents. Like Miriam, Hannah's symptoms decreased to normative levels, with occasional flare-ups that she developed the skills to manage. She is now in the maintenance phase of treatment and has been working to place the old relationships with her parents as they are now (as opposed to the internalized versions) on new and healthier footing. Hannah provided the ratings shown in Figure 10.8, separated by a period of 6 months. At time 1, Hannah reported being at her best 50% of the time, and 30% at worst. Her self-treatment was largely in the therapy goal region, but with progress still to be made in terms of (a) self-acceptance when at best (3-2: *Self-Affirm*) and (b) increasing how often she is in her at-best (i.e., green) states. Hannah's relationship with the family in the head (lower-left graph) showed her experiencing them as controlling and blaming (1-5: **Control** and 1-6: **Blame**), while she responded to them with 2-1: Separate.

At time 2, Hannah reported being at her best 40% of the time, but only 10% at worst. Her self-treatment at best occupies the therapy goal region; when at worst, her levels of self-attack and self-neglect are lower than at time 1. Hannah's family-in-the-head picture (lower-right graph) contains substantial hostility, with the important persons or their internalized representations engaging in hostile control, while Hannah recoils but also stays in differentiated space. The content discussed in therapy around the time Hannah made

Tracking Change and Assessing Outcomes • 257

FIGURE 10.8. Hannah's Self-Treatment and Family in the Head

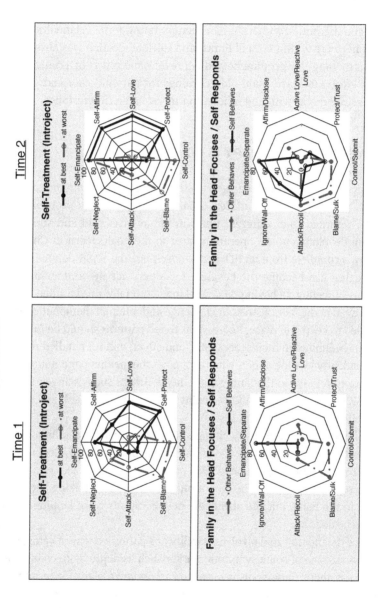

258 • *Treatment: Connecting With Patients and Optimizing Interventions*

the second set of ratings is based on her conversation with family about holiday travel plans. She felt the need to be on guard for signs of their criticism (an old theme) but managed the interaction well. Afterward, internally, she was aware of recoiling away from their perceived attacks but managed this without becoming hostile to herself. On therapy rating forms, Hannah's anxiety symptoms were within normal limits, and suicidal ideation was absent. Subsequent therapy conversation helped her review and reflect in a centered way on her efforts to leave aside old yearnings for parental care and, instead, relate as she might with any other adult in the same circumstance.

## KNOWING WHEN THERAPY IS COMPLETE

Therapy can be undertaken as a discrete project with a beginning and end, such as to understand and address a particular symptom or problem. It can also be returned to at different times in life as a scaffold and support for ongoing development. As operationalized in the goal speech in Chapter 5, therapy is complete from an IRT perspective once the SASB-defined therapy goal region has become the baseline for a person's life and spans across domains of feeling, behaving, and thinking. Optimally, this baseline is maintained even in the face of stress or challenge and minimal therapeutic support is needed to keep it in place. Regressions to red patterns should be (a) rare or absent; (b) limited in their scope, time, and effect; and (c) handled relatively independently by the patient, who recognizes the meaning and nature of the red pattern relative to the family in the head. Affects such as anger, fear, and sadness, when present, should be reality based, correctly cued, and effective in mobilizing adaptive responses.

An important part of many change processes involves installation of the therapist as a new internalization that helps counteract problematic messages from the family in the head. One patient who hears voices remarked to her therapist that she now hears not only her own voice talking back to her family in the head, but she also hears her therapist's voice helping support her as she does so.

Since the therapy goal involves stability of a patterned way of being, rather than an absence of some symptom marker such as depression, collaborative discussion about these goals is necessary to optimize plans for termination. Plans may include tapering off sessions, moving to as-needed contact, or ending treatment when a major life transition occurs to "graduate" the patient on to the new life pursuit.

## OUTCOMES CONSIDERED MORE BROADLY: IRT RESEARCH

Following the model of problem-treatment-outcome congruence, SASB has been used to address multiple aspects of IRT theory and practice. As described in prior chapters, research to validate copy process theory shows that these kinds of behavioral parallels can be reliably detected and are near ubiquitous in both clinical and nonclinical samples. Clinical samples copy maladaptive degrees of hostility, distance, and/or enmeshment at greater rates than non-clinical groups who, by and large, copy a secure attachment profile. Copy process patterns can be reliably assessed via questionnaire at the individual level (Conroy & Pincus, 2006; Critchfield & Benjamin, 2008, 2010; Woehrle et al., 2023) or by codes applied to clinical interviews (Critchfield et al., 2015).

As a method of treatment, IRT allows the use of techniques from any tradition so long as they are consistent with the patient's case formulation and support progress toward green therapy goals. Research shows that adherent IRT therapists indeed incorporate methods from multiple orientations in their sessions, sometimes in creative combinations, such as assigning homework and assertiveness skills in a manner reminiscent of CBT approaches but directing them toward internalized figures (Critchfield et al., 2017). This process unfolds using the core algorithm and five steps of IRT as a guide. Within these guidelines, therapists are encouraged to be responsive in the use of discernment, critical thinking, and empathy to tailor interventions relative to unique patient learning needs and case formulation patterns.

The IRT approach defies easy testing via randomized controlled trial (RCT) methods because it seeks to optimize treatment variability to meet the needs of diverse profiles. This contrasts with the RCT approach of standardizing the application of treatment to address a specific disorder type. To test the underlying theory, IRT research has instead emphasized rated adherence to the model's principles. These have been operationalized and shown to be reliable when applied to individual sessions at the level of each element of the core algorithm and the five steps of IRT (rated for patient and therapist contributions; Critchfield et al., 2008). A measure of GOL awareness and stages of change has also been developed and can be reliably applied at the session level (Critchfield et al., 2008).

IRT adherence can also be assessed when other therapeutic orientations are the focus, so long as enough data are available to develop a case formulation based on copy process patterns (Critchfield, Dobner-Pereira, & Stucker, 2021). It is expected that when therapeutic interventions are effective, they can be shown to be consistent with IRT principles. In other words, we believe that effective therapy sessions share in common some method for enhancing green ways of being and leaving red ones behind, while attending to ways in which love and loyalty to prior learning in close relationships might interfere.

Most IRT research to date has focused on CORDS cases. These patients typically have complex diagnostic profiles involving personality disorder, have had multiple prior treatment attempts without substantial progress, and show signs of high risk. As a result, they tend to be ruled out of research studies. Even so, most clinicians know the profile well. Some CORDS patients have been informally identified as "frequent fliers" through hospital systems, whereas others suffer without adequate care "off the grid." When in treatment, they occupy many supervisory and consultation sessions. Given the historical track record for this group, it is heartening to see many of these patients make progress in IRT treatments. Our preliminary data suggest strong support for the IRT approach, particularly regarding the importance of relinquishing the GOL in order for symptoms to resolve and functioning to improve. In preliminary work thus far, IRT adherence has been linked with (a) retention in treatment, (b) fewer rehospitalizations, (c) symptom reduction, and (d) improved self-treatment (Benjamin et al., 2018; Karpiak et al., 2011). Manuscripts about this work are being prepared for peer review.

At a deeper level, the theory suggests that IRT adherence will be linked to outcome through a successful process of helping patients let go of the GOL in favor of more adaptive ways of being. Figure 10.9 presents SASB-based outcomes for a sample of 12 CORDS patients. As shown, change in self-treatment from the beginning to end of therapy is predicted by the highest GOL stages of change rating achieved across the sessions. The pattern is consistent with the expectation that progress in recognizing and letting go of the GOL is associated with a green therapy goal pattern that includes positive correlations for friendliness to the self, peaking on enhanced self-affirmation (3-2: *Self-Affirm*). It also includes mostly negative correlations with hostile self-treatment. A significant negative correlation with 3-5: *Self-Control* is understood in this sample to be a function of CORDS patients working very hard at baseline to manage and monitor themselves in order to function. This need substantially decreases when there is progress in relinquishing the GOL.

Our findings also show that IRT adherence strongly predicts symptomatic outcomes (i.e., anger, anxiety, and depression) among therapy completers in a CORDS sample ($r = .59$). As predicted by theory, this link is mediated by change in the GOL (Critchfield, Dobner-Pereira, et al., 2019; Critchfield & Benjamin, 2024). That is, the attachment-based mechanism of change appears to play a key role in linking therapist activity to outcomes. Additional analysis suggests that the therapist's influence is largely a function

**FIGURE 10.9. Pre–Post Change in Self-Concept (at Best) Predicted by Progress With GOL**

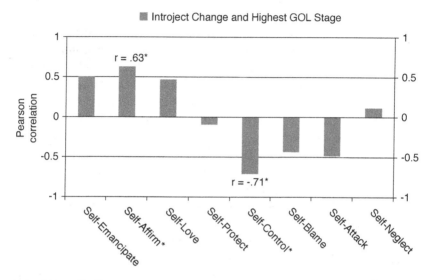

Note. GOL = gift of love.
*p < .05.

of enhancing the patient's use of IRT principles in service of relinquishing the GOL. If reliable, such observations are key evidence validating the conceptual core of IRT theory—that psychopathology reflects "attachment gone awry" and that lasting change is not expected until or unless a patient is able to differentiate from internalized attachment figures sufficient to allow usual and customary interventions to finally have an effect.

## CONCLUSION AND FUTURE DIRECTIONS

It has been 50 years since the first publication of the SASB model (Benjamin, 1973). SASB has had a good deal of use and application in clinical practice and research since that time, far more than could be summarized in this book. As noted at the outset and illustrated across all chapters of this book, SASB can be used to help map and describe a wide range of settings, contexts, and domains for human relating. SASB is used to describe instances of behavior, interactive sequences, and repeating patterns and also change in each of these. IRT builds on clinical observations using SASB to bring clarity to how and why relationship patterns are learned and internalized, how they can produce and maintain psychopathology, and how change is often possible for treatment-resistant problems.

Although there is a great deal of complexity in "what humans get up to," SASB consists of just three dimensions: focus, affiliation, and interdependence. This book provides extensive practice locating all kinds of clinical material in SASB's coordinate system. When applied in real time during sessions, it can feel like a heavy lift to evaluate all the possibilities, even in only three dimensions. The sense of complexity in seeing through the SASB lens fades with time and practice. A good way to begin is to keep the quadrant model in mind while listening to patient narratives. This is the model with just a binary choice for each dimension: (a) other versus self, (b) friendly versus hostile, and (c) independent versus interdependent. Additional nuance and methods discussed in this book can be added as that initial process begins to feel more natural.

Future directions for SASB include continuing to support a tradition of practice and investigation using an interpersonal and attachment-based lens. It also includes increasing the accessibility and ease of use of the Intrex questionnaire and other training materials. Consultation, training, and access to resources, including scoring programs, are available through the Interpersonal Reconstructive Therapy Institute (https://irtinstitute.com).

# References

Ahmed, M., Westra, H. A., & Constantino, M. J. (2012). Early therapy interpersonal process differentiating clients high and low in outcome expectations. *Psychotherapy Research, 22*(6), 731–745. https://doi.org/10.1080/10503307.2012.724538

Alexander, F., & French, T. M. (1946). *Psychoanalytic therapy: Principles and application*. Ronald Press.

Alpher, V. S. (1996). Identity and introject in dissociative disorders. *Journal of Consulting and Clinical Psychology, 64*(6), 1238–1244. https://doi.org/10.1037/0022-006X.64.6.1238

American Psychiatric Association. (1994). *Diagnostic and statistical manual of mental disorders* (4th ed.).

American Psychiatric Association. (2013). *Diagnostic and statistical manual of mental disorders* (5th ed.). https://doi.org/10.1176/appi.books.9780890425596

Arata, C. M. (2002). Child sexual abuse and sexual revictimization. *Clinical Psychology: Science and Practice, 9*(2), 135–164. https://doi.org/10.1093/clipsy.9.2.135

Armelius, K., & Granberg. (2000). Self-image and perception of mother and father in psychotic and borderline patients. *Psychotherapy Research, 10*(2), 147–158. https://doi.org/10.1080/713663671

Bakan, D. (1966). *The duality of human existence: Isolation and communion in Western man*. Beacon Press.

Barnett, B., & Parker, G. (1998). The parentified child: Early competence or childhood deprivation? *Child Psychology and Psychiatry Review, 3*(4), 146–155. https://doi.org/10.1017/S1360641798001695

264 • *References*

Beck, A. T., & Freeman, A. M. (1990). *Cognitive therapy of personality disorders*. Guilford Press.

Bedics, J. D., Atkins, D. C., Comtois, K. A., & Linehan, M. M. (2012a). Treatment differences in the therapeutic relationship and introject during a 2-year randomized controlled trial of dialectical behavior therapy versus nonbehavioral psychotherapy experts for borderline personality disorder. *Journal of Consulting and Clinical Psychology, 80*(1), 66–77. https://doi.org/10.1037/a0026113

Bedics, J. D., Atkins, D. C., Comtois, K. A., & Linehan, M. M. (2012b). Weekly therapist ratings of the therapeutic relationship and patient introject during the course of dialectical behavioral therapy for the treatment of borderline personality disorder. *Psychotherapy, 49*(2), 231–240. https://doi.org/10.1037/a0028254

Bedics, J. D., Henry, W. P., & Atkins, D. C. (2005). The therapeutic process as a predictor of change in patients' important relationships during time-limited dynamic psychotherapy. *Psychotherapy, 42*(3), 279–284. https://doi.org/10.1037/0033-3204.42.3.279

Benjamin, L. S. (1961). The effect of bottle and cup feeding on the nonnutritive sucking of the infant rhesus monkey. *Journal of Comparative and Physiological Psychology, 54*(3), 230–237. https://doi.org/10.1037/h0041831

Benjamin, L. S. (1973). A biological model for understanding the behavior of individuals. In J. Westman (Ed.), *Individual differences in children* (pp. 215–241). Wiley.

Benjamin, L. S. (1974). Structural analysis of social behavior. *Psychological Review, 81*(5), 392–425. https://doi.org/10.1037/h0037024

Benjamin, L. S. (1979). Structural analysis of differentiation failure. *Psychiatry, 42*(1), 1–23. https://doi.org/10.1080/00332747.1979.11024003

Benjamin, L. S. (1986). Operational definition and measurement of dynamics shown in the stream of free associations. *Psychiatry, 49*(2), 104–129. https://doi.org/10.1080/00332747.1986.11024313

Benjamin, L. S. (1987). Use of the SASB dimensional model to develop treatment plans for personality disorders: I. Narcissism. *Journal of Personality Disorders, 1*(1), 43–70. https://doi.org/10.1521/pedi.1987.1.1.43

Benjamin, L. S. (1989). Is chronicity a function of the relationship between the person and the auditory hallucination? *Schizophrenia Bulletin, 15*(2), 291–310. https://doi.org/10.1093/schbul/15.2.291

Benjamin, L. S. (1993). Every psychopathology is a gift of love. *Psychotherapy Research, 3*(1), 1–24. https://doi.org/10.1080/10503309312331333629

Benjamin, L. S. (1995). Good defenses make good neighbors. In H. R. Conte & R. Plutchik (Eds.), *Ego defenses: Theory and measurement* (pp. 53–78). John Wiley & Sons.

Benjamin, L. S. (1996). *Interpersonal diagnosis and treatment of personality disorders* (2nd ed.). Guilford Press.

Benjamin, L. S. (Host). (1997). *Interpersonal reconstructive therapy for passive–aggressive personality disorder* [Video/DVD]. American Psychological Association. https://www.apa.org/pubs/videos/4310830

Benjamin, L. S. (2000). *Intrex user's manual*. Interpersonal Reconstructive Therapy Institute.

Benjamin, L. S. (2003). *Interpersonal reconstructive therapy: Promoting change in nonresponders*. Guilford Press.

Benjamin, L. S. (2005). Interpersonal theory of personality disorders: The structural analysis of social behavior and interpersonal reconstructive therapy. In M. F. Lenzenweger & J. F. Clarkin (Eds.), *Major theories of personality disorder* (pp. 157–230). Guilford Press.

Benjamin, L. S. (2006). *Interpersonal reconstructive therapy: An integrative personality-based treatment for complex cases*. Guilford Press.

Benjamin, L. S. (2008). What is functional about functional autonomy? *Journal of Personality Assessment, 90*(5), 412–420. https://doi.org/10.1080/00223890802248596

Benjamin, L. S. (2018). *Interpersonal reconstructive therapy for anger, anxiety, and depression: It's about broken hearts, not broken brains*. American Psychological Association. https://doi.org/10.1037/0000090-000

Benjamin, L. S. (2022). A brief history of "me." In C. J. Hopwood (Ed.), *The evolution of personality assessment in the 21st century: Understanding the people who understand people*. Routledge. https://doi.org/10.4324/9781003036302

Benjamin, L. S. (2023). Die realität der endlichkeit von arbeit [The reality of the finiteness of work]. In B. Strauss & C. Spitzer (Eds.), *Psychotherapeuten und das altern [Psychotherapists and aging]* (pp. 235–237). Springer.

Benjamin, L. S., & Critchfield, K. L. (2010). An interpersonal perspective on therapy alliances and techniques. In J. C. Muran & J. P. Barber (Eds.), *The therapeutic alliance: An evidence-based guide to practice* (pp. 123–149). Guilford Press.

Benjamin, L. S., Critchfield, K. L., Karpiak, C. P., Smith, T. L., & Mestel, R. (2018). Using interpersonal reconstructive therapy to select effective interventions for comorbid, treatment-resistant, personality-disordered individuals. In W. J. Livesley & R. Larstone (Eds.), *Handbook of personality disorders: Theory, research, and treatment* (pp. 394–416). Guilford Press.

Benjamin, L. S., & Cushing, G. (2000). *Reference manual for coding social interactions in terms of structural analysis of social behavior*. Interpersonal Reconstructive Therapy Institute.

Benjamin, L. S., Rothweiler, J. C., & Critchfield, K. L. (2006). The use of structural analysis of social behavior (SASB) as an assessment tool. *Annual Review of Clinical Psychology, 2*(1), 83–109. https://doi.org/10.1146/annurev.clinpsy.2.022305.095337

Benjamin, L. S., Wamboldt, M. Z., & Critchfield, K. L. (2006). Defining relational disorders and identifying their connections to Axes I and II. In S. R. H. Beach, M. Z. Wamboldt, N. J. Kaslow, R. E. Heyman, M. B. First, L. G. Underwood,

& D. Reiss (Eds.), *Relational processes and DSM-V: Neuroscience, assessment, prevention, and treatment* (pp. 157–173). American Psychiatric Association.

Benjamin, L. S., & Wonderlich, S. A. (1994). Social perceptions and borderline personality disorder: The relation to mood disorders. *Journal of Abnormal Psychology, 103*(4), 610–624. https://doi.org/10.1037/0021-843X.103.4.610

Bennett, D., & Parry, G. (1998). The accuracy of reformulation in cognitive analytic therapy: A validation study. *Psychotherapy Research, 8*(1), 84–103. https://doi.org/10.1093/ptr/8.1.84

Beveridge, R. M., & Berg, C. A. (2007). Parent-adolescent collaboration: An interpersonal model for understanding optimal interactions. *Clinical Child and Family Psychology Review, 10*(1), 25–52. https://doi.org/10.1007/s10567-006-0015-z

Björck, C., Clinton, D., Sohlberg, S., Hällström, T., & Norring, C. (2003). Interpersonal profiles in eating disorders: Ratings of SASB self-image. *Psychology and Psychotherapy, 76*(Pt. 4), 337–349. https://doi.org/10.1348/147608303770584719

Bodlund, O., & Armelius, K. (1994). Self-image and personality traits in gender identity disorders: An empirical study. *Journal of Sex & Marital Therapy, 20*(4), 303–317. https://doi.org/10.1080/00926239408404380

Bowlby, J. (1969). *Attachment and loss: Vol. 1. Attachment.* Basic Books.

Bowman, M. (2018). Contributory factors of well-being in new mothers: An exploratory study. *Dissertations, 2014–2019*, 184. https://commons.lib.jmu.edu/diss201019/184

Brewin, C. R., Andrews, B., & Gotlib, I. H. (1993). Psychopathology and early experience: A reappraisal of retrospective reports. *Psychological Bulletin, 113*(1), 82–98. https://doi.org/10.1037/0033-2909.113.1.82

Canate, R. R. (2012). Change in group therapy: A grounded theory inquiry into group and interpersonal patterns in a community sample. *Theses and Dissertations*, 2986. https://scholarsarchive.byu.edu/etd/2986

Carr, J. L., & VanDeusen, K. M. (2002). The relationship between family of origin violence and dating violence in college men. *Journal of Interpersonal Violence, 17*(6), 630–646. https://doi.org/10.1177/0886260502017006003

Carson, R. C. (1969). *Interaction concepts of personality.* Routledge.

Chermack, S. T., & Walton, M. A. (1999). The relationship between family aggression history and expressed aggression among college males. *Aggressive Behavior, 25*(4), 255–267. https://doi.org/10.1002/(SICI)1098-2337(1999)25:4<255::AID-AB2>3.0.CO;2-U

Clarkin, J. F., Levy, K. N., Lenzenweger, M. F., & Kernberg, O. F. (2007). Evaluating three treatments for borderline personality disorder: A multiwave study. *American Journal of Psychiatry, 164*(6), 922–928. https://doi.org/10.1176/ajp.2007.164.6.922

Clarkin, J. F., Yeomans, F. E., & Kernberg, O. F. (1999). *Psychotherapy for borderline personality.* John Wiley & Sons.

Coady, N. F. (1991a). The association between client and therapist interpersonal processes and outcomes in psychodynamic psychotherapy. *Research on Social Work Practice, 1*(2), 122–138. https://doi.org/10.1177/104973159100100202

Coady, N. F. (1991b). The association between complex types of therapist interventions and outcomes in psychodynamic psychotherapy. *Research on Social Work Practice, 1*(3), 257–277. https://doi.org/10.1177/104973159100100303

Cohen, J. (1968). Weighted kappa: Nominal scale agreement with provision for scaled disagreement or partial credit. *Psychological Bulletin, 70*(4), 213–220. https://doi.org/10.1037/h0026256

Cole, P. M., Tamang, B. L., & Shrestha, S. (2006). Cultural variations in the socialization of young children's anger and shame. *Child Development, 77*(5), 1237–1251. https://doi.org/10.1111/j.1467-8624.2006.00931.x

Conroy, D. E. (2003). Representational models associated with fear of failure in adolescents and young adults. *Journal of Personality, 71*(5), 757–784. https://doi.org/10.1111/1467-6494.7105003

Conroy, D. E., & Pincus, A. L. (2006). A comparison of mean partialing and dual-hypothesis testing to evaluate stereotype effects when assessing profile similarity. *Journal of Personality Assessment, 86*(2), 142–149. https://doi.org/10.1207/s15327752jpa8602_03

Constantino, M. J. (2000). Interpersonal process in psychotherapy through the lens of the structural analysis of social behavior. *Applied & Preventive Psychology, 9*(3), 153–172. https://doi.org/10.1016/S0962-1849(05)80002-2

Critchfield, K. L. (2002). *An empirical analysis and initial taxonomy of patient reported relational patterns based on interpersonal case formulation* (UMI No. 3064849) [Doctoral dissertation, The University of Utah]. ProQuest. https://www.proquest.com/openview/05a148b7963fd7001ab1d57eb8657253/1?pq-origsite=gscholar&cbl=18750&diss=y

Critchfield, K. L., & Benjamin, L. S. (2008). Internalized representations of early interpersonal experience and adult relationships: A test of copy process theory in clinical and non-clinical settings. *Psychiatry: Interpersonal and Biological Processes, 71*(1), 71–92. https://doi.org/10.1521/psyc.2008.71.1.71

Critchfield, K. L., & Benjamin, L. S. (2010). Assessment of repeated relational patterns for individual cases using the SASB-based Intrex questionnaire. *Journal of Personality Assessment, 92*(6), 480–489. https://doi.org/10.1080/00223891.2010.513286

Critchfield, K. L., & Benjamin, L. S. (2016). *The Relational Cognitions and Affects Questionnaire (RCA-Q)*. Interpersonal Reconstructive Therapy Institute.

Critchfield, K. L., & Benjamin, L. S. (2024). *The "gift of love" as a mechanism of psychopathology and change in interpersonal reconstructive therapy for CORDS patients* [Manuscript submitted for publication]. Ferkauf Graduate School of Psychology, Yeshiva University.

Critchfield, K. L., Benjamin, L. S., & Levenick, K. (2015). Reliability, sensitivity, and specificity of case formulations for comorbid profiles in interpersonal reconstructive therapy: Addressing mechanisms of psychopathology. *Journal of Personality Disorders, 29*(4), 547–573. https://doi.org/10.1521/pedi.2015.29.4.547

Critchfield, K. L., Davis, M. J., Gunn, H. E., & Benjamin, L. S. (2008, June 18–21). *Measuring therapist adherence in interpersonal reconstructive therapy (IRT): Conceptual framework, reliability, and validity* [Poster presentation]. International Society for Psychotherapy Research, Barcelona, Spain.

Critchfield, K. L., Dobner-Pereira, J., Panizo, M., & Benjamin, L. S. (2019, August 8). The gift of love as a key mechanism of change in interpersonal reconstructive therapy. In L. S. Benjamin (Chair), *Effective psychotherapy using principles from attachment theory and developmental psychopathology* [Panel presentation]. American Psychological Association Annual Convention, Chicago, IL, United States.

Critchfield, K. L., Dobner-Pereira, J., & Stucker, E. (2021). The case of Sharon considered from the vantage point of interpersonal reconstructive therapy. *Pragmatic Case Studies in Psychotherapy, 17*(1), 42–62. https://doi.org/10.14713/pcsp.v17i1.2087

Critchfield, K. L., Henry, W. P., Castonguay, L. G., & Borkovec, T. D. (2007). Interpersonal process and outcome in variants of cognitive-behavioral psychotherapy. *Journal of Clinical Psychology, 63*(1), 31–51. https://doi.org/10.1002/jclp.20329

Critchfield, K. L., Karpiak, C., & Benjamin, L. S. (2011, June 29–July 2). *Copy process assessment and case formulation in interpersonal reconstructive therapy* [Paper presentation]. Society for Psychotherapy Research, Bern, Switzerland.

Critchfield, K. L., & Mackaronis, J. E. (2016). Use of empirically grounded relational principles to enhance clinical decision making. In J. J. Magnavita (Ed.), *Clinical decision making in mental health practice* (pp. 193–221). American Psychological Association. https://doi.org/10.1037/14711-008

Critchfield, K. L., Mackaronis, J. E., & Benjamin, L. S. (2017). Characterizing the integration of CBT and psychodynamic techniques in interpersonal reconstructive therapy for patients with severe and comorbid personality pathology. *Journal of Psychotherapy Integration, 27*(4), 460–475. https://doi.org/10.1037/int0000092

Critchfield, K. L., Mackaronis, J. E., Thapa, P., & Cechak, P. (2022). A brief overview of safety planning in interpersonal reconstructive therapy. *Psychotherapy, 59*(2), 168–173. https://doi.org/10.1037/pst0000415

Critchfield, K. L., Panizo, M. T., & Benjamin, L. S. (2019). Formulating key psychosocial mechanisms of psychopathology and change in interpersonal reconstructive therapy. In U. Kramer (Ed.), *Case formulation for personality disorders: Tailoring psychotherapy to the individual client* (pp. 181–201). Elsevier Academic Press. https://doi.org/10.1016/B978-0-12-813521-1.00010-2

Critchfield, K. L., Pempek, T. A., Stucker-Rozovsky, E., Dobner-Pereira, J., & Thapa, P. (2021, June 23–26). *Refining the Relational Cognitions and Affects Questionnaire (RCA-Q)* [Poster presentation]. Society for Psychotherapy Research 52nd Annual International Meeting.

Crits-Christoph, P., Gibbons, M. B. C., Temes, C. M., Elkin, I., & Gallop, R. (2010). Interpersonal accuracy of interventions and the outcome of cognitive and interpersonal therapies for depression. *Journal of Consulting and Clinical Psychology, 78*(3), 420–428. https://doi.org/10.1037/a0019549

Cushing, G. (2003). *Interpersonal origins of parenting among addicted and non-addicted mothers* (UMI No. 3084582) [Doctoral dissertation, The University of Utah]. ProQuest Dissertations Publishing. https://www.proquest.com/openview/5e48f0bf9e957e82beccff395dbe5cf0/1?pq-origsite=gscholar&cbl=18750&diss=y

Desai, S., Arias, I., Thompson, M. P., & Basile, K. C. (2002). Childhood victimization and subsequent adult revictimization assessed in a nationally representative sample of women and men. *Violence and Victims, 17*(6), 639–653. https://doi.org/10.1891/vivi.17.6.639.33725

Dobner-Pereira, J. (2021). Healing attachment wounds: Drama therapy within an interpersonal theoretical frame as a group treatment modality. *Dissertations, 2020–Current,* 40. https://commons.lib.jmu.edu/diss202029/40

Eastwick, P. W., Saigal, S. D., & Finkel, E. J. (2010). Smooth operating: A structural analysis of social behavior (SASB) perspective on initial romantic encounters. *Social Psychological and Personality Science, 1*(4), 344–352. https://doi.org/10.1177/1948550610373402

Elliott, R., Bohart, A. C., Watson, J. C., & Murphy, D. (2018). Therapist empathy and client outcome: An updated meta-analysis. *Psychotherapy, 55*(4), 399–410. https://doi.org/10.1037/pst0000175

Ellis, A. (1994). *Reason and emotion in psychotherapy* (Rev. ed.). Birch Lane.

Erickson, T. M., & Pincus, A. L. (2005). Using structural analysis of social behavior (SASB) measures of self- and social perception to give interpersonal meaning to symptoms: Anxiety as an exemplar. *Assessment, 12*(3), 243–254. https://doi.org/10.1177/1073191105276653

Essex, M. J., Klein, M. H., Lohr, M. J., & Benjamin, L. S. (1985). Intimacy and depression in older women. *Psychiatry, 48*(2), 159–178. https://doi.org/10.1080/00332747.1985.11024277

Eubanks, C. F., Lubitz, J., Muran, J. C., & Safran, J. D. (2019). Rupture Resolution Rating System (3RS): Development and validation. *Psychotherapy Research, 29*(3), 306–319. https://doi.org/10.1080/10503307.2018.1552034

First, M. B., Gibbon, M., Spitzer, R. L., Williams, J. B. W., & Benjamin, L. S. (1996). *Structured Clinical Interview for DSM-IV Axis II Personality Disorders (SCID-II).* American Psychiatric Press.

Florsheim, P., & Moore, D. R. (2008). Observing differences between healthy and unhealthy adolescent romantic relationships: Substance abuse and interpersonal process. *Journal of Adolescence, 31*(6), 795–814. https://doi.org/10.1016/j.adolescence.2007.09.005

Forsén Mantilla, E., Clinton, D., & Birgegård, A. (2019). The unsafe haven: Eating disorders as attachment relationships. *Psychology and Psychotherapy, 92*(3), 379–393. https://doi.org/10.1111/papt.12184

Forsén Mantilla, E., Norring, C., & Birgegård, A. (2019). Self-image and 12-month outcome in females with eating disorders: Extending previous findings. *Journal of Eating Disorders, 7*(1), 15. https://doi.org/10.1186/s40337-019-0247-1

Freedman, M. B., Leary, T. F., Ossorio, A. G., & Goffey, H. S. (1951). The interpersonal dimension of personality. *Journal of Personality, 20*(2), 143–161. https://doi.org/10.1111/j.1467-6494.1951.tb01518.x

Frick, E., & Halevy, C. (2002). Is structural analysis of social behavior (SASB) suitable for the content analysis of dreams? *Sleep and Hypnosis, 4*(2), 58–69.

Fromm, L. M. (1981). Parental responses to anorexia nervosa adolescents' attempts at individuation [ProQuest Information & Learning]. *Dissertation Abstracts International: Section A. Humanities and Social Sciences, 42*(3-A), 1007.

Giesen-Bloo, J., van Dyck, R., Spinhoven, P., van Tilburg, W., Dirksen, C., van Asselt, T., Kremers, I., Nadort, M., & Arntz, A. (2006). Outpatient psychotherapy for borderline personality disorder: Randomized trial of schema-focused therapy vs transference-focused psychotherapy. *Archives of General Psychiatry, 63*(6), 649–658. https://doi.org/10.1001/archpsyc.63.6.649

Gladstone, G. L., Parker, G. B., Mitchell, P. B., Malhi, G. S., Wilhelm, K., & Austin, M. P. (2004). Implications of childhood trauma for depressed women: An analysis of pathways from childhood sexual abuse to deliberate self-harm and revictimization. *American Journal of Psychiatry, 161*(8), 1417–1425. https://doi.org/10.1176/appi.ajp.161.8.1417

Goedken, J. R. (2004). *Representation of self and important others in depression: Exploration of unique and qualitative distinctions using structural analysis of social behavior* [Unpublished master's thesis]. University of Utah.

Goldman, R., & Greenberg, L. S. (1997). Case formulation in process-experiential therapy. In T. D. Eells (Ed.), *Handbook of psychotherapy case formulation* (pp. 402–429). Guilford Press.

Gorlin, E. I., & Békés, V. (2021). Agency via awareness: A unifying meta-process in psychotherapy. *Frontiers in Psychology, 12,* 698655. https://doi.org/10.3389/fpsyg.2021.698655

Graham, D. T., Lundy, R. M., Benjamin, L. S., Kabler, J. D., Lewis, W. C., Kunish, N. O., & Graham, F. K. (1962). Specific attitudes in initial interviews with patients having different "psychosomatic" diseases. *Psychosomatic Medicine, 24*(3), 257–266. https://doi.org/10.1097/00006842-196205000-00007

Greenberg, J. R., & Mitchell, S. A. (1983). *Object relations in psychoanalytic theory.* Harvard University Press.

Greenberg, L. S. (1979). Resolving splits: Use of the two chair technique. *Psychotherapy, 16*(3), 316–324. https://doi.org/10.1037/h0085895

Greenberg, L. S. (2017). *Emotion-focused therapy* (Rev. ed.). American Psychological Association. https://doi.org/10.1037/15971-000

Greenberg, L. S., & Foerster, F. S. (1996). Task analysis exemplified: The process of resolving unfinished business. *Journal of Consulting and Clinical Psychology, 64*(3), 439–446. https://doi.org/10.1037/0022-006X.64.3.439

Greenberg, L. S., Ford, C. L., Alden, L. S., & Johnson, S. M. (1993). In-session change in emotionally focused therapy. *Journal of Consulting and Clinical Psychology, 61*(1), 78–84. https://doi.org/10.1037/0022-006X.61.1.78

Greenberg, L. S., & Malcolm, W. (2002). Resolving unfinished business: Relating process to outcome. *Journal of Consulting and Clinical Psychology, 70*(2), 406–416. https://doi.org/10.1037/0022-006X.70.2.406

Gunn, H. E., Critchfield, K. L., Mackaronis, J. E., Rau, H. K., Cribbet, M. R., Troxel, W. M., & Williams, P. G. (2017). Affiliative interpersonal behaviors during stress are associated with sleep quality and presleep arousal in young, healthy adults. *Sleep Health, 3*(2), 98–101. https://doi.org/10.1016/j.sleh.2016.12.004

Gurvits, I. G., Koenigsberg, H. W., & Siever, L. J. (2000). Neurotransmitter dysfunction in patients with borderline personality disorder. *Psychiatric Clinics of North America, 23*(1), 27–40. https://doi.org/10.1016/S0193-953X(05)70141-6

Guttman, L. (1954). A new approach to factor analysis: The radex. In P. F. Lazarsfeld (Ed.), *Mathematical thinking in the social sciences* (pp. 258–348). Free Press.

Hara, K. M., Westra, H. A., Coyne, A. E., Di Bartolomeo, A. A., Constantino, M. J., & Antony, M. M. (2022). Therapist affiliation and hostility in cognitive-behavioral therapy with and without motivational interviewing for severe generalized anxiety disorder. *Psychotherapy Research, 32*(5), 598–610. https://doi.org/10.1080/10503307.2021.2001069

Harder, S. (2006). Self-image and outcome in first-episode psychosis. *Clinical Psychology & Psychotherapy, 13*(5), 285–296. https://doi.org/10.1002/cpp.498

Harlow, H. F. (1958). The nature of love. *American Psychologist, 13*(12), 673–685. https://doi.org/10.1037/h0047884

Harrist, R. S., Quintana, S. M., Strupp, H. H., & Henry, W. P. (1994). Internalization of interpersonal process in time-limited dynamic psychotherapy. *Psychotherapy, 31*(1), 49–57. https://doi.org/10.1037/0033-3204.31.1.49

Harvell-Bowman, L. A., Critchfield, K. L., Ndzana, F., Stucker, E., Yocca, C., Wilgus, K., Hurst, A., & Sullivan, K. (2022). Of love and death: Death anxiety, attachment, and suicide as experienced by college students. *Omega: Journal of Death and Dying.* Advance online publication. https://doi.org/10.1177/00302228221100636

Heider, F. (1958). *The psychology of interpersonal relations.* John Wiley & Sons. https://doi.org/10.1037/10628-000

Henry, W. P. (1996). Structural analysis of social behavior as a common metric for programmatic psychopathology and psychotherapy research. *Journal of Consulting and Clinical Psychology, 64*(6), 1263–1275. https://doi.org/10.1037/0022-006X.64.6.1263

Henry, W. P. (1997). Interpersonal case formulation: Describing and explaining interpersonal patterns using the structural analysis of social behavior. In T. D. Eells (Ed.), *Handbook of psychotherapy case formulation* (pp. 223–259). Guilford Press.

Henry, W. P., Schacht, T. E., & Strupp, H. H. (1986). Structural analysis of social behavior: Application to a study of interpersonal process in differential psychotherapeutic outcome. *Journal of Consulting and Clinical Psychology, 54*(1), 27–31. https://doi.org/10.1037/0022-006X.54.1.27

Henry, W. P., Schacht, T. E., & Strupp, H. H. (1990). Patient and therapist introject, interpersonal process, and differential psychotherapy outcome. *Journal of Consulting and Clinical Psychology, 58*(6), 768–774. https://doi.org/10.1037/0022-006X.58.6.768

272 • *References*

Heyman, R. E., & Slep, A. M. S. (2002). Do child abuse and interparental violence lead to adulthood family violence? *Journal of Marriage and Family, 64*(4), 864–870. https://doi.org/10.1111/j.1741-3737.2002.00864.x

Higgins, D. J., & McCabe, M. P. (2000). Multi-type maltreatment and the long-term adjustment of adults. *Child Abuse Review, 9*(1), 6–18. https://doi.org/10.1002/(SICI)1099-0852(200001/02)9:1<6::AID-CAR579>3.0.CO;2-W

Hill, C. E. (1989). *Therapist techniques and client outcomes: Eight cases of brief psychotherapy*. Sage.

Hilliard, R. B., Henry, W. P., & Strupp, H. H. (2000). An interpersonal model of psychotherapy: Linking patient and therapist developmental history, therapeutic process, and types of outcome. *Journal of Consulting and Clinical Psychology, 68*(1), 125–133. https://doi.org/10.1037/0022-006X.68.1.125

Horowitz, L. M. (2004). *Interpersonal foundations of psychopathology*. American Psychological Association. https://doi.org/10.1037/10727-000

Humes, D. L., & Humphrey, L. L. (1994). A multimethod analysis of families with a polydrug-dependent or normal adolescent daughter. *Journal of Abnormal Psychology, 103*(4), 676–685. https://doi.org/10.1037/0021-843X.103.4.676

Humphrey, L. L., & Benjamin, L. S. (1986). Using structural analysis of social behavior to assess critical but elusive family processes. A new solution to an old problem. *American Psychologist, 41*(9), 979–989. https://doi.org/10.1037/0003-066X.41.9.979

Ichiyama, M. A., Zucker, R. A., Fitzgerald, H. E., & Bingham, C. R. (1996). Articulating subtype differences in self and relational experience among alcoholic men using structural analysis of social behavior. *Journal of Consulting and Clinical Psychology, 64*(6), 1245–1254. https://doi.org/10.1037/0022-006X.64.6.1245

Jeanneau, M., & Armelius, K. (2000). Self-image and burnout in psychiatric staff. *Journal of Psychiatric and Mental Health Nursing, 7*(5), 399–406. https://doi.org/10.1046/j.1365-2850.2000.00321.x

Jørgensen, C., Hougaard, E., Rosenbaum, B., Valbak, K., & Rehfeld, E. (2000). The dynamic assessment interview (DAI), interpersonal process measured by structural analysis of social behavior (SASB) and therapeutic outcome. *Psychotherapy Research, 10*(2), 181–195. https://doi.org/10.1093/ptr/10.2.181

Karpiak, C., Critchfield, K. L., & Benjamin, L. S. (2011, June 29–July 2). *Empathy, adherence, and outcome in interpersonal reconstructive therapy with treatment-resistant patients* [Paper presentation]. Society for Psychotherapy Research, Bern, Switzerland.

Karpiak, C. P., & Benjamin, L. S. (2004). Therapist affirmation and the process and outcome of psychotherapy: Two sequential analytic studies. *Journal of Clinical Psychology, 60*(6), 659–676. https://doi.org/10.1002/jclp.10248

Kaslow, N. J., Wamboldt, F. S., Wamboldt, M. Z., Anderson, R. B., & Benjamin, L. S. (1989). Interpersonal deadlock and the suicidal adolescent: An empirically based hypothesis. *American Journal of Family Therapy, 17*(3), 195–207. https://doi.org/10.1080/01926188908250767

Kernberg, O. F. (1984). *Severe personality disorders: Psychotherapeutic strategies*. Yale University.

Kiesler, D. J. (1983). The 1982 Interpersonal Circle: A taxonomy for complementarity in human transactions. *Psychological Review, 90*(3), 185–214. https://doi.org/10.1037/0033-295X.90.3.185

Kiesler, D. J. (1996). *Contemporary interpersonal theory and research: Personality, psychopathology, and psychotherapy*. John Wiley & Sons.

Klein, M. H., Wonderlich, S. A., & Crosby, R. (2001). Self-concept correlates of the personality disorders. *Journal of Personality Disorders, 15*(2), 150–156. https://doi.org/10.1521/pedi.15.2.150.19214

Knobloch-Fedders, L. M., Caska-Wallace, C., Smith, T. W., & Renshaw, K. (2017). Battling on the home front: Posttraumatic stress disorder and conflict behavior among military couples. *Behavior Therapy, 48*(2), 247–261. https://doi.org/10.1016/j.beth.2016.08.014

Knobloch-Fedders, L. M., Critchfield, K. L., Boisson, T., Woods, N., Bitman, R., & Durbin, C. E. (2014). Depression, relationship quality, and couples' demand/withdraw and demand/submit sequential interactions. *Journal of Counseling Psychology, 61*(2), 264–279. https://doi.org/10.1037/a0035241

Knobloch-Fedders, L. M., Critchfield, K. L., & Staab, E. M. (2017). Informative disagreements: Associations between relationship distress, depression, and discrepancy in interpersonal perception within couples. *Family Process, 56*(2), 459–475. https://doi.org/10.1111/famp.12201

Laing, R. D., Phillipson, H., & Lee, A. R. (1966). *Interpersonal perception: A theory and a method of research*. Springer.

Leary, T. (1957). *Interpersonal diagnosis of personality: A functional theory and methodology for personality evaluation*. Ronald Press.

Leppmann, W. (1984). *Rilke: A life*. Fromm.

Levy, K. N., Meehan, K. B., Kelly, K. M., Reynoso, J. S., Weber, M., Clarkin, J. F., & Kernberg, O. F. (2006). Change in attachment patterns and reflective function in a randomized control trial of transference-focused psychotherapy for borderline personality disorder. *Journal of Consulting and Clinical Psychology, 74*(6), 1027–1040. https://doi.org/10.1037/0022-006X.74.6.1027

Linehan, M. M. (1993). *Cognitive-behavioral treatment of borderline personality disorder*. Guilford Press.

Lorr, M., Bishop, P. F., & McNair, D. M. (1965). Interpersonal types among psychiatric patients. *Journal of Abnormal Psychology, 70*(6), 468–472. https://doi.org/10.1037/h0022766

Lorr, M., & Strack, S. (1999). A study of Benjamin's eight-facet structural analysis of social behavior (SASB) model. *Journal of Clinical Psychology, 55*(2), 207–215. https://doi.org/10.1002/(SICI)1097-4679(199902)55:2<207::AID-JCLP8>3.0.CO;2-O

Luborsky, L. (1976). Helping alliance in psychotherapy. In J. L. Cleghhorn (Ed.), *Successful psychotherapy* (pp. 92–116). Brunner/Mazel.

Luborsky, L., & Crits-Christoph, P. (1998). *Understanding transference: The core conflictual relationship theme method* (2nd ed.). American Psychological Association. https://doi.org/10.1037/10250-000

Lynch, T. R., Chapman, A. L., Rosenthal, M. Z., Kuo, J. R., & Linehan, M. M. (2006). Mechanisms of change in dialectical behavior therapy: Theoretical and empirical observations. *Journal of Clinical Psychology, 62*(4), 459–480. https://doi.org/10.1002/jclp.20243

MacDonald, J., Cartwright, A., & Brown, G. (2007). A quantitative and qualitative exploration of client-therapist interaction and engagement in treatment in an alcohol service. *Psychology and Psychotherapy, 80*(2), 247–268. https://doi.org/10.1348/147608306X156553

MacKenzie, K. R. (1996). *Time-managed group psychotherapy: Effective clinical applications.* American Psychiatric Association.

Maramba, G. J. K. (2005). *Early alliance and dropout* [Doctoral dissertation, Pennsylvania State University]. ProQuest Dissertations Publishing.

Marble, A., Høglend, P., & Ulberg, R. (2011). Change in self-protection and symptoms after dynamic psychotherapy: The influence of pretreatment motivation. *Journal of Clinical Psychology, 67*(4), 355–367. https://doi.org/10.1002/jclp.20771

McGonigle, M. M., Smith, T. W., Benjamin, L. S., & Turner, C. W. (1993). Hostility and nonshared family environment: A study of monozygotic twins. *Journal of Research in Personality, 27*(1), 23–34. https://doi.org/10.1006/jrpe.1993.1003

McLemore, C. W., & Benjamin, L. S. (1979). Whatever happened to interpersonal diagnosis? A psychosocial alternative to *DSM-III. American Psychologist, 34*(1), 17–34. https://doi.org/10.1037/0003-066X.34.1.17

Messer, S. B. (2021). How do we decide which of two case formulations is correct? Commentary on Westerman and Critchfield et al. *Pragmatic Case Studies in Psychotherapy, 17*(1), 104–108. https://doi.org/10.14713/pcsp.v17i1.2090

Moe, B. K., King, A. R., & Bailly, M. D. (2004). Retrospective accounts of recurrent parental physical abuse as a predictor of adult laboratory-induced aggression. *Aggressive Behavior, 30*(3), 217–228. https://doi.org/10.1002/ab.20019

Monell, E., Clinton, D., & Birgegård, A. (2020). Self-directed behaviors differentially explain associations between emotion dysregulation and eating disorder psychopathology in patients with or without objective binge-eating. *Journal of Eating Disorders, 8*(1), 17. https://doi.org/10.1186/s40337-020-00294-4

Muran, J. C., Safran, J. D., Eubanks, C. F., & Gorman, B. S. (2018). The effect of alliance-focused training on a cognitive-behavioral therapy for personality disorders. *Journal of Consulting and Clinical Psychology, 86*(4), 384–397. https://doi.org/10.1037/ccp0000284

Murray, H. A. (1938). *Explorations in personality.* Oxford University Press.

Ness, E., Dahl, H.-S. J., Critchfield, K. L., & Ulberg, R. (2018). Exploring in-session process with qualitative and quantitative methods in psychotherapy with an adolescent. *Journal of Infant, Child, and Adolescent Psychotherapy, 17*(4), 310–327. https://doi.org/10.1080/15289168.2018.1526021

Noll, J. G., Horowitz, L. A., Bonanno, G. A., Trickett, P. K., & Putnam, F. W. (2003). Revictimization and self-harm in females who experienced childhood sexual abuse: Results from a prospective study. *Journal of Interpersonal Violence, 18*(12), 1452–1471. https://doi.org/10.1177/0886260503258035

Norcross, J. C., & Lambert, M. J. (Eds.). (2019). *Psychotherapy relationships that work: Vol. 1. Evidence-based therapist contributions* (3rd ed.). Oxford Academic. https://doi.org/10.1093/med-psych/9780190843953.001.0001

Paddock, J. R., Terranova, S., & Giles, L. (2001). SASB goes Hollywood: Teaching personality theories through movies. *Teaching of Psychology, 28*(2), 117–121. https://doi.org/10.1207/S15328023TOP2802_11

Paivio, S. C., & Greenberg, L. S. (1995). Resolving "unfinished business": Efficacy of experiential therapy using empty-chair dialogue. *Journal of Consulting and Clinical Psychology, 63*(3), 419–425. https://doi.org/10.1037/0022-006X.63.3.419

Paivio, S. C., & Nieuwenhuis, J. A. (2001). Efficacy of emotion focused therapy for adult survivors of child abuse: A preliminary study. *Journal of Traumatic Stress, 14*(1), 115–133. https://doi.org/10.1023/A:1007891716593

Panizo Jansana, M. T. (2020). An interpersonal view of personality disorders. *Dissertations, 2020–Current, 5*. https://commons.lib.jmu.edu/diss202029/5

Park, J. H. (2005). A validation study of the structural analysis of affective behavior: Further development and empirical analysis. *Dissertation Abstracts International: Section B. The Sciences and Engineering, 65*(10-B), 5418.

Parker, G. (1990). The parental bonding instrument: A decade of research. *Social Psychiatry and Psychiatric Epidemiology, 25*(6), 281–282. https://doi.org/10.1007/BF00782881

Parker, G., Tupling, H., & Brown, L. B. (1979). A parental bonding instrument. *British Journal of Medical Psychology, 52*(1), 1–10. https://doi.org/10.1111/j.2044-8341.1979.tb02487.x

Pincus, A. L., Dickinson, K. A., Schut, A. J., Castonguay, L. G., & Bedics, J. (1999). Integrating interpersonal assessment and adult attachment using SASB. *European Journal of Psychological Assessment, 15*(3), 206–220. https://doi.org/10.1027//1015-5759.15.3.206

Pincus, A. L., Gurtman, M. B., & Ruiz, M. A. (1998). Structural analysis of social behavior (SASB): Circumplex analyses and structural relations with the interpersonal circle and the five-factor model of personality. *Journal of Personality and Social Psychology, 74*(6), 1629–1645. https://doi.org/10.1037/0022-3514.74.6.1629

Plutchik, R., & Conte, H. R. (Eds.). (1997). *Circumplex models of personality and emotions*. American Psychological Association. https://doi.org/10.1037/10261-000

Prochaska, J. O., & DiClemente, C. C. (1983). Stages and processes of self-change of smoking: Toward an integrative model of change. *Journal of Consulting* and *Clinical Psychology, 51*(3), 390–395. https://doi.org/10.1037/0022-006X.51.3.390

Quintana, S. M., & Meara, N. M. (1990). Internalization of therapeutic relationships in short-term psychotherapy. *Journal of Counseling Psychology, 37*(2), 123–130. https://doi.org/10.1037/0022-0167.37.2.123

Ruiz, M. A., Pincus, A. L., & Bedics, J. B. (1999). Using the structural analysis of social behavior (SASB) to differentiate young adults with borderline personality disorder features. *Journal of Personality Disorders, 13*(2), 187–198. https://doi.org/10.1521/pedi.1999.13.2.187

Safran, J. D., Muran, J. C., Samstag, L. W., & Stevens, C. (2002). Repairing alliance ruptures. In J. C. Norcross (Ed.), *Psychotherapy relationships that work: Therapist contributions and responsiveness to patients* (pp. 235–254). Oxford University Press.

Schaaf, K. K., & McCanne, T. R. (1998). Relationship of childhood sexual, physical, and combined sexual and physical abuse to adult victimization and posttraumatic stress disorder. *Child Abuse & Neglect, 22*(11), 1119–1133. https://doi.org/10.1016/S0145-2134(98)00090-8

Schacht, T. E., & Henry, W. P. (1994). Modeling recurrent patterns of interpersonal relationship with structural equation analysis of social behavior: The SASB-CMP. *Psychotherapy Research, 4*(3–4), 208–221. https://doi.org/10.1080/10503309412331334042

Schaefer, E. S. (1959). A circumplex model for maternal behavior. *Journal of Abnormal and Social Psychology, 59*(2), 226–235. https://doi.org/10.1037/h0041114

Schaefer, E. S. (1965). A configurational analysis of children's reports of parent behavior. *Journal of Consulting Psychology, 29*(6), 552–557. https://doi.org/10.1037/h0022702

Schut, A. J., Castonguay, L. G., Flanagan, K. M., Yamasaki, A. S., Barber, J. P., Bedics, J. D., & Smith, T. L. (2005). Therapist interpretation, patient–therapist interpersonal process, and outcome in psychodynamic psychotherapy for avoidant personality disorder. *Psychotherapy, 42*(4), 494–511. https://doi.org/10.1037/0033-3204.42.4.494

Shearin, E. N., & Linehan, M. M. (1992). Patient–therapist ratings and relationship to progress in dialectical behavior therapy for borderline personality disorder. *Behavior Therapy, 23*(4), 730–741. https://doi.org/10.1016/S0005-7894(05)80232-1

Shrout, P. E., & Fleiss, J. L. (1979). Intraclass correlations: Uses in assessing rater reliability. *Psychological Bulletin, 86*(2), 420–428. https://doi.org/10.1037/0033-2909.86.2.420

Skowron, E. A., Loken, E., Gatzke-Kopp, L. M., Cipriano-Essel, E. A., Woehrle, P. L., Van Epps, J. J., Gowda, A., & Ammerman, R. T. (2011). Mapping cardiac physiology and parenting processes in maltreating mother–child dyads. *Journal of Family Psychology, 25*(5), 663–674. https://doi.org/10.1037/a0024528

Smetana, J. G. (2017). Current research on parenting styles, dimensions, and beliefs. *Current Opinion in Psychology, 15*, 19–25. https://doi.org/10.1016/j.copsyc.2017.02.012

Smith, B. E. (2018). An exploration of the collegiate coach–athlete relationship and its impact on female athlete attitudes and behaviors toward disordered eating and body image. *Dissertations, 2014–2019*, 186. https://commons.lib.jmu.edu/diss201019/186

Smith, T. L., Klein, M. H., & Benjamin, L. S. (2003). Validation of the Wisconsin Personality Disorders Inventory-IV with the SCID-II. *Journal of Personality Disorders, 17*(3), 173–187. https://doi.org/10.1521/pedi.17.3.173.22150

Smith, T. W., Baron, C. E., Deits-Lebehn, C., Uchino, B. N., & Berg, C. A. (2020). Is it me or you? Marital conflict behavior and blood pressure reactivity. *Journal of Family Psychology, 34*(4), 503–508. https://doi.org/10.1037/fam0000624

Smith, T. W., Baron, C. E., & Grove, J. L. (2014). Personality, emotional adjustment, and cardiovascular risk: Marriage as a mechanism. *Journal of Personality, 82*(6), 502–514. https://doi.org/10.1111/jopy.12074

Soenens, B., Elliot, A. J., Goossens, L., Vansteenkiste, M., Luyten, P., & Duriez, B. (2005). The intergenerational transmission of perfectionism: Parents' psychological control as an intervening variable. *Journal of Family Psychology, 19*(3), 358–366. https://doi.org/10.1037/0893-3200.19.3.358

Stein, D. J. (2021). *Problems of living: Perspectives from philosophy, psychiatry, and cognitive-affective science.* Elsevier Academic Press.

Stern, R. S., King, A. A., & Diamond, G. (2023). Repairing attachment in families with depressed adolescents: A task analysis. *Journal of Clinical Psychology, 79*(1), 201–209. https://doi.org/10.1002/jclp.23399

Strupp, H. H., Schacht, T. E., & Henry, W. P. (1988). Problem–treatment–outcome congruence: A principle whose time has come. In H. Dahl, H. Kächele, & H. Thomä (Eds.), *Psychoanalytic process research strategies* (pp. 1–14). Springer. https://doi.org/10.1007/978-3-642-74265-1_1

Stucker, E. I., Critchfield, K. L., Bonilla, K., Mischinski, M., & Benjamin, L. S. (2020, June 17–20). Differential therapist responsiveness to attachment-based mechanisms of change in interpersonal reconstructive therapy. In K. L. Critchfield (Organizer), *Relational patterns in psychopathology and its treatment: Studies using SASB as a clarifying lens* [Poster presentation]. International Society for Psychotherapy Research, Amherst, MA, United States.

Stucker-Rozovsky, E. (2022). Operationalizing the gift of love (GOL) in interpersonal reconstructive therapy (IRT): An examination of the role of meaning reconstruction in therapeutic change. *Dissertations, 2020–Current*, 64. https://commons.lib.jmu.edu/diss202029/64

Sullivan, H. S. (1938). Introduction to the study of interpersonal relations: The data of psychiatry. *Psychiatry, 1*(1), 121–134. https://doi.org/10.1080/00332747.1938.11022177

Sullivan, H. S. (1939). A note on formulating the relationship of the individual and the group. *American Journal of Sociology, 44*(6), 932–937. https://doi.org/10.1086/218180

Sullivan, H. S. (1940). *Conceptions of modern psychiatry* (2nd ed.). W. W. Norton & Co. https://doi.org/10.1080/00332747.1940.11022272

Sullivan, H. S. (1953). *The interpersonal theory of psychiatry.* W. W. Norton & Co.

Swann, W. B., Jr. (1997). The trouble with change: Self-verification and allegiance to the self. *Psychological Science, 8*(3), 177–180. https://doi.org/10.1111/j.1467-9280.1997.tb00407.x

Tasca, G. A., Foot, M., Leite, C., Maxwell, H., Balfour, L., & Bissada, H. (2011). Interpersonal processes in psychodynamic-interpersonal and cognitive behavioral group therapy: A systematic case study of two groups. *Psychotherapy, 48*(3), 260–273. https://doi.org/10.1037/a0023928

Teti, D. M., Heaton, N., Benjamin, L. S., & Gelfand, D. M. (1995, May 29). Quality of attachment and caregiving among depressed mother–child dyads: Strange situation classifications and the SASB coding system. In S. Petrovich (Chair), *Patterns of early socialization: Behavioral ecology of attachment* [Paper presentation]. Society for Applied Behavioral Analysis Annual Meeting, Washington, DC, United States.

Thomas, N., McLeod, H. J., & Brewin, C. R. (2009). Interpersonal complementarity in responses to auditory hallucinations in psychosis. *British Journal of Clinical Psychology, 48*(4), 411–424. https://doi.org/10.1348/014466509X411937

Tscheulin, D., & Glossner, A. (1993). Die Deutsche übertragung der INTREX "longform questionnaires": Validität und auswertungsgrundlagen der SASB-fragebogenmethode [The German transmission of the INTREX "longform questionnaires": Validity and evaluation principles of the SASB questionnaire method]. In W. Tress (Ed.), *SASB: Die strukturale analyse sozialen verhaltens: Ein arbeitsbuch für forschung, praxis und weiterbildung in der psychotherapie* [SASB: The structural analysis of social behavior: A workbook for research, practice and further training in psychotherapy] (pp. 123–155). CIP-Medien.

Ulberg, R., Amlo, S., Critchfield, K. L., Marble, A., & Høglend, P. (2014). Transference interventions and the process between therapist and patient. *Psychotherapy, 51*(2), 258–269. https://doi.org/10.1037/a0034708

Ulberg, R., Høglend, P., Marble, A., & Sørbye, Ø. (2009). From submission to autonomy: Approaching independent decision making: A single-case study in a randomized, controlled study of long-term effects of dynamic psychotherapy. *American Journal of Psychotherapy, 63*(3), 227–243. https://doi.org/10.1176/appi.psychotherapy.2009.63.3.227

Vespa, A., Spatuzzi, R., Fabbietti, P., Penna, M., & Giulietti, M. V. (2021). Association between care burden, depression and personality traits in Alzheimer's caregiver: A pilot study. *PLOS ONE, 16*(9), e0251813. https://doi.org/10.1371/journal.pone.0251813

Vespa, A., Spatuzzi, R., Merico, F., Ottaviani, M., Fabbietti, P., Meloni, C., Raucci, L., Ricciuti, M., Bilancia, D., Pelliccioni, G., & Giulietti, M. V. (2018). Spiritual well-being associated with personality traits and quality of life in family caregivers of cancer patients. *Supportive Care in Cancer, 26*(8), 2633–2640. https://doi.org/10.1007/s00520-018-4107-3

Vittengl, J. R., Clark, L. A., & Jarrett, R. B. (2004). Self-directed affiliation and autonomy across acute and continuation phase cognitive therapy for recurrent depression. *Journal of Personality Assessment, 83*(3), 235–247. https://doi.org/10.1207/s15327752jpa8303_07

von der Lippe, A. L., Monsen, J. T., Rønnestad, M. H., & Eilertsen, D. E. (2008). Treatment failure in psychotherapy: The pull of hostility. *Psychotherapy Research, 18*(4), 420–432. https://doi.org/10.1080/10503300701810793

Walker-Barnes, C. J., & Mason, C. A. (2001). Ethnic differences in the effect of parenting on gang involvement and gang delinquency: A longitudinal, hierarchical linear modeling perspective. *Child Development, 72*(6), 1814–1831. https://doi.org/10.1111/1467-8624.00380

Westerman, M. A. (2005). What is interpersonal behavior? A post-cartesian approach to problematic interpersonal patterns and psychotherapy process. *Review of General Psychology, 9*(1), 16–34. https://doi.org/10.1037/1089-2680.9.1.16

Westerman, M. A. (2021). The case of Sharon considered from the vantage point of interpersonal defense theory. *Pragmatic Case Studies in Psychotherapy, 17*(1), 19–41. https://doi.org/10.14713/pcsp.v17i1.2086

Westerman, M. A., & Muran, J. C. (2017). Investigating an approach to the alliance based on interpersonal defense theory. *Psychotherapy Research, 27*(5), 620–641. https://doi.org/10.1080/10503307.2016.1152407

Wiggins, J. S. (1979). A psychological taxonomy of trait-descriptive terms: The interpersonal domain. *Journal of Personality and Social Psychology, 37*(3), 395–412. https://doi.org/10.1037/0022-3514.37.3.395

Wiggins, J. S., Trapnell, P., & Phillips, N. (1988). Psychometric and geometric characteristics of the Revised Interpersonal Adjective Scales (IAS-R). *Multivariate Behavioral Research, 23*(4), 517–530. https://doi.org/10.1207/s15327906mbr2304_8

Williams, D. C., & Levitt, H. M. (2007). Principles for facilitating agency in psychotherapy. *Psychotherapy Research, 17*(1), 66–82. https://doi.org/10.1080/10503300500469098

Woehrle, P. L., Critchfield, K. L., Anolik, S., Bobal, C., Pempek, T. A., & Skowron, E. A. (2023). Multigenerational patterns of parenting-at-risk: A test of interpersonal specificity using copy process theory. *Journal of Clinical Psychology, 79*(1), 186–200. https://doi.org/10.1002/jclp.23412

Wonderlich, S., Klein, M. H., & Council, J. R. (1996). Relationship of social perceptions and self-concept in bulimia nervosa. *Journal of Consulting and*

*Clinical Psychology, 64*(6), 1231–1237. https://doi.org/10.1037/0022-006X. 64.6.1231

Wong, K., & Pos, A. E. (2014). Interpersonal processes affecting early alliance formation in experiential therapy for depression. *Psychotherapy Research, 24*(1), 1–11. https://doi.org/10.1080/10503307.2012.708794

Young, J. E., Klosko, J. S., & Weishaar, M. E. (2003). *Schema therapy: A practitioner's guide*. Guilford Press.

Zahn, B. S., Zehrung, D. L., & Russo-Innamorato, L. (2010). Cognitive interventions in primary care. In R. A. DiTomasso, B. A. Golden, & H. Morris (Eds.), *Handbook of cognitive behavioral approaches in primary care* (pp. 223–246). Springer.

Zinbarg, R. E., Barlow, D. H., Brown, T. A., & Hertz, R. M. (1992). Cognitive-behavioral approaches to the nature and treatment of anxiety disorders. *Annual Review of Psychology, 43*(1), 235–267. https://doi.org/10.1146/annurev.ps. 43.020192.001315

# Index

## A

**Active love**, 41, 64, 94, 169, 208–209
*Active Self-Love,* 44
Adherence, to IRT, 259
Affective behavior models, 56–58
Affiliation, 12, 17, 25, 27, 64–66, 85, 168
**Affirm**, 41, 74, 169, 172–174, 201–205
Affirmation, therapist, 108
AG (attachment group), 52
Aggression, 12
Alexander, F., 223
Alienation, 105–106
Alliance ruptures, 71, 212
American Psychological Association (APA), 71
Analysis of interpersonal narratives, 131
Analysis of sequences, 79
Anger, 121, 169, 187, 255
Antithesis (predictive principle), 49, 51–52
Anxiety and anxiety disorders, 22, 121, 168, 169, 205
APA (American Psychological Association), 71
Applications, process-experiential, 113–117
Attachment, 120, 125, 127
Attachment figures, internalized, 127, 217, 249. *See also* Family in the head; IPIRs; Key figures
Attachment group (AG), 52
**Attack**, 42, 69–70, 104, 182
Attack (ATK) pattern coefficient, 85–86
Autonomy, 15–16, 19, 85, 168

## B

Baseline for behavior, 52–56
Beck, A. T., 103–105

Beck Depression Inventory, 242
Bedics, J. D., 107–108, 204
Behavioral genetics, 22
Behaviors
  baseline for, 52–56
  capture of, 65
  focus on other, 26–28, 32, 52
  focus on self, 26–27, 29, 33, 52
  simple vs. complex, 38, 46–47
Benjamin, L. S.
  on anger, 255
  on blockers to change, 247
  on defense functions, 113
  on depression, 169
  on dynamic crisis management, 144, 236
  on Five R's, 227
  on focus distinction, 26
  on green parts of the self, 123
  on hospitalization, 233–234
  on immune system analogy, 141
  on important early relationships, 6
  on interpersonal reconstructive therapy approach, 117
  on interview process, 128
  *Intrex User's Manual,* 82n5, 85n6, 151, 167
  on IRT, 119–120
  on links between symptoms and patterns, 187
  on parallel conceptual models, 20
  on personality disorders, 103–104, 190–192, 227
  on primate social behavior, 10
  on relationship disorders, 94
  on SASB model structure, 35, 56, 58–60

on Shaurette principle, 54
on therapist affirmation, 108
Best fit. *See* goodness of fit
Birthright self. *See* Green parts of the self
**Blame**, 42, 51, 69, 100–104, 111, 241
Blockers to change, 247
Blocking maladaptive patterns, 138
Borderline personality disorder (BPD),
    108, 192, 204, 240
Bowlby, J., 10, 52, 120
BPD. *See* Borderline Personality Disorder

## C

Capture of behaviors, 65
Case conceptualization, 22
Case formulations
    individual, 114
    interview process, 128–135
    and IRT, 125, 171, 220–238, 259
    research on, 194–195
    using SASB and copy processes, 241
Category definition, 22
CBT. *See* Cognitive Behavior Therapy
CFL (Conflict) pattern coefficient, 85
Chair technique, 113, 117
Change. *See also* Stages of Change model
    Five R's for, 227
    in IRT, 136–144
    motivation for, 138
    in symptoms, 240
    tracking of, 240–258
Change blockers, 247
Childhood relationships with parents,
    224–227
Child-like prototype, 32
Chronic pain, 240
Circular order of concepts, 59–60
Circumplex (term), 59
Clarification, 112
Clarkin, J. F., 109–110
Client (term), 6n2
Clinical group outcome prediction, 79
Clusters, 82
Coding, observational. *see* Observational
    coding of interactions
Cognitive behavior models, 56–58
Cognitive Behavior Therapy (CBT), 21,
    102–108, 200, 202, 205
Cohen's weighted k, 78
Collaboration, 138
Comorbid diagnoses, 136

Complementarity (predictive principle),
    48–50, 91
Complex behavior, 46
Complex codes, 36n2, 46n3, 50n5, 65
Complex communications, 79
Conceptual models, parallel, 20
Conflict (CFL) pattern coefficient, 85
Conflicts, wish-fear, 112
Content codes and coding, 66–68, 72–73,
    110, 195
**Control**, 41, 126, 173, 191n2
Control (CON) pattern coefficient, 85–86
Convergent validity, 79
Copy processes, 54–55, 123, 125–130,
    188–192, 194–195, 241–243
Copy process formulation, 177–189
Copy process speech, 130, 132
CORDS acronym, 136, 239, 260
Core algorithm, 137
Core-conflictual relationship theme method,
    114
Correlations, within-subject, 91
Couples therapy, 22, 113
Crisis management, dynamic, 144, 236
Critchfield, K. L., 78, 211, 221
Cultural diversity, 151n2
Cushing, G., 55

## D

DAG (disrupted attachment group), 52
Dating, 22
DBT (dialectical behavior therapy), 107, 204
Defense theory, interpersonal, 111–112
Depression, 121, 169
Detail, interpersonal, 70
*Diagnostic and Statistical Manual of Mental
    Disorders*, 94
*Diagnostic and Statistical Manual of Mental
    Disorders, 4th ed. (DSM-IV)*, 103,
    105, 190, 191n3, 227
*Diagnostic and Statistical Manual of Mental
    Disorders, 5th ed. (DSM-5)*, 227
Dialectical behavior therapy (DBT), 107
Differential diagnosis, 22
Differentiation, 27, 31, 52, 199, 217–220
Dimensional ratings approach, 58–59
Dimensions, 82
Disclose, 42, 72–74, 200–201, 211n2
Disrupted attachment group (DAG), 52
Dissociative disorders, 168
Distance, 33, 34

Diversity, cultural, 151n2
Domination, 16
*DSM-IV. See Diagnostic and Statistical Manual of Mental Disorders, 4th ed.*
*DSM-5 (Diagnostic and Statistical Manual of Mental Disorders, 5th ed.)*, 227
Dyadic process, 113
Dyadic roles, 109
Dynamic crisis management, 144, 236
Dysfunctionality, 136

### E

Early interpersonal schema, 105
Early patterns, 126
Eating disorders, 22, 168
EFT (emotion-focused therapy), 21
Ellis, A., 102
**Emancipate**, 41, 85, 92, 107, 125, 173–176
Emancipation of others, 31–32
Emotion-focused therapy (EFT), 21
Empathy, 137
Enmeshment, 27, 31, 199
Existential therapy, 99, 202

### F

Failure, 105–106
Family in the head, 23, 121–122, 142–144, 236, 246, 255, 257. *See also* Attachment figures, internalized; IPIRs; Key figures
Family processes, 79
Family systems therapy, 120
Family therapy, 22
Father, childhood relationship with, 226–227
Fit. *See* Goodness of fit
Five R's, 227
Fluency, in observational coding, 78
Focus, 25–27, 64, 66, 210–212
"Focus on other" behaviors, 26–28, 32, 52
"Focus on self" behaviors, 26–27, 29, 33, 52
Freedman, M. B., 12
Freedom, 18
Freeman, A. M., 103–105
French, T. M., 223
Fromm, L. M., 78

### G

Genetics, behavioral, 22
Gift of love (GOL)
    articulating, 187, 189
    awareness of, 243–244, 254–256

copy process as, 125, 127–128
formulating hypothesis of, 132–133
relinquishment of, 217–220, 255–256, 260–261
as term, 122–123
Gift of Love Awareness and Choice scale, 242
Goals. *See also* Green goals
    in the head, 215–216
    of therapy, 133–135, 193–194, 217–220
    in the world, 215
Goal speech, 133
Goedken, J. R., 169
GOL. *See* Gift of love
Goldman, R., 113–117
Goodness of fit, 82, 85
Graham, D. T., 120
Graphical representations of relationships, 91
Greenberg, L. S., 113–117
Green goals, 136–138, 143, 199, 214–222, 259–260
Green parts of the self, 121–124, 211, 220–222, 232–235, 238
Green patterns, 127
Group therapy, 22, 167
Growth collaborator. *See* Green parts of the self
Gunn, H. E., 120
Guttman, L., 59

### H

Harlow, H. F., 18, 59, 120
Hate, 31
Healing image, 138
Heart disease, 120
Heider, F., 10, 12
Henry, W. P., 209
Hospitalization, 136, 232–237
Hostility, 32, 33–34, 55, 70
Humanistic therapy, 99, 202
Humor, 46

### I

Identification (copy process), 54–55, 109, 123
**Ignore**, 42, 65–69, 125–126, 188, 241
Immune system analogy, 141
Impact on self, 177, 184
Important persons or their internalized representations (IPIRs). *See also* Attachment figures, internalized; Family in the head; Key figures

284 • Index

Impulsivity, 187
Independence, warmth-neutral, 32
Individual case formulations, 114
Individual therapy, 22
Inference, 68, 72
Input, 177, 184
Input-response nature, of interactive
  patterns, 20–21
Integrative therapy, 21
Interactions
  coding of. *See* Observational coding of
    interactions
  elements of, 64
Interaction states, 80
Interactive patterns, 20–21, 47–52
Interdependence, 17, 25, 27, 61, 64–66, 85
Intergenerational patterns of relating, 22
Internal consistency, 87
Internalized attachment figures, 127, 217,
  249
Internal object relations, 109
Interpersonal defense theory, 111–112
Interpersonal detail, 177
Interpersonal patterns. *See* Linking
  symptoms to interpersonal patterns
Interpersonal profile, sinusoidal, 82
Interpersonal prototype-matching, 190
Interpersonal Reconstructive Therapy (IRT),
  10, 117–144
  adherence to, 259
  case formulations, 125, 171, 220–238
  change in, 136–144
  and copy process formulation, 128–136
  five steps of, 138–141
  goals, 135–136
  major concepts in, 120–128
  progress notes, 252–253
  research on, 259–261
Interpersonal Reconstructive Therapy
  Institute, 262
Interpersonal relating, 79
Interpersonal schema, early, 105
Interpretation, reflective, 202
Interrater reliability, 78–79
Interviewing style, 172–176
Interview process, 128–135
Intrex questionnaires, 80–91, 147–170
  case studies, 149–167
  and change tracking, 240
  levels of analysis, 148
  and outcomes research, 113
  perspective and context in, 80–82

presenting findings to patients, 167–168
research findings, 168–169
summary reports, 87–91
understanding the basic output, 82–87
Intrex ratings, 250
*Intrex User's Manual* (Benjamin), 82n5,
  85n6, 151, 167
Introject, 27, 30, 33, 56n6
Introjection (copy process), 54–55, 125
Introjection (predictive principle), 50–51
IPC (interpersonal circle), 12, 14–15, 17
IPIRs (important persons or their
  internalized representations). *See also*
  Attachment figures, internalized;
  Family in the head; Key figures
IRT. *See* Interpersonal Reconstructive Therapy

## J

Jansana, P., 191n2

## K

Karpiak, C. P., 108
Key figures, 195. *See also* Attachment figures,
  internalized; Family in the head; IPIRs
Klute syndrome, 247–248
Knobloch-Fedders, L. M., 53
Knowing, 12

## L

Laing, R. D., 5
Lambert, M. J., 70
Learning, 121–123
Leary, T., 12, 81
Linehan, M. M., 107
Linking symptoms to interpersonal
  patterns, 120–121, 130, 185, 187
Links between symptoms and key figures,
  195
Love, 31, 32, 121–123, 200, 208–209
Loyalists, regressive, 123
Loyalty, 121–123

## M

Mackaronis, J. E., 211, 221
Maladaptive patterns, blocking of, 138
Manic symptoms, 187
Mead, G. H., 11
Measures of personality, 79

Medical health problems, 22
Mistrust/abuse, 105–106
Mood disorders, 22, 168
Mothers, 91, 93, 224–225, 227
Motivation for change, 138
Murray, H. A., 12–14

## N

Narrative detail, 100–102
Narrative interpersonal detail, 177
Needs, primary vs. secondary, 12
Nervous system, 127
Neurobiology of attachment, 120
Nonsuicidal self-injury (NSSI), 107–108
Nonverbal communication, 65n2, 72
Norcross, J. C., 70
Normative data, 151n2, 161n3
Normative development, 22
Norms, 92, 94–95
NSSI (non-suicidal self-injury), 107–108

## O

Object relations, 109, 110, 120
Observational coding of interactions, 63–80
content coding, 66–68
in-session process, 73–77
process coding, 70–72
putting process and content coding together, 72–73
reliability and validity of, 77–80
summarizing codes, 68–70
Opposition (predictive principle), 49, 51
Optimal relating, 214
Optimal therapy session, 220–222
Outcomes, 79, 113

## P

PAG (Passive-aggressive personality disorder), 191–192
Pain, chronic, 240
Panic disorder, 240
Parallel affective model, 201
Parallel structure analysis of affective and cognitive behavior, 56–58
Paranoid personality disorder, 103–105, 191n2
Parental Bonding Instrument (PBI), 16
Parent–child interaction research, 16
Parenting, 22

Parentlike image, 32
Parents, childhood relationships with, 224–227
Parts of the self. *See* Green parts of the self; Red parts of the self
Passive-aggressive personality disorder (PAG), 191–192
Past relationships, 183, 185
Patient (term), 6n2
Patient case formulations, 79
Patient-centered therapy, 21
Patient history, 73–76
Patient safety, 232
Pattern(s)
awareness of, 138
blocking maladaptive, 138
coefficients, 82
repetition, 121–122
tracking of, 127
Patterning of the therapy relationship, 199–214
Pattern/symptom linking, 120–121, 185, 187
PBI (Parental Bonding Instrument), 16
Pearson *r* values, 79, 91, 103–104
Personality, measures of, 79
Personality disorders, 22, 168, 189–193, 227, 260. *See also* Paranoid personality disorder; Passive-aggressive personality disorder
Personality symptom reports, 80
Pond water theory, 70
Posttraumatic stress disorder (PTSD), 22, 240
Power, 12, 33
Predictive principles, 48–52
Predictive validity, 79
Primary needs, 12
Primate social behavior, 10, 17–18
Primitive basics, 35
Process coding, 70–73, 78
Process-experiential treatment, 113–117, 200
Process skills, 137
Profile differences, 169
**Protect**, 41, 94, 107, 169, 173–176, 205–208
Prototype-matching, internalized, 190
Psychodynamic therapy, 99, 108, 200, 202
Psychogenic (secondary) needs, 12
*The Psychology of Interpersonal Relations* (Heider), 10
Psychopathology, 11–12, 79
Psychosis, 22, 168
Psychotherapy outcomes, 79

286 • *Index*

Psychotherapy Video Series (APA), 71
PTSD (posttraumatic stress disorder), 22, 240

**R**

RCA-Q (Relational Cognitions and Affects
    Questionnaire), 58
Reactive Love, 43, 208
Recapitulation (copy process), 54–55, 93,
    109, 123
Recognition of patterns, 138
Recoil, 43, 152
Recuing, 141–142
Recurrent theme identification, 75
Red goals, 204, 221
Red parts of the self, 121–125, 137,
    142–144, 211, 216, 220–222
Referents, 47, 64, 66
Reflective interpretation, 202
Regressive loyalists, 123
Relating
    intergenerational patterns of, 22
    interpersonal, 79
    optimal, 214
    setting of, 80
Relational Cognitions and Affects
    Questionnaire (RCA-Q), 58
Relational context, 22
Relational disorders, 94–95
Relational patterns, self-reported, 59–60
Relationships
    early, 6
    sequential patterning of, 71
Reliability, test-retest, 82
Repeating themes across relationships,
    91–95
Revenge of the red, 143
Reversed focus, 210–212
Rilke, R. M., 16
Rules, from attachment figures, 127
Rules of engagement, 136–137

**S**

SAAB. *See* Structural Analysis of Affective
    Behavior
SACB. *See* Structural Analysis of Cognitive
    Behavior
Sarcasm, 46
SASB. *See* Structural Analysis of Social
    Behavior
SASBQuest scoring program, 82

Schaefer, E. S., 16–17, 33
Schema-focused therapy, 105
Schizophrenia, 168, 169
Secondary needs, 12
*Self-Affirm*, 44, 51
*Self-Attack*, 45, 69–70, 87
*Self-Blame*, 45, 50–51, 69–70, 87–88,
    115–116, 181–182
Self-concept, 240
*Self-Control*, 45, 104, 115–116, 241
*Self-Emancipate*, 44, 82
Self-focused separation, neutral, 32
Self-harm, 204
*Self-Neglect*, 9, 45, 50–51, 67–70, 115–116,
    181–182, 241
*Self-Protect*, 44–45, 67–70
Self-reported relational patterns, 59–60
Self-sacrifice, 105–106
Separate, 19, 42, 181–183
Separateness, 15
Sequential patterning of relationships, 71
Setting of relating, 80
Severity, spectrum of, 135–136
Sexual abuse, 55, 178, 240, 247
Sexuality, 17, 158, 182, 247–248. *See also*
    Klute syndrome
Shaurette principle, 54
Shearin, E. N., 107
Similarity (predictive principle), 48
Sinusoidal interpersonal profile, 82
Skowron, E. A., 143
Sleep, 120
Smith, T. W., 120
*Social isolation/alienation*, 105–106
Specificity hypothesis, 120
Spectrum of severity, 135–136
Spirituality, 22
Sports performance, 22
Stages of Change model, 242
Status, 12
Structural Analysis of Affective Behavior
    (SAAB), 58, 102, 133, 201
Structural Analysis of Cognitive Behavior
    (SACB), 58, 133, 201
Structural Analysis of Social Behavior
    (SASB)
    basic structure of, 26–27
    and CBT, 102–108
    and copy processes, 241
    full model of, 26–30
    history of, 21–22
    interactive context of, 20–21

learning, 7–11
logic of the diamond structure, 34–36
and narrative detail, 100–102
as precise description, 99–117
and process-experiential applications, 113–117
and transference-focused psychotherapy, 108–113
underlying dimensional structure, 31
validation of structure of, 58–61
Structural Analysis of Social Behavior (SASB) models, 25–38
basic, 26–27
circular order of concepts, 59–60
cluster, 8, 38–45
full, 27–36
quadrant, 36–38, 262
structure of, 35, 56, 58–60
Structured Clinical Interview for *DSM-IV* Axis II Personality Disorders, 240
Submission, 16, 18
Submit, 43, 50n5, 68–70, 181–183, 241
Substance use and abuse, 22, 168
Suicidality, 22, 136, 193, 204, 209, 236–237, 245
Sulk, 43, 73, 241
Sullivan, H. S., 11–12
Symptom change, 240
Symptom/pattern linking, 120–121, 185, 187
Symptoms/key figures links, 195

## T

Teaching of psychology, 22
Test-retest reliability, 82
TFP (transference-focused psychotherapy), 108–113
Thematic tracks, 35n1, 37–38
Therapist affirmation, 108

Therapy completion, 258
Therapy goals, 133–135, 193–194, 217–220
Thought units, 64
Tone of voice, 72, 114
Tracking change, 240–258
Tracking of patterns, 127
Training, for observational coding, 77–78
Traitlike processes, 80
Transference-focused psychotherapy (TFP), 108–113
Treatment goal operationalizing, 113–114
Trust, 205–208
Trust, 43, 73–74, 104, 181
Two-chair technique, 113, 117

## U

Ulberg, R., 112

## V

Validity, predictive, 79
Viscerogenic (primary) needs, 12
Vocal tone, 72, 114

## W

Wall-Off, 19, 44, 50n5, 101, 104, 201
Warmth, 33, 34, 52
Wiggins, J. S., 81
Will to change, 249
Within-subject correlations, 91
Woehrle, P. L., 55

## Y

Yearning self, 123
Young, J. E., 105–106

# About the Authors

**Kenneth L. Critchfield, PhD,** is a tenured associate professor and program director of the Clinical Psychology Program of the Ferkauf Graduate School of Psychology at Yeshiva University. Dr. Critchfield's research, teaching, and clinical work all emphasize interpersonal and attachment-based principles of change implemented in Interpersonal Reconstructive Therapy (IRT). He was codirector of the IRT clinic at the University of Utah Neuropsychiatric Institute until 2014. Dr. Critchfield is an American Psychological Association Fellow (Division 29, Society for the Advancement of Psychotherapy) and has long been a member of both the Society for the Exploration of Psychotherapy Integration and the Society for Psychotherapy Research. He is the director of the IRT Institute, which provides training in the use of Structural Analysis of Social Behavior and certification in IRT, while also maintaining an independent practice.

**Lorna Smith Benjamin, PhD,** is professor emerita of psychology at the University of Utah and founder of the IRT [Interpersonal Reconstructive Therapy] Clinic at the University of Utah Neuropsychiatric Institute. She is now in full retirement. She is the creator of Structural Analysis of Social Behavior (SASB) for describing interactions with the self and others and of IRT, which was developed for patients with "treatment-resistant" psychiatric disorders on the basis of what she learned after decades of using SASB in research and clinical practice. Dr. Benjamin is a past president of the International Society for Psychotherapy Research and an American Psychological Association Fellow (Division 29, Society for the Advancement of Psychotherapy). Her honors include the Distinguished Research Career Award from the International Society for Psychotherapy Research; an honorary doctorate (FDHC) from the University of Umea, Sweden; the Society for Personality Assessment Bruno Klopfer Award for outstanding, long-term professional contribution; and the Distinguished Psychologist Award for Contributions to Psychology and Psychotherapy from the Society for the Advancement of Psychotherapy.